AF518381

CUTTING EDGES

Biology of Experience in the Poetry of Kamala Das

CUTTING EDGES

Biology of Experience in the Poetry of Kamala Das

Jayakrishnan Nair

ADHYAYAN

ADHYAYAN PUBLISHERS & DISTRIBUTORS
New Delhi-110002

Published by
ADHYAYAN PUBLISHERS & DISTRIBUTORS
4378/4B, 105, J.M.D. House, Murari Lal Street
Ansari Road Darya Ganj, New Delhi - 110002
Ph.: 011-23263018, 011-23277156, Fax: 23280028
Email: adhyayanpublishers@yahoo.com

Cutting Edges:
Biology of Experience in the Poetry of Kamala Das

© Author
Edition 2009
ISBN 978-81-8435-123-1

The responsibility for facts stated, opinion expressed are conclusions reached and plagiarism, if any, in this book is entirely that of the author/ editor. The publishers bears no responsibility for them whatsoever.

Printed in India

Published by Harish Chandra Yadav for Adhyayan Publishers & Distributors, Delhi. Laser Typesetting at V. M. Graphics and Printed at Tarun Offset Printers, Delhi

To my parents

Preface

To assert that Kamala Das is one of the few most important living English poets in India is almost a critical commonplace. Though Das's poetry is not easily available for literary interpretations, yet an attempt to analyse it is an exciting task, particularly when she has been variously interpreted owing to her unabashed tone of anger and violence in expressing the feminine concerns, and demands for feminine freedoms and choices. For all such readers whose reading habits are soaked in the centuries of representative writings, all kinds of suggestions through delicate gestures of language and life become puzzling matters. While the writer intends to indicate, just indicate, towards a certain abstract essence of life, the reader in vain searches for a literal label for all such assertions. Gone are the eras of assertions. Only we have indications of inner anxieties to be evacuated through the same old botched language nurtured by a botched culture. Manipulating the subtleties of language for the purpose of artistic expertise is the unique privilege of the creative writers. Kamala Das, for whom English is a second language, could acquire for herself a first rate creative expertise in handling English language for her enviable poetic purpose. Since all the tell tale stories of cultures and societies are half-truths pleasantly fabricated into plasticized facets of language, the whole truth, as and when uttered, as in Kamala Das, becomes an unwithstandable fact that undercuts the superstructure, and pulls down the multi-storeyed mansions built on bleak plinths or no plinths at all.

Kamala Das had picked up most of the forward-looking ideas concerning women's liberation from the European *avant-garde* feminist writers like Simone de Beauvoir and Virginia Woolf. Insofar as her poetry takes its life-blood from the European feminist liberation movement, there is a profound point, that too an urgent one, in what all she talks and chatters ragingly like an inspired schizophrenic. In fact her schizophrenia is not a psychological deformity. On the other hand, it is a poetic fact that conformed her poetic themes into the most urgent issues that needed apt resolutions and answers. In her poetry she untiringly argues that there is a great need for a humanistic and humanized reformation in the attitudes and dispositions of men towards their women, and that only such an understanding atmosphere can ultimately pave way for a better state of happiness for humanity in the future. Therefore, it is high time an altogether different readership was built up for Kamala Das's poetry for her poetry demands a serious and sympathetic attempt on the part of the reader to assume upon himself the actor's trunk of interior paramour in being one with her subtle and vibrant exposition of woman's psyche.

This work is a concentrated study on Kamala Das's treatment of her psychic violence in her poetry. Here it becomes pertinent to clarify that in the whole work, the word 'violence' is taken as a syndrome representing a sort of metaphysical rebellion, anger, and angst, manifesting itself as vehement poetic fury with the help of powerful images and symbols. Violence as such can be understood as fallout of inexpressible emotions and the ensuing suffocation.

The work is in a seven chapter format. The first chapter is an attempt to introduce Kamala Das as one of the few living Indian poets of substance, and also as the only woman poet of international standing in the Indo-Anglian poetic milieu. A brief study of the feminist movement of the West is also attempted so as to project Das as the Indian counterpart of the feminist writers of the West. Also a succinct historical perspective of the earlier Indian women poetry in English is taken up in order to show how Das distances herself from the earlier poets. This chapter also attempts to view Das as a modern poet displaying all the properties of modernism in her poetry. A small biographical sketch and her quantitative achievements in Indian writing in English are given at the end of the chapter.

The second chapter discusses the main sources of her poetic

violence from both the angles of Indian woman's predicament and from the poet's own biographical particulars. The third chapter is a natural sequel of the previous chapter in the sense that after the 'sources,' it instantly becomes pertinent to look at the targets towards which her poetic violence is directed. So it is tried to juxtapose at the receiving end the two main targets of her poetic violence, viz., nature and fellowmen. The fourth chapter puts a glance at the journey of the poet's own self through the labyrinthine grooves of life, and the frustration she has had in her experiments with love and lust. The fifth chapter explores the essential philosophy behind violence and rebellion in general and also as to how this philosophy works in Das's poetry. It is tried to base her poetic violence on instinctive aberrations and also on theories of metaphysical rebellion as suggested by Albert Camus. The sixth chapter takes up a new but essential question as to how all this poetic anger and violence is converted into a profound aesthetic formula of expression in Kamala Das. An attempt has been made to explore and unveil the poetic self struggling between the creaturely dispositions of earthly life and the unattainable transcendental heights. The seventh and concluding chapter initially deals with some unfounded charges of pornography and exhibitionism on the author by her critics. However, the chapter sums up the overall discussion with a suggestion to look at the entire poetic property of Kamala Das as a humanistic and aesthetic document intended to enlighten and educate the fellowmen for a better understanding of feminine predicaments and demands, and thereby pave way for a better future of humanity.

I am deeply indebted to my teachers Late Prof. S.B.K. Murthy and Prof. Dr. A. Q. Khan whose unflinching support, affection and encouragement helped my work to a great extent. I also thank my colleague Prof. Narendra Dev for the help and encouragement for bringing out this book. I am also grateful to M/s Adhyayan Publishers and Distributors, New Delhi, for their positive response and efforts in publishing this book. I must also express my gratitude to my wife and my two daughters, whose love and co-operation always stood as an impetus to complete this work.

—Jayakrishnan Nair

List of Abbreviations

Titles	*Abbreviations*
The Descendants	D
The Old Playhouse and Other Poems	OP
Tonight This Savage Rite	TSR
Collected Poems	CP
The Best of Kamala Das	BK
Only the Soul Knows How to Sing	OSK
My Story	MS
"My Instinct, My Guru."	My Instinct
"I Needed to Disturb Society."	I Needed
"Of Masks and Memories."	Of Masks
"I Have Kept Myself Away From Books . . ."	I Have Kept
The Path of the Columnist	*Path*

Contents

I

Introduction

Kamala Das as a creative artist progressively involves herself into the modern fundaments of thought and action: scepticism, opposition, and criticism. Ever since Frederick Nietzsche envisaged these three characteristic properties of modern thought and action, many revolutionary ideologies like the leftist philosophy and the feminist revolution in the European countries came to the forefront. Kamala Das successfully poetises the modern Indian feminine psyche's violence and rebellion in accordance with the celebrities of the twentieth century Western women's liberation movement, like Simone De Beauvoir and Virginia Woolf. Being an Indian, Das progressively introduces the Indian woman's predicament by taking into consideration four prominent aspects differentiating women: biological, linguistic, psychoanalytic, and cultural. Her sensibility is filled with agonizing circumstances of feminine predicament and the ensuing anxiety and angst. This anxiety and angst eventually transform into violent poetic outcries which are directed towards a society that constantly and continuously cold-shouldered the feminine sensibilities, and violated the freedoms and aspirations of women. In the context of modern India, hers is a unique poetic innovation and experiment of superimposing the violent and revolutionary ideas of the Western women's liberation movement upon the Indian women's world of rigid and unbending traditions.

Kamala Das, in fact, is concerned with the exclusive problems faced by women in general in the context of the traditional life-giving institutions. When it comes to the question of taking issues and conducting a quarrel with man and his masculine preoccupations, Kamala Das is certainly justified in her violent fury against the autocratic manner in which man behaves in his relations both with woman and with nature. Needless to say, certain amount of self-centredness, hypocrisy, envy, and hate entered into the ego-centric province of man, and it is very difficult to say since when he started becoming a grudging rival of the very essence of femininity. As a matter of safe conjecture, it is Renaissance man duly appended with egocentric individualism that progressively contributed for a kind of authoritarian manner of taking decisions and executing them. This authoritarian manner of man reached its pinnacle towards the end of the nineteenth century. This male-centred authoritarian dogma had to be met with opposition and criticism. The feminist cause itself emerged as a rival critical social phenomenon and took the form of a furious liberation movement. Kamala Das partakes herself in this process of liberating women by way of openly declaring her grievances and concerns about the self-centred nature of man in being an authority for himself without analytically understanding the relative importance and prerogatives of woman as a person and as a social being.

Very often Das's poetry prominently verges upon making a sort of concerned confessional declarations about the superior credentials of woman in nature and about her equal credentials in the matters concerning social and cultural contexts of existence. Das prominently believes that in nature's strict parameters femininity occupies a very important place of superiority because nature has entrusted woman with greater responsibilities and with higher credentials in awarding her the status of an essential base in the process of evolution. So her grievance is based on the fact that this naturalistic superiority and supremacy of woman was never allowed to take the form of a culture by man and his crushing tendencies of authoritarianism. This subdued existence breeds in woman a typical manner of being a critic in opposition of all that goes in the society in the name of traditions. In this context, she acts like an interior grudging paramour with the prime purpose of setting the things right in the structural complexities of social systems. Therefore, feminine property in a given society always acts as a concerned critic in order to set right man and his egocentric autonomy. Kamala Das enhances this feminist feud by way of poetically expressing the true texts and contexts of Indian woman and her suffering because of the authoritarian onslaughts of the post-Renaissance man. Her entire poetic property has since been an evidence of her unique personal temper and temperament.

A. The Ordeal of Kamala Das

Kamala Das is of the opinion that given the opportunity of freedom and transparency in thought and action, Indian woman too can come out of the seemingly unassertive and submissive calm and quietude of her world, and go hand in hand with her Western counterparts in aspiring and exacting for a dignified status for women rather than putting up with the humiliations of sexual exploitations and subservience that they undergo in the Indian social milieu. What she violently pleads for is a possible understanding between man and woman as equally interdependent personalities struggling to measure each other's personality mutually in an atmosphere of what the Christian fathers call agape or Christ-like charity. The modern mechanized and industrial life-styles do not allow a place for that agape. So her real rebellion is against the modern 'botched culture' (to borrow the expression of Ezra Pound), which does not allow interpersonal free and frank transparency in the affairs concerning the mutual joys and sublimations of man and woman as partners in life. The categorical distinction and differentiation between man and woman as naturalistic creatures put man as a self-serving conservative agent, serving his own purposes and cold-shouldering his feminine counterpart into a state of negligence and unwanted state. As Das says in the poem "An Introduction," against woman's longing for a transparent and sympathetic interpersonal relations, the man "is tightly packed like the / Sword in its sheath" (OP 26). Again, as she says in "The Old Playhouse," he unsheathes the 'sword' only to serve "his love in lethal doses" (OP 1).

In fact the whole poetic rebellion in Kamala Das is just a way of recording her protest against a culture that has rendered both man and woman into mutual non-entities in being life-partners.

Generations of traditions and conventions verbally dubbed women in a state of passivity and in course of time quite innocuously and ungrudgingly women reconciled to their so-called state of passivity, and gradually got conditioned to the strategically proposed systems and traditions. Justifying Das's concerns as a woman-poet, K. Satchidanandan rightly observes:

> She [Das] refuses to glorify the historical past . . . . She rejects the patriarchal value system that is based on egoism, greed for power, expansionism, hero-cult, violence, war, mindless exploitation of man and nature, the misuse of intelligence and the supremacy of reason and theory over sensitiveness and experience. (16-17)

Kamala Das's poetry, with its absolute transparencies of what it means by being a woman, particularly as a life partner, creates in man a sort of stirring sensibility. Her poetry just initiates a fret and fever in man to revalidate his rigid, uncompromising stance on woman. It is here that she becomes a precious poetic voice bent upon rectifying everything that went wrong for centuries together in a man-made world that does not really offer any substantial progress in being human. The real progress of humanity does not lie in its material gains, and personal profits thereof; the real nature of living beings in a gregarious set needs a concern and consideration for others. If only man compounds in himself the basic idea as to how it looks like being the other in all the interpersonal transactions and commerce, there is scope for a humanistic harmony. Such harmony is the most desired state according to Kamala Das. At the same time, she also fervently pleads for recognition of the uniqueness of woman as an all-encompassing compassionate entity in a given society. This plea for recognition of woman's uniqueness, since she proposes to the same in most clear terms added with a sense of emotional fury, often provokes in the readers a sort of immediate initial response of discord. But in her poetry she simultaneously provides a rational and realistic proposition concerning the state and status of women in the Indian system; and, after a calm and cool thinking, the readers wholeheartedly consent and conform themselves to what she says as something quite sensible, even laudable.

Das's poetry is more and more informed by the use of conversational language, a prominent manner of performing in the accentual verse pattern and *verse libre* 'free verse.' The very technique of Kamala Das's poetry is associated with challenging tonalities full of angst born of looking at woman as a mere tool or mechanical instrument. Das spells out her anguish over this gender dichotomy in unequivocal terms with such intrepidity and audacity as was hitherto unheard of in the Indian women's literary traditions. In the following lines of the poem "The Old Playhouse," she expresses this anguish very powerfully:

> You called me wife,
> I was taught to break saccharine into your tea and
> To offer at the right moment the vitamins. Cowering
> Beneath your monstrous ego I ate the magic loaf and
> Became a dwarf. . . . (OP 1)

The expression 'You called me wife' is very important because of the implied social compulsiveness on which the husband-wife relationship stands, for nothing transpires between the two hearts. The 'magic loaf' and 'dwarf' metaphors are very powerful, which are indicative of man's fulfilling woman's survival necessities and woman's dwindling of personality. It is the collective psyche of women speaking out from a sudden awakening. If so, Kamala Das's real rebellion is against a culture that has instituted every socially interactive counter on the inherent principle of gender dichotomy. With her accurate poetic temper she identifies herself with the whole humanity, and conducts her poetic activity in such a manner that she would gain for herself the honorific credentials of being a citizen of the world. Her poetic fight on behalf of women is not at all narrowed down to the Indian context alone. In the whole world, the manner in which women are discriminated and sidelined for centuries together pained her a lot. In the poem "The Suicide" she expresses this pain over women's historical role:

> I must pose.
> I must pretend,
> I must act the role

Of happy woman,
Happy wife. (D 2)

Posing what she is not, and pretending what she is expected to be is precisely acting. The same agent ['You'] of the lines 'You called me wife' in the "The Old Playhouse" (OP 1), here forces her to pretend to be a 'happy woman' and a 'Happy wife.' It is here that she painfully realizes her loss of identity. She is not only compelled by the civilization and its patriarchal agents to wear the garbs of many roles but is also not allowed to express her dissent over this imposition ('I must act the role / Of a happy woman / Happy wife').

Kamala Das freely borrows most of the forward-looking ideas concerning women's liberation from the European avant-garde feminist writers like Simone de Beauvoir and Virginia Woolf. In spite of the fact that her poetic temperament tilts towards the liberation of women, her natural credentials for poetry is because of her abundant love for life, liberty, and progress. In fact it is these factors along with her longing for happiness and joy that render her into a rebel when she finds that the heartless social mills of religion, tradition, morality, and conventions ruthlessly crush the genuine naturalistic credentials of feminine supremacies. The urgency that pervades over her poems springs from the firm belief that life is only one, and that it is meant to be much happier. The slipping away of the 'only one' without granting the naturalistic perquisites is all the more painful. In the poem "The Seashore" she expresses her pain over this passing away of life without awarding the aspired fulfilment: "I sense / The tug of time, I see you go away from me / And feel the loss of love I never once received" (BK 33). The poetic fervour of Kamala Das's confessional rhetoric here is comparable to that of Sylvia Plath. Kamala Das had an urgency to speak out her mind freely and frankly. In this process, she involves herself in poetic creativity quite fearlessly. Her missionary zeal for poetically compacting the exclusive concerns of women is really commendable.

As far as what Kamala Das wants to assert through her poetry is concerned, she comes very near to the observations made by Western feminist liberators about the position of women in society. In the articulation of feminist concerns through literary aesthetic dimensions, thus, Kamala Das is not a beginner, but an Oriental link in the train of such strong European women writers as Simone de Beauvoir and Virginia Woolf, and such astounding feminist confessional poets as Anne Sexton and Sylvia Plath of America. A brief look at the evolution of women's movement into a profound aesthetic formula of exacting feminine concerns, therefore, instantly becomes pertinent here.

Evolution of Feminist Literary Genre

1. *Predicament of Women*

As a matter of fact, the gender inequities are not associated with any particular race; this evil has travelled in space and time from the primordial period to the present day. Since human civilization itself has evolved incessantly ignoring the vital half of its race, i.e. women, the concerns voiced in the modern feminist writings are as relevant and momentous as the question of man's existence itself. This fact has prompted Helen Cixous to say: "If women were to set themselves to transform History, it can safely be said that every aspect of History would be completely altered" (487). Quite ironically, the sidelining of this 'better half' by generations together is head-on with the nature's blue print of evolution, for nature trusts femininity, and bestows on it the maximum responsibility of advancing evolution towards progressive directions. Nevertheless, since the dawn of civilization, the male principle has been overacting itself as a phenomenal exploiter that sabotaged the female principle at all practical counters. In this context, the following words of Gerda Lerner on women's predicament are worth quoting:

> Women have been left out of history not because of the evil conspiracies of men in general or male historians in particular, but because we have considered history only in male centered [sic] terms. We have missed women and their activities, because we have asked questions of history, which are inappropriate to women. (qtd. in Showalter 470)

Whether or not it is because of 'the evil conspiracies of men in general or male historians in particular,' it remains a fact that the feminine consciousness is one of alienation, non-recognition, and loss of identity.

2. *Towards Equal Dignity of Being-in-the World*

Woman becoming conscious of her natural rights is of recent origin. Freudian psychology with its emphasis on instincts, more particularly on *libido* ("sexual instinct") gave a sort of open challenge and sanction for the transparency of the exclusive feminine concerns. In the West, the post Freudians, with a prominent stress on primary activity, further hastened the feminist spoke-persons to give a call for the liberation of women. The primary activity essentially concerns with self-preservation and preservation of the race. Needless to say, nature primarily depends on femininity in its choice of evolution and progress. For an introspective analysis, the traditional woman's conditions in the context of family as well as society had turned to be that of a veritable slave without any independent and individual sanction of freedoms for her feelings, emotions, and desires.

Under the functional properties of democratic complexities that had entered in social life of late, a passionate desire for asserting equality as a given property for humanity entered into human psyche. The feminists, having felt the humiliation of male chauvinism and aggressiveness for centuries together, discovered for themselves a unique opportunity to give vent to their exploited and suppressed egos in exacting for equality even in the context of sharing the male-female intimate relations. Though the root of the feminist plea for equality lay embedded in the principle of humanism as propounded by the Renaissance writers like Thomas More and Erasmus, feminist introspection in terms of seeking a real and adequate identity for woman began with the eighteenth century European enlightenment, with writers like Mary Wollstonecraft. Her Book, *A Vindication of the Rights of Women,* published in 1792, was a milestone in this direction. Then, the pioneer nineteenth century feminists, considered radical for their belief in the equality of the sexes, included Emmeline Pankhurst in the UK; and Susan B Anthony and Elizabeth Cady Stanton in the USA. Thus, with the advent of the Western women's liberation movement, women progressively started pleading for equal dignity and equal prominence for women, more particularly in the familial context. Since these women revolutionaries considered femininity as equally dignified, they started making a vociferous tract against men on behalf of women.

Thus dawned the era of man-woman strife and struggle. Equality and equal dignity of being-in-the world was the original exacting ground for women. In course of time, woman gradually understood her naturalistic superiorities and supremacies as a prime creative agent in the progressive evolution of human Homo sapiens. This gave her an additional edge over man in the natural counters, and gradually she started vociferously asserting for her superiority and domination even in the domestic and familial environments. Though Feminism grew as an ideology alongside the concept of Humanism, feminist writings evolved as a literary genre at a later stage. Many women writers have contributed to this genre of literature, and through their articulations of feminist unrest, it has evolved as a cogent medium of expression of the modern feminine psyche with its fears and anxieties. Susheela Singh rightly says, "Through the long line of women writers who protested against the inequities from Christine de Pisan to Mary Wollstonecraft, and through Simone de Beauvoir to present day feminist thinkers, an outlook, a 'theory,' a feminist thought system evolves" (33). In fact it is the Twentieth century writers like Simone de Beauvoir of France and Virginia Woolf of England that made conscious analysis of the patriarchal traditions and conventions that go to defeat the ultimate purpose of woman in being woman. The feminist liberation movement with due transparency virtually dawned in the writings of these women. The following observation of Beauvoir, for instance, very powerfully expresses the need for woman to counter the prejudice of patriarchy:

> Masculine claims are contradictory; authority no longer works. Woman must judge and be critical, she cannot remain a mere docile echo . . . what she is able to agree with in her husband's way of thinking she should agree with only through an independent act of judgment . . . she cannot borrow from another her own reasons for existing. (208)

What all Beauvoir summates in the above context is a fervent plea on behalf of women for a proper understanding of their needs. It is obvious that the enlightenment begotten by these Western writers suggest at the fundamental idea that women can no more tolerate the chauvinist exploitations by men as executors of the familial strategy. However, with the advent of phenomenal personalities like Woolf and Beauvoir in the feminist literary scene, laying the very bricks for the foundation of modern feminist literature, the inhibitions that had hung over the feminine experiences like a veil have cleared themselves off. Women's cause that was hitherto a movement has now been elevated to aesthetic heights in their hands; here is unravelled a new world of feminine experiences both at physical and psychological counters. The basic metaphysics of the feminine psyche started becoming outspoken and vibrant in this act of de-caging of women.

The feminist confessional poetry is almost synonymous with the American poets, Anne Sexton and Sylvia Plath. Their poetic articulations of feminine anxieties paved way for an unprecedented revelation of the vibrant presence of an existential conflict in the feminine psychic response to the patriarchal social systems. Their poetic personae have become the protagonists of the collective consciousness of women. Their poetry is a far cry from the lullabies, the only kind of poetry women were traditionally expected (or permitted?) to write. They reject the select vocabulary meant for women in the name of social civilities and decencies, and adopt for themselves a sublime rhetoric of violence without the anticipated feminine concealments. The poetic outbursts of these modern women-poets stamp the patriarchal society as a cruel manipulator, which strategically subdued women and sidelined their freedoms and choices.

3. *Feminism and Feminist Literature in India*

However, the 'feminist thought system' that Sushila Singh suggests above was somewhat not native for India. To uplift women from the rock bottom of her socially depraved condition, emergence of a vibrant thought was a timely necessity. The revolutionary upheavals on the Western part of the world notwithstanding, the Indian women still had little opportunity to board the train of the modern feminist thinkers, chiefly due to the peculiar nature of Indian social set up emerging out of its abnormal demographic variations and social and cultural expansions and differences. In a rigid social structure like India's, revolting against any accepted values would mean risking an existential conflict with the society as a whole. Thus, with the awareness of the comparatively freer existence of women on the other side of the globe, Indian women felt themselves to be like caged animals. The partly emancipated women of the West functioned as teasers for these 'caged animals.' To break the stronger social bars around themselves than those around their Western counterparts, women needed extra energy and intrepidity in the Indian context. It is in the post-Independence era, particularly in the late fifties and the sixties, that Indian women's writings in English abundantly revealed a hitherto unravelled feminine psyche, thanks to the spread of learning and awareness in the country. More and more women writers began expressing their anger articulately against the vile social situation they live in. The tone and tenor of Indian women's writing in English, particularly fiction and poetry, gradually revealed a consciousness of alienation, deprivation, and a quest for a new identity for women. These writings, with their vibrant presence in the Indian literary scenario, are living evidences of the Indian woman's modern temperament, a rapid growth in their awareness, and the resultant urgency revealed in re-writing the man-woman interpersonal relationships in their typical Indian political, ethical, and socio-cultural background settings. Veena Noble Dass evaluates this awakening among Indian women writers:

> Very often these works do not offer a tangible solution for the feminists. But the experiences rendered through the feminine consciousness invariably point to an inner exhilaration suggesting the beginning of a fresh awakening, a much sought-after precept of the feminists. Indian English Fiction, Poetry, and Drama are replete with the male-female confrontation, problems of adolescence, and coming of age, with special reference to women, explicit and latent pleadings for equality, liberty and self preservation, even risking the normal safe-guarding of hallowed tradition. (11-12)

The essential poetic subject of Kamala Das ultimately concerns with this 'hallowed tradition.' But more than the details of 'the male-female confrontation' Das's poems do reveal even the most intimate experience of a very sensitive feminine psyche. She wants to present a new transparency, a new articulate vision of understanding woman and her depraved state of survival in the Indian familial context. Through her poetry, she initiates that long-awaited vibrancy and transparency in the Indian mainland. In this context, she is the leading floodlight in the Indian subcontinent. In her ferocious poetic forms, she is at pains to suggest that even after the glorious feminist liberation programme, the fundamental problems of woman and her province of personal experience remain tentative, obscure, and unappreciated.

Kamala Das's Poetic Contribution

1. *The Feminist Mouthpiece*

Kamala Das plays a very significant role in making the feminine concerns and points of view violently clarified and made transparent through her poetry. In our times she is probably the only poetic voice of India, which attracted a wide critical acclaim all over the world. As far as the Indian novel in English is concerned, there are many names to reckon with. Bharati Mukherjee, Anita Desai, Nayantara Sehgal, Ruth Praver Jhabhwalla, and Shashi Deshpande are some such Indo-Anglian fiction writers in addition to innumerable creative fiction writers in the regional languages. With these writers, Indian Novel has evolved into a respectable genre of literature in terms of thematic complexities and idiomatic innovativeness. Nevertheless, the advancement has not been so rapid in other genres of Indian writings in English including poetry. Kamala Das is a loner in poetry in the sense that no feminist revolutionary, more particularly in the Indian English poetic milieu, is as important as Kamala Das either in terms of structural and thematic complexities or in terms of aesthetic dimensions. If one endeavours to examine the Indian woman poetry in English in the last fifty years or so, only Kamala Das stands apart as a woman poet of international stature. This fact prompts Sunanda P. Chavan to say, "Kamala Das embodies the most significant stage of development of Indian feminine poetic sensibility not yet reached by her contemporaries" ("Moderns" 60).

Kamala Das's poetry is more of a familial nature than social or cultural. It does not mean that her social and cultural concerns are in any way less important. It only means to imply that she progressively arrives at her social and cultural concerns after making a meticulous analysis of the familial interpersonal relations, particularly of men and women in their ideological thrust for a greater and perfect involvement and understanding of human relations. Since she is taking the mature woman's point of view for her poetic creative analysis, it is quite natural that she is bound to be prominently of partisan perception on behalf of women. The tone of violent outcry in her poetry is a poetic strategy; in fact her poetry is a call for humanistic understandings born of mercy, pity, peace, love, and charity. Somehow, the lopsided and even one-sided progress that humanity made in the scientific and technological directions ultimately contributed for a confusion rather than clarity of human relations. Kamala Das makes a humble but violent poetic effort in order to highlight the feminine problems and predicaments in the context of our times.

The cultural crisis that Kamala Das personally underwent in the biographical context is greatly responsible for her being violent in the tone and tenor of her poetry. It is not altogether untenable to state that her poetry is most prominently personal in nature. The entire amalgam of it conforms to the prime credentials of a confessional document, wherein utmost attention is paid to the fundamental feminine demands and privileges in being a woman endowed with a sort of prime individuality, independence, and self-introspection coupled with enviable judicious assertions. It is in Das that modern Indian feminist poetry acquired for itself a real substantitalness that matches equally with the creative contributions of the Western confessional poets like Sylvia Plath and Anne Sexton of America.

2. *Traditional Women Poetry in India vis-a-vis Kamala Das's Poetry*

Referring to Kamala Das's poetic temper, K.R.S. Iyengar says,

"There is no doubt, Kamala Das is a new phenomenon in the Indo-Anglian Poetry, a far cry indeed from Toru Dutt or even Sarojini Naidu" (680). There is relevance in Iyengar's bringing in the names of Toru Dutt and Sarojini Naidu in the context of Kamala Das because the former two represent one important aspect of Indian women's poetry—the Indian Romantic tradition. Before Kamala Das took to writing poetry, the tradition of Indian woman-poetry ran along a different path; it had the ancient tradition of transcendental poetry of Avvayyar and Mirabai, and the Romantic tradition of poetry written by Toru Dutt and Sarojini Naidu. Das's modern poetic temperament did not lead her to any of these traditional manners of poetry. Her world was not colourful; her mission was different. In fact she did not have any Indian role model to emulate in her poetic endeavours. In a 'Meet the Author Programme' thus spoke Das: "Till recent times, women lacked the social and intellectual authority to write seriously. There were certain prescribed norms for a woman's writing. When I was growing up, there was no tradition to fall back on, no model to emulate" ("My Instinct" 156). Both in the thematic and structural aspects of her poetry, Das absolutely distances herself from these Indian Romanticists. The Romanticists displayed an imitative tendency on the structural front, and penned beautiful poetry in soft chiselled words tacitly hailing the patriarchal culture and its ancillaries, whereas the dynamics of Das's poetry are promptly endowed with the angst born of woman in general being neglected. No traditional Indian woman-poet, she felt, had ever endeavoured to question the legitimacy of their own fosterage as social beings. They had written a kind of poetry that customarily tried to lure their own class to the feet of man-made gods or man-gods. In Das's own words:

> The prescribed themes for women's writings were God and domestic bliss. Nothing else. This body, this physicality was to be ignored. We had Avvayyar, Mirabai, but they wrote of God, they sang of God. That was allowed. But what happens to you, what happens to a woman, when a man becomes her god, her living god? Has she no right to write about that god? ("My Instinct" 156)

Right from her early childhood, Kamala Das appears to have

had a sublime awareness of her exact role. This awareness, this firm commitment, made her look at the surroundings in a different perspective. She felt the need to redefine beauty and ugliness in the feminine world, was determined to upset the apple-cart of the complacent world of male autocracy. For the same reason she rejects, but gracefully, the kind of poetry her predecessors wrote. She would certainly not come under their influence. Her perspective of beauty and ugliness is different from theirs. Says she: "I see a beauty of horrible kind in people. I see a kind of beauty which Sarojini Naidu did not see, and she had seen a kind of beauty I do not see. We have two separate visions" ("My Instinct" 158-159). Sarojini Naidu is a lyric voice, but her lyrical thrust merely comprehends what the *Rasa* School of poetry in India proposed as an aesthetic exposition. But Das, on her own acknowledgement, belongs altogether to a different category. As she had found exploitation of women at the social and psychological levels of Indian social system, she felt the compelling need of poetically opposing the feminine sufferings. If so, she has taken upon herself the province of tragic emotions born of centuries of neglect and suffering of women. This subjective tone and modality that she attributes for this suffering of women becomes the essential poetic figuration. Therefore, she considers her perception of 'beauty' as altogether different from that of a traditional lyric poet like Sarojini Naidu. While the 'beauty' of performing oneself as a traditional woman is the subject of Sarojini Naidu's poetry, altogether a compelling passion to express the anxieties and concerns of modern woman in all her troubled states of mind is the poetic province of Kamala Das. In other words, Kamala Das is a poet of tragic dimensions, while Sarojini Naidu is a votary of plastic dimensions of beauty.

3. *The Quintessential Modern Poet*

The revolting instinctive manner of looking at the gross creaturely nature of human survival, particularly in the context of male-female transactions, gives Kamala Das's poetry a sort of modernistic harrowing, agonizing dimensions. There is that nerves-fretting imposing manner of life constantly and continually contributing for a sort of shattering of the very naturalistic dignity of being woman in the context of our traditions. With a fervent zeal, she hopes to establish through her poetry altogether a new way of looking at woman as an entity created with a rare and unique prerogative in the naturalistic context. If so, her rebellion in itself contains that unique sense of modernism.

Then, modernism in literature is an ambiguous term. J.A. Cuddon defines "modernism" as a term "which describes the element of rebellion and innovation in new work which attempts to break from tradition." According to *Hutchinson Educational Encyclopaedia*, "modernism in art and literature" is "the conscious rejection of traditional forms and use of new forms of expression" ("Modernism"). However, the attempts 'to break from tradition' in the modern literature do not merely manifest in 'the conscious rejection of traditional forms,' but it also tries to express the collective sensibility of the time and space in which the author exists. In other words, the modern literature not only spells out the personal agonies of writers, but it also has a collective tonal vibrancy. As Wilbur Scott observes rightly, "Art is not created in a vacuum; it is the work not simply of a person, but of an author fixed in time and space, answering to a community of which he is an important because articulate part" (123). This is what Albert Camus had clarified by saying: "The unhappiness experienced by a single man becomes collective unhappiness . . . . I rebel—therefore we exist" (28).

The modern literature of Europe is experimental in nature, innovative in temper, and considerately humanistic in spirit as against the traditional egocentric heroic boastings of man as the centre of the universe. In this context, writers like N. Mallarme, Baudlaire, are the plinth makers of the modern temper or temperament. Precisely speaking, according to modernism, a poem is not an imitation of an action or an expression of the authentic interiority of the maker or the poet. Poets like T.E. Hulme, Ezra Pound, and T.S. Eliot, the avant-garde innovators of what we call modernism in poetry, had said that the modern poetic movement had on its stead Imagism, use of Symbolism, and the formula of audible and visual excitations.

The fact about modernism in general and modern poetry in

particular lies in the conscious realization of the exact human predicaments in the naturalistic, ideological, and social counters of existence and survival. Gone are the days where man-hero and his worship ruled the roost; in his place 'man-concerned' came to the forefront. As it had been suggested by Aldous Huxley, the twentieth century would not be remembered in future for its aeroplanes, its sky-scrapers, or for its atomic weaponry, but it would be remembered as an age in which man for the first time started thinking in terms of how it looks like being the other. Needless to say, the other, just as the self, is bound by physical, metaphysical, and cosmic limitations of being-in-the world; and a concerned and apt realization of these limitations is the true text of modern man's formula of understanding. This understanding in all its vibrant dimensions takes the form of an experimental poetic genre. In fact modernism in literature is more a matter of temper or temperament than the strategy of exposition. Even in the poetic strategies, the moderns are out and out experimental in nature. But the uniqueness of modern temper lies in comprehending life in a distinctly deviated angle. This way of perceiving life from a deferred angle in the moderns, while it is progressively attuned with enlightened humanistic impulses, readily contributes for a new and quickening experience that stands as unique in being a matter of perception.

With the advent of modernism, the Indian English poetry also came out of the Western classical imitation counters (Aristotle), as well as the expressionistic formulas. It also freed itself from the tedium of over-spirituality of the Aurobindian School of poetry, and embraced more relevant themes concerning the creaturely instinctive experiences of man. To quote Iyengar:

> The consciousness of the verbal medium, where it doesn't degenerate into a mere play with words, semantic pyrotechnics or promiscuous image-hunting, and where it doesn't dispense with the need for emotional or intellectual content, has given to the poetry of the moderns a freshness, a crispness, an immediacy and a vitality . . . (688)

Kamala Das's poetic temper is exactly born of frustration. What all that strikes modern in her poetry is revealed in the violent, irrepressible 'cry' of the occasion. Anger and fury are voluptuous emotions, which have their short rise and sudden fall in the inner authentic feeling self. The texture of her poems is aptly matched to the extent of the rouse of anger and fury, and, therefore, the poems envelope in themselves those harsh moments of serious reactions born of her stricken and shattered psyche. Hopelessness, condescending to cynicism, even pessimism, is the tonal significance. But this pessimism is not owing to a Hardian view of life against the backdrop of providential freaks. As Kurup points out, it is the articulation of "the universal angst of the modern feminine sensibility" (144). This is evident in the following lines of her poem "A Request":

> When I die
> Do not throw the meat and bones away
> But pile them up
> And
> Let them tell
> By their smell
> What life was worth
> On this earth
> What love was worth
> In the end. (D 5)

It is a stock taking, in a highly personalized style, of the sum total of achievements a woman has had in the process called 'life.' As a woman, life and its most vital ingredient i.e. love, gave her only memories of pain and disgust. For her, even before death life turns out to be as nauseating as the decaying flesh and bones. She speaks out her mind in the rhythmic onslaughts exactly as her feeling heart experiences them. Of all the Romantic poets, John Keats is the only poet who had given supreme importance for feelings. According to Helen Cixous, the modern women's writings directly appeal to feeling: "Let's look not at syntax but at fantasy, at the unconscious: all the feminine texts I've read are very close to the voice, very close to the flesh of language . . . perhaps because they don't rush into meaning, but are straightaway at the threshold of feeling" (489). True to Cixous' observation, Kamala

Das considers feelings as all-important. The stricken feelings of her heart are profoundly confessed into furious eruptions in her poems. Therefore, most of her poetry is conversational in form and lyrical in structure.

Judicious introspection and intense re-evaluation of the inherent human strengths and weaknesses is the ideological leap that the Renaissance humanism acquired for itself in our time; and the period after eighteen ninety, with its seriously concerned interrogative temper contributed for a dispassionate and honest search for the very nuances of being-in-the world and being-in-the universe. According to Kamala Das, being-in-the world is a matter of insufferable existential crisis, for woman particularly, in the male-predominant social environments. If being human is a unique privilege, being woman is a matter of greater concern and still greater responsibility in this world. Although Das borrowed her feminist ideological properties from the furious liberation movement of the West, her intimate knowledge and understanding of the Indian woman, and her special grievances born of centuries of neglect and subservience of women culminated into a serious and uncontrollable volcanic fury in her. This tinge of collective concern on behalf of woman in general, and Indian woman in particular makes her essentially a modern poetic voice.

4. *The Unique Poetic Voice*

Referring to Das's uniqueness as a modern Indian poet writing in English, K. Satchidanandan says:

> She is an Indian poet writing in English when Indian poetry in English is breaking free from the rhetorical and romantic traditions, when her male counterparts like Nissim Ezekiel and A. K. Ramanujan are struggling hard to form a dense, pithy and ironic idiom in their poems, and Jayanta Mahapatra is trying to relate his poetry to his immediate environment with pain and anger. (9)

The phenomenon of British poetry extricating itself from the 'rhetorical and romantic traditions' started with T.E. Hulme, Ezra Pound, and T.S. Eliot. Before this, Gerard Manley Hopkins and W.B. Yeats progressively contributed to make poetic imagery out of conversational language. Needless to say, the conversational language in any speech island is divided into various strata of operation; dialectic variations and the variations of their implementations in the kitchen, in the drawing room, in the market place, and even in the closed walls of the bedroom are significantly distinct. Taking the lead from T.S. Eliot [of *The Waste Land*], Kamala Das compounds her poetic strategies in the drawing room and bedroom jingo. That way, she is an earnest confessional poet speaking to herself in mono-logic monotones and complacent musings. As such, there is no place for 'rhetorical and romantic traditions' in her poetry. But then, interpersonal relations between man and woman being her principal theme, love as a certain phenomenon of human existence (not of the romantic sublime sort) becomes all-important in her poetry. Love, according to Kamala Das, is a sort of invitation by two competent personalities inviting each other for the purpose of mutually measuring the depth of their personalities. It does not mean that the so-called depth of the personalities is readily available for rational and mechanical mensurations. The depth of a personality has to be intuitively apprehended and instinctively conformed or confectioned into certain expressive verbal images. These verbal images in Kamala Das, which adumbrate themselves in a clear conversational language, take their origin in the instinctive manner of apprehending interpersonal gestures and relations. In this instinctive phenomenon of her poetic innovations in imagery, to the extent that it is related to the sublime aspirations of the British Romanticists (John Keats and P.B. Shelley prominently influenced her imagery filled with Romantic agony), there is a profound inbreeding of melancholy and frustration. Frustrated love and failing love-partner being the central themes of her poems, she is in close affinity to D.H. Lawrence and his mystic of love in its creaturely dimensions. Further, the 'dense, pithy, and ironic idiom' that Ezekiel and Ramanujan 'are struggling hard to form,' as suggested by Satchidanandan, came to Das as a spontaneous verbal force. So far as relating her poetry to the immediate environment is concerned, she is a better success than Mahapatra, as her environment is located in her authentic self as far serious self-reflective, self-emanating, self-evident, and self-fulfilling ideas concerning man-woman encounters in the familial as well as social counters. These ideas sometimes are so profound and strong that they become absolute confessional demonstrations of her inner most thoughts and feelings. The extra-vibrant and violent manner in which Kamala Das expresses her feelings and volitions finds equivalence in no other Indian English poets.

The influence of the feminists like Simone de Beauvoir and Virginia Woolf is far too obvious to make extended elaborations. Some modern American poets like William Carlos Williams also influence her poetry. The delicate and sensitive manner in which her poetic images spiral themselves into certain inverted and introverted imaginative interminable and never-ending reflections particularly designate her as a poet in a serious quest for meaning of being and becoming-in-the world.

No other voice in Indian literature could ever revolt with such tribal fury and violence as has been sounded in Das's poems against traditions and conventions. She has daringly defied the phallus as in the following lines of her poem "Conflagration":

> Woman, is this happiness, this lying buried
> Beneath a man? It's time again to come alive,
> The world extends a lot beyond his six foot frame.
> (D 20)

She is vibrantly declaring here her inner most feeling that the six foot male frame is not only insufficient for her aspirations, but also incapable of subjugating her identity which, she feels, is as profound and mysterious as nature itself. Das just wants to show the unlimited vibrancy of feminine creative principle as against what man thought it to be a suppressible living entity. She exhorts woman to realize her real significance as a being-in-the world. In a sense she wants to suggest that man can neither control, nor fulfil her personal needs of identity as a woman and as a creative principle. The expression 'again' in the second line is notable, for it stands as a pointer towards the prehistoric past when femininity had received the requisite eulogy in being the most important aspect in the schemes of nature in the matrilineal context. So Kamala Das's outcry, which appears to be a fervent furious personal onslaught, is really an invitation for a proper understanding of the feminine sentiments. It is all as though she is speaking as an official mouthpiece of every woman and her depravities. The tone of the above lines expresses a sort of uncontrolled and uncontrollable violence and fury, which is an assertion of uninhibited feminine freedoms and choices.

The modern sense of alienation, the nostalgic sentiments—both in spatial and temporal contexts, the anxiety syndrome, the nausea arising out of the girdling ugliness, all find a fuller and a more meaningful expression in Das than in any of her older or younger Indian poets writing in English. Nissim Ezekiel, as Iyengar comments, is a poet "who is willing to take pains, to cultivate reticence, to pursue the profession of poetry with a sense of commitment . . . " (657). Ezekiel turns around and writes with a sense of frustration and despondency about the poverty, deprivation, and the dirt and squalor of urban India, of course in a mocking tone, in lines such as the following from "Poverty Poems—2":

> I lifted up my eyes
> near the railway station
> and saw a leper standing
> against a poster-ridden wall (L. 1- 4)

But in Kamala Das, the objective pathetic pictures of social and cultural complexities of poverty and deprivation in India are substituted by the objectification of subjective animations of unfulfilled desires and the frustrations thereof. The following lines from the poem "The Seashore" will illustrate this point:

> On some evenings I drive past the cremation ground
> And seem to hear the crunch of bones in those vulgar
> Mouths of fire, or at times I see the smoke, in strands
> Slowly stretch and rise, like serpents, satiated
> Slow, content and, the only face I remember
> Then is yours, my darling, and the only words, your
> Oft-repeated plea, give me time, more time and I
> Shall learn to love. . . (BK 33)

The 'crunch of bones' in the 'vulgar / Mouths of fire' and 'the smoke / Slowly stretch(ing) and ris(ing), like serpents, satiated / Slow, content,' bringing the memory of the 'face' of the 'darling' has definitely undertones of the cruel satiation of carnal hunger by him who has still not learnt to 'love.'

A. K. Ramanujan's poetry revolves round his cultural past and the loss of ethnic roots. About Ramanujan's thematic concerns, Iyengar's observation is pertinent: "He [Ramanujan] is like one caught in the crossfire between the elemental pulls of his native culture and the aggressive compulsions of the Chicago milieu" (714). Both Ramanujan and Kamala Das are evidently caught 'in the crossfire between the elemental pulls' of their 'native culture and the aggressive compulsions' emerging out of the European enlightenment and progress. Particularly in the case of Kamala Das, the crumbled ethnic roots of her culture born out of East-West encounter become inflated poetic material. Here her poetry is typically informed by both the Freudian and Jungian dreams. It is true that all the poets are conscious of their personalities that go to drive and dive them into their creative manner of expressions. It is the vibrant presence of this personality in whatever they create that becomes poetically enthusing. If so, Kamala Das has a complex personality as a woman, which very often proposes itself as an unabashed 'schizoid.' In her the vibrant conscious self seeks a constant regress into libidinal ego, and the machismo in her reverts fiercely against it. In her poem "Summer in Calcutta" we have a rare fire of passion that drinks the "April sun":

> What is this drink but
> the April sun, squeezed
> like an orange in
> my glass? . . .
> . . . .
> What noble
> venom flows through
> my veins and fills my
> mind with unhurried
> laughter?. . .

. . . .
Dear, forgive
this moment's lull in
wanting you, the blur
in memory. How
brief the term of my
devotion, how brief
your reign. . . . (OP 24)

The 'April sun' being 'squeezed / like an orange in my glass' becomes an expression of contempt for feminine weakness. Therefore, a 'noble / venom flows through / my veins and fills my / mind with unhurried laughter.' This 'unhurried laughter' is born of her irrepressible machismo and 'this moment's lull in wanting you' (A hot desire for companionship) coming into a conflict with each other as split personalities in her, contending for supremacies and victory. Further, the "Wee bubbles ring / my glass like a bride's / nervous smile" (OP 24) explains her concern for the flimsy momentary nature of the pleasures of meeting. It all becomes a 'blur in memory' since the 'term of my / devotion, how brief your reign' ends when the drinking glass is still in her hand, with the 'wee bubbles ring / my glass' (A profound poetic analogy for John Keats' "beaded bubbles winking at the brim" ["Nightingale," L.17]). She ultimately implores her partner to 'forgive / this moment's lull in / wanting you' (a sharp stabbing irony) for "drink, drink, / And drink again this / juice of April suns" (OP 24). Here, the 'April sun' metaphor, in which the male counterpart is conceived, substantiates the idea for its fierceness as well as brief nature.

"Summer in Calcutta" is one of the early poems of Kamala Das, and it bears the autobiographical personal experience of her adolescence in Calcutta. The poem depicts a passionate infatuation for companionship, and the consequent half-fulfilled and frustrating manner in which the affairs end up. "Summer in Calcutta" very artistically blends the Jungian archetypes ('juice of April suns') with the Freudian agony ('Dear, forgive / this moment's lull in / wanting you, the blur / in memory').

R. Parthasarthy's poetry too compels a comparison with that of Kamala Das in the context of the influence of T.S. Eliot and his modern verve of imagery and symbols. In the poem "Homecoming," Parthasarthy writes:

This afternoon I dusted my table.
Arranged everything in order
in a desperate attempt to get hold of myself.
Later, I watched my forty years
swim effortlessly ashore in a glass of beer.
However, there is no end
to the deceptions I practise on myself:
I have, for instance, lived off friends.
Told the usual lies. (L. 94-102)

The intimate evocations towards T.S. Eliot's "Alfred J. Prufrock" and his 'insidious' rhetoric are obvious in the above lines. The squeaking voices of exploitation of her privacy, and the consequent unrest of the 'Lady Prufrock' are obviously present in the following lines of Das in the poem "The Freaks":

He talks, turning a sun-stained
Cheek to me, his mouth, a dark
Cavern, where stalactites of
Uneven teeth gleam, his right
Hand on my knee, while our minds
Are willed to race towards love;
But, they only wander, tripping
Idly over puddles of
Desire.... (OP 11)

'But, they only wander, tripping / Idly over puddles of / Desire...' has a suggestive and symbolic echo to the lines: 'the women come and go / Talking of Michelangelo' of Eliot's Prufrock.

However, in the midst of the Indo-Anglian poets touched upon above, the uniqueness of Das's poetic arguments lies in the fact that none of her contemporary poets, male or female, has shown the courage to directly assault the traditions, and question the legitimacy of culture and its antecedents. Kamala Das, on the other hand, confronts like a rebel, the glorified nastiness of human culture. To her the entire gamut of the history of human civilization and progress looks like a grotesque edifice of Gothic horrors. This denunciation, this defiance of human advance and progress finds expression in her poem 'Daughter of the Century':

> We ate our forefathers
>
> To gather the vigour for living.
>
> Our grandchildren shall perhaps eat us
>
> When their turn arrives. (BK 140)

The 'eat' metaphor used to express the manner in which we ate the tradition, and in turn hope our children to do the same is inflated and cannibalistic. But then, for Das, nothing short of cannibalism can serve the purpose of expressing her fury and agony. In the above cannibal metaphor she implies that one generation flourishes after having massacred and smashed the earlier one. If so, from generation to generation what perspires is not progress. On the other hand, it is all a vain show of failure in standing up to the credentials of the hopes and desires. In effect she wants to confirm poetically that generations after generations, it is always this failure to be that stares into the eyes of the individuals. The whole edifice of culture all through the ages shows the same symptoms of failure and distress. Therefore, there is nothing to be really proud of the human traditions that invariably hurdle the women folk to a marginalized status of being non-entities.

Thus, at more places than one, Kamala Das hints that the evolution of human society is strictly in contrast to the self-reflecting, self-fulfilling idealized greatness of human birth. She throws a question directly on to the face of human civilization: "Who can say for certain that we are superior / To the maggots that eat us in the end?" (BK 141). The macabre self-image of the individual here conflicts with the reality of the disciplined society. All kinds of animosity seep through the interstices of modern life, a sort of maggot culture feeds upon it, transforming the pragmatism of hatred into an essential commodity of every day existence. What differentiates Kamala Das from other Indian poets of her times also is this existential concern, this expression of anger against the set values of the present times. While it is true that her whole poetic property is against the backdrop of woman's concerns, she rather takes a broader view of human life and its tribulations, and argues out her cause with relevant questions that cover the whole of humanity. Whatever she utters poetically is immediately connectable to its human significance. Thus, Das's poetic personae represent the 'essential woman' in her manifold aspects, rebelling against traditions and conventions, with an underlying reminder of what should be true of humanity. When it comes to the crushing of the very natural felicities, her poetic personae experience an inordinate crisis of agony and restlessness, which in effect turns out to be an inconsolable 'cry' of the occasion. When a sense of self-pity attends such a 'cry,' her poetry becomes a vibrant symbolic gesture of showing a rebellious will to fight for her cause. The metaphors that she creates are highly charged with a sort of robust complexities. She confesses in "Loud Posters":

> I am today a creature turned inside
> Out. To spread myself across wide highways
> Of your thoughts, stranger, like a loud poster
> Was always my desire. . . . (OP 47)

In her autobiography *My Story* also Das expresses somewhat the same wish: "I have often wished to take myself apart and stick all the bits, the heart, the intestines, the liver, the reproductive organs, the skin, the hair and all the rest on a large canvas to form a collage which could then be donated to my readers" (217). Such a 'wish' arises from a passionate inner urge to metamorphose into something else out of the self. As Vincent O' Sullivan rightly points out: "It is the story of how a woman takes herself apart, so that when she is reassembled she has become her own creation. She *wants* that to be disturbing–as if *Nude Descending a Staircase* were a self-portrait that stepped from its frame and insisted on doing the living" (181). This poetic transmutation of the self is not for the sake of rhetoric, but it is an attempt to perceive oneself more objectively; and, when this is done, it puts her on verbal excruciations flaring into abject ravings of a creature wriggling and spiralling under the ideological pressures of life, like Kafka's cockroach. Hence, life as a given for Kamala Das is a Kafkaish unending agony through a trial. So far as the modern human predicament is concerned, Franz Kafka created the insufferable boils and blisters, and Albert Camus wriggled the wounds. Kamala Das peeps at these boils, blisters, and wounds with an assiduous intention of revealing the very pain of being an ever-neglected woman. This sui generis quality, this creaturely approach towards one's being, against the backdrop of institutional pressures, is what makes Kamala Das the unique voice of Indian English poetry.

D. ***Formative Years***

Kamala Das was born in *Punnayurkulam*, Northern Kerala in 1934 to a poet-mother (Her mother Balamani Amma is a well known Malayalam poet) and a businessman-father. Her father migrated to Bengal, and thereby his children got an enviable exposure to multicultural parameters. Das's childhood spent in the Missionary School of Bengal greatly contributed for her individualism, as yet a child, whereby she had an opportunity to learn the primary lessons of Individualism and Humanism as propagated by the European Renaissance and the eighteenth century European enlightenment. The ideas of European enlightenment and progress supplemented the streak of inborn trenchant individualism in her. In spite of the fact that the European enlightenment and the ideas of material progress are a natural fall-out of British Imperialism and Colonialism, Das never developed any inhibition or hatred in adopting for herself the progressive ideas of Enlightenment and Individualism. The foreign rule and cultural exploitation do not appear to have bothered her much. She progressively attached herself to the modern British poetic experimentations that started from T.E. Hulme, Ezra Pound, W. B. Yeats, and T.S. Eliot.

As far as Das's formal education is concerned, she did not have a regular school education and never attended any college. After the short-lived European missionary school education in

Calcutta, she was sent to an elementary school at her native place in North Kerala, and was subsequently admitted to a Boarding school run by Catholic nuns. However, she was again removed to Calcutta when she fell ill in the Boarding school, and was put under home-tuition. The school years, however, were a period for moulding of Kamala's very sensitive poetic sensibility.

Apart from the experience of racial discriminations she encountered in the European missionary school, another factor which might have made a deep scar in her already hurt sensibility is the discord between her father and mother as a couple, who, as she tells in her autobiography, "were dissimilar and horribly mismated" (MS 5). This discord, however, did not develop to reach a stage of serious conflict or divorce owing to the timidity of the mother, thus creating an "illusion of domestic harmony" (MS 5). This parental conflict in the family with an upper hand of the father is the starting point of her feministic views and grievances.

Although her father had not much time for his children, he very prudently and mechanically discharged his duties as a father. In the poem "Next to Indira Gandhi" Das hints at the kind of restriction he must have imposed on his children, particularly on Kamala as a female child: "You chose my clothes for me / My tutors, my hobbies, my friends, / And at fifteen with my first saree you picked me a husband" (OSK 118). Her father originally implanted in her a permanent sore and scare towards men and their manners, and in course of time the same scare grew in her psyche to assume alarming dimensions with the unloving manners of her husband, and remained a lifetime sore. The result is her autobiographical painful poetry. But the autobiographical status is a mere poetic ploy. Her real feminine anxieties are prominently inherited from the autocratic, chauvinistic systems in which she was forced to live as a marginalized, self-denigrated woman.

However, the sparks of fire really went ablaze within her with the very early marriage (at the age of sixteen) with a relative, living with whom she saw all her adolescent dreams crumble to the ground. As she tells in her autobiography, and also as her many poems suggest, her husband was an unkind, unloving man who had had sexual encounters with his maidservants. He used his wife only to show the sexual acrobatics he had learnt from his earlier bouts, "veteran that he was in his rowdy ways of sex which he had practised with the maids who worked for his family" (MS 93). The abnormal manner of diverting and directing her anger towards the issues speaks for the painful manner in which she suffered the companionship of her perennially failing partner in love. From here onwards, her life, if we take her autobiography *My Story* as factual record of events in her life, was a tale of woes and illness. But it is interesting to note that her autobiography, like many of her poems, is a mixture of facts and fiction. Her expectations in life were idealized and her experiences romanticized, but the ultimate outcome is her very vibrant, and emotionally charged poems expressed in extraordinary and powerful language, revealing the interiorities of a very sensitive feminine psyche, responding aggressively to the Indian familial and socio-cultural complexities.

Finally, as regards Kamala Das's quantitative achievements, it becomes pertinent to briefly look at her major works. Das is a bi-lingual writer, writing both in Malayalam and English. (In Malayalam she writes under the pseudonym *Madhavikutty*; has produced many volumes of short stories and novelettes). She is the winner of the Poetry Award of the Asian PEN Anthology in 1963, and the Kerala Sahitya Akademi Award in 1969 for her Collection of Short Stories in Malayalam *Thanuppu*, ("Cold"). She has published six Collections of Poems in English, viz., *Summer in Calcutta* (1965), *Descendants* (1967), *Old Playhouse And Other Poems* (1973), *Collected Poems* (1984), *The Best of Kamala Das* (1991), and *Only the Soul Knows How to Sing* (1996). She has also collaborated with Pritish Nandy, another notable Indian poet in English, in bringing out a volume of love poems, viz., *Tonight This Savage Rite* (1979). Her most controversial book, her fictional autobiography, *My Story*, was first published in Malayalam (*Ente Katha*), and was later translated by herself into English (1976). She has also published a novel, *The Alphabet of Lust* (1976), and three volumes of translations of her short stories viz., *A Doll for the Child Prostitute* (1977), *Padmavati, the Harlot and Other Stories* (1992) and *The Sandal Trees and Other Stories* (1998). Apart from these works she has written many articles in journals and periodicals, a few of which are: "I Studied All Men" (*Love and Friendship*, Sterling, 1973), "What Women Expect out of Marriage, and What They Get" (*Femina*, July 1974), "Why Not More Than One Husband" (*Eve's Weekly*, May 1972), and "I Have Lived Beautifully" (*Debonair*, May 1974). In the year 2000, she published a collection of articles entitled *The Path of the Columnist*.

Kamala Das's poetry has established a fervent ground for poetic expression of the feminine freedoms and choices, which she considers as the urgent necessities of existence with due dignity and honour in the context of our times. At the same time, she is painfully aware that the real predicament of being woman in the male-chauvinistic counters of modern civilization concerns with the impossibility of reconciling her creaturely survival against the backdrop of spiritual heights theoretically sanctioned to the dignity of being human. Her argumentations are perpetually haunted by the sense of this impending failure at the end. Her poetry, therefore, abounds in feminine angst and violence. Her women protagonists assume the role of herself, the Indian woman, and eventually, overcoming geographical and ethnic considerations, go to identify with the essential womanhood. As S. C. Harrex puts it, "In stressing the personal tenor and texture of Kamala Das's poetic voice the extra-personal elements in her idiom should not be overlooked" (165). Here, the expression 'extra-personal elements' clarifies that her overall assessment of the feminine predicaments are born of the women's liberation movement of the West, and her poetry is not a mere outcome of her autobiographical counters. In fact the subjectively compounded 'personal voice' gives a rare authenticity to her irrepressible feminine transparencies.

Before summing the discussion in this chapter it is worth recalling a statement by Elaine Showalter on George Eliot, which reads, ". . . most ninteenth century women novelists seem to have found [Eliot] a troubling and demoralizing competitor, one who had created an image of the woman artist they could never equal" (qtd. in Gilbert 493). On the same analogy one çan evaluate Kamala Das as a poet in the context of Indian women poetry in English. Das's achievement of the absolute rebellious dimensions in her poetry places her as the only voice of its kind in the milieu of Indian women-poetry in English. In fact she has revolutionized the conventional notions about the definition and scope of Indian women-poetry in its structural, thematic, and tonal aspects. The women poets preceded and came after her have never shown such intrepidity and audacity in stretching their "two dimensional / Nudity on sheets of weeklies, monthlies, Quarterlies . . . ("Loud Posters," OP 47). With no model to emulate, Das invented her own stylistic manner of expressions most suitable to the thematic concerns that she wanted to handle. As Bruce King remarks, "Das opened areas in which previously forbidden or ignored emotions could be expressed in ways which reflect the true voice of feeling; she showed how an Indian woman poet could create a space for herself in the public world" (152). She has set a tradition of a new generation-women-poetry in the Indian poetic scene that would definitely continue to kindle the fire in the women poets of the coming times.

In the foregoing pages, an attempt has been made to examine the uniqueness and significance of Kamala Das as a modern feminist poet in the Indian context. But any attempt to pigeonhole a poet of her stature within the framework of a particular philosophy would be tantamount to undermining her creative achievements. As Vincent O' Sullivan rightly comments, "there is much in Das that will not be herded into the clear boundaries we may try to erect. She is no more worried than was Walt Whitman that she contradicts herself, omits, exaggerates. It might be argued that her texts offer no bonding centre of control" (193). Sullivan's statement is true in the light of what Das herself says in one of her answers: "I have not chosen any particular philosophy to guide me in life. I change too fast for any philosophy. I move too fast for any message to catch up with me" (qtd. in Saha 16). Here we are reminded of Camus' lines: "The true philosophy is the negation of philosophy. No religion is my religion. No philosophy is my philosophy" (118).

The attempt in the foregoing pages, however, was to determine Kamala Das's standing (certainly not an inconsequential one) in the overall scenario of Indian English poetry of our times.

Having done this, an attempt has been made in the following chapters to analyse the sources of the exclusive feminine violence in her poetry, and the significance and relevance thereof against the backdrop of socio-cultural and aesthetic parameters.

2

Sources of Violence

Taking upon herself the mantle of being a mouthpiece of Indian women, Kamala Das looks at the predicament of gender inequity as an incurable canker that struck the human civilization and spread its tentacles to the body politic in India and its decadent tradition. She is aware that this disease affects the whole of humanity, and that the same has to be recognized and diagnosed beyond the immediate socio-cultural and ethnic boundaries. Therefore, she superimposes through her violent poetic expressions the ideas of the Western women's liberation movement mutatis mutandis in the Indian scenario in her fight against the social, familial, linguistic, and cultural subservience of women both in the physiological and psychological contexts. She tries to understand the deeply hidden woes of average Indian woman, and poetically expresses her concern in all their verbal manifestations. Of all the women poets of the present in India, she projects herself as a fervent feminist poetic voice always exacting for a dignified place of honour, a respect for the naturalistic freedoms and choices of woman. Thus, Das's poetry contributes for the strong reactions and justifications for the most needful awakening of woman as a living entity in being-in-the world. The element of violence and angst in her poetry emerges chiefly from her concern on woman's loss of personality as a result of the conditioned and passive state in which she is destined to exist in almost all the counters of human interaction. As she says in her poem "The Siesta," the world she lives in looks like an "alien world which talks / of Gods and casual sins," where she longs

to pick herself an average
identity, to age
through years of earthy din
gently, like a cut flower until
it's time to be removed. . . . (BK 9)

So in this 'alien world which talks / of Gods and casual sins,' she, being a woman, is hardly recognized to be a person. Thus, a major source of violence in Kamala Das's poetry can be attributed to the personality crisis that she as a woman faces in our biased social system.

Personality Crisis

Personality is a concept that needs explanation. Personality and ego are commonly used synonyms, though they do not have exactly the same meaning. According to G.W. Allport, personality is "the dynamic organization within the psychophysical systems that determine his or her unique adjustment to his or her environment" (48). According to modern psychology and psychiatry, personality is a reflection of the inner self of a person. Since the goal of the self is continuous victory achieved through liberating experiences, whenever this sense of victory is crushed mercilessly by the institutional prerogatives in the society, it struggles to reconcile to such despondency, and confronts them restlessly. This restlessness is born out of the apprehension by the ethical, moral, and religious surroundings that always make ominous inroads into the familial interpersonal dimensions of life, and contribute for a sort of checkmating the personality. As a result, a desperate longing for freedom is born within the self out of a keen desire for liberation, not of the sort that is prominently projected by religion, called *moksha* ("redumption"), but significantly evolved by psychology as 'sublimation.' Insistence on this sublimation accordingly in the man-woman intimate affairs is a coveted necessity. But this sublimation comes only in a free and frank atmosphere of transparency and dependency on the mutual attitudes and dispositions. Modern feminists argue that achievement of this sublimation, technically called orgasm, is a birthright of all women, which is cognate with what the modern psychologists call the 'aha' experience achieved by the human organic system in the course of the interpersonal involvements.

1. *Interpersonal Relations and Personality Crisis*

Kamala Das gives vent to the intense feelings of frustration born out of the discrimination imposed upon the feminine counterpart in the process of her achieving the finite ultimate sublime 'aha' experience. The word 'sublime' also in its original context smacks of the esoteric and religious phenomenal context. But then, the act of love between man and woman conforms itself to offering an infelt highest satisfaction, again, by the 'person,' in its intense desire for assertion of its liberation through freedom from the outward clutches that hold it tight and unassertive. This process of imposing checks on achieving the ultimate 'sublime' experience is consistently rebelled at by Das in her poetry. In her poetic rebellion she never hesitates to destroy and demolish the age-old conventions and traditions insofar as they become boulders and speed-breakers in the process of her personality aspiring for the most requisite liberation through sublimation. This kind of free and frank achievement of sublimations, again, is a matter of personal necessity. Life for Kamala Das is a personal affair. The immense charm of this personal affair emerges out of transparent, clear, and uninhibited interpersonal engagements of men and women. But in the patriarchal egoistic world, these requisite transparencies are brutally effaced due to sheer ignorance and neglect of feminine needs by the male partner. There is a very moving suggestion of this kind of neglect on the part of the male partner in the poem "The Motif in the Mirror":

> How shall I describe that first embrace, you have not seen
>
> The many mirrors in his room. When we embraced, we fell in their
>
> Cerulean pools as a deathless motif, repeating, repeating,
>
> Repeating this reflection of a reflection, this shadow of
>
> A shadow, this dream of a dream, and I knew him then by knowing who

> I was, and knew myself more by knowing who he was, but he said,
>
> Rising from my side, it is eight, get up 'sweet wife' I'll take you home.
>
> (OSK 37)

What is presented here is the brutal imposition of the male ego on the female partner, which comes in the way of her attaining a sublime satisfaction in 'that first embrace.' The exhilaration and ecstasy experienced by the female persona suddenly collapses with such interference that creates in the sensibility virtually a vacuum as if someone stoned down and splintered in one flash the 'many mirrors in his room.' If so, the intense Freudian overtones and undertones are obvious. Woman's quest for emotional involvement with the partner in the act of love invariably ends up in a sort of enslaving herself under his autonomous impositions. Woman desperately needs liberation from this traumatic experience of "lying buried / beneath a man" (Conflagaration, D 20). Woman particularly suffers from a sort of colossal denial of her due when her male counterpart absolutely lacks the necessary objectivity and sensibility to be a love partner. Engagement with such a partner is certainly a matter of 'lying buried' as an unfeeling deadwood as though she does not have any genetic living responses to offer. Das rightly points out that the woman's world and the woman's necessities, in being love-partners, have really a great vibrancy that goes unattended to by men.

2. *Indian Women and the Personality Crisis*

Kamala Das as a feminist poet realizes the personality crisis of the Indian women strategically perpetrated and perpetuated by the unbending patriarchal traditions, and she violently reacts to this situation. In the characteristically unrelenting Indian socio-cultural milieu, where any surface commotion does not percolate very easily, particularly when it is against traditions and conventions, Das makes a poetic revolt by way of introspectively pondering upon the unfortunate state of existence in which Indian women conduct themselves. Like a seasoned artist, she penetrates her imaginative insight to sympathetically understand the possible average grievances of the Indian woman as extremely exploited agent in the social, ethical, moral, and existential circumstances.

The Indian woman, in spite of the classical eulogies paying to her in the literary traditions, was allotted a place of negligence even in the practical domestic circumstances from time to time. This kind of biased treatment meted out to women irked Kamala Das to the extreme. The invisible agony that woman suffers as a mother, as a wife, and as a daughter, particularly in the Indian familial context, is the proper subject of her poetic activity. As a poet she presents herself as a crusader in revolt against this kind of injustice. Das's concept of freedom leads her to an existential conflict with the traditional social institutions like marriage, family, and the society as a whole, which put on woman shackles of domesticity where she is required to play the pre-determined roles of "happy woman" and "happy wife" as she says in "The Suicide" (D 2). This concern further finds violent and moving expressions in poems like "The Old Playhouse," "The Stone Age," "I Shall Some Day." In the "Old Playhouse," she indicts her man for his brutal manners in the companionship:

> You planned to tame a swallow, to hold her
> In the long summer of your love so that she would forget
> Not the raw seasons alone, and the homes left behind, but
> Also her nature, the urge to fly, and the endless
> Pathways of the sky. (OP 1)

Here Das appears to be vociferously bargaining for a sort of colossal appeasement of her instinctive needs for freedom as a woman. She attributes for herself symbolically the personality of a 'swallow,' and in the very first line there is a suggestion that a great plan or scheme was made in order 'to tame a swallow.' Swallow is not a tameable bird like a parrot. In its 'season' it makes its own joyful unrestrained flights in the sky. The irony in the expression 'the long summer of your love' is notable. In the tropical countries 'summer' is attributed to anything unbearable, but here, the poet attributes it to 'love.' But no 'long summer of love' can hold a 'swallow' imprisoned, as the rainy season is bound to come. In a sense she wants to suggest that men have grossly erred in considering woman as a tameable entity.

She already makes it clear to reawaken in herself the 'raw seasons' and 'the homes left behind.' She also wants to acquaint herself with her 'nature.' In a very complacent and loving manner she confirms that her nature (i.e. woman's nature) is in the 'urge to fly' along 'the endless pathways of the sky.' The childlike autistic daydreaming is hinted at. But at the same time she is very clear that nature had awarded her with immense potentialities, and the exploration of those potentialities is the only purpose of woman opting man as her momentary partner in love.

Interpersonal love, in the sense of two concerned partners struggling to arrive at a harmonious sublimation, is a matter of serious mutual responsibility. But Kamala Das's experience in life warrants her that the partners' sharing of a common purpose of sublimation detracts themselves on the opposite directions. Her self-love and the urgency of concerns for herself on the one hand, and his Narcissistic inversion into himself with a great urgency of serving his own sublime purpose on the other bring forth a sort of emotional conflict. This is further clarified in the following lines:

> The strong man's technique is
>
> Always the same, he serves his love in lethal doses
>
> For, love is Narcissus at the water's edge, haunted
>
> By its own lonely face. . . . (OP 1)

In the above lines male love that was like a 'long summer' in the beginning of the poem transforms into a slow poison served 'in lethal doses.' As S.C. Harrex puts it, "The narcissistic picture of love in "The Old Playhouse" introduces an interesting perspective on the themes in Kamala Das's poetry that are concerned with the quest for identity through sexual passion and through the giving and receiving of love" (171). But the aspirations of attaining orgasm and sublimation, and the 'identity' of being human 'through sexual passion and through the giving and receiving of love' do not ever gain success in the patriarchal concept of familial relationships, where the female partner either becomes a tamed 'swallow,' or a "granite / Dove" into whose dreaming eye the barbarous husband "stick a finger" as she suggests at in the poem "The Stone Age" (OP 51). How a woman's personality shrinks in the man's totalitarian state called family is poignantly revealed in "The Stone Age." She indicts her husband for what he is, but at the same time suggestively does a sobbing bargain for kindness from him:

> Fond husband, ancient settler in the mind,
> Old fat spider, weaving webs of bewilderment,
> Be kind. You turn me into a bird of stone, a granite
> Dove, you build round me a shabby drawing room,
> And stroke my pitted face absent-mindedly while
> You read. With loud talk you bruise my pre-morning sleep,
> You stick a finger into my dreaming eye. . . . (OP 51)

At the outset, the very title of the poem "The Stone Age" alludes to the barbarous nature of her man in their mutual transactions. Thus the 'swallow' image of the "Old Playhouse" and the 'granite / Dove' image of "The Stone Age" assume the same status, trapped in the 'webs of bewilderment' woven by her man ('Old fat spider'). In this context, Ramachandran Nair rightly observes: "'The Stone Age' is, thematically, a continuation of 'The Old Playhouse.' The condemnation of male insensitivity is in more fierce terms and the glorification of an extra-marital affair imparts it a strange significance as one of the crucial poems in Kamala Das's contrived system of male-abhorrence" (39). In "The Stone Age" she suggests at this 'extra marital affair,' apparently imaginary, in order to avenge the inconsiderate nature of her own man:

> When you leave, I drive my blue battered car
> Along the bluer sea. I run up the forty
> Noisy steps to knock at another's door.
> Through peep-holes, the neighbours watch,
> they watch me come
> And go like rain. . . . (OP 51)

Here there is a broad confessional statement concerning the feminine needs of sublimation. Modern sexologists confirm that there is a substantial difference in the orgasmic experience in man and woman. Man arrives at it at one jolt towards the end of the coitus, while woman has the inherent physical potency to arrive at it innumerable times during one session of love-play. Quite naturally, after man single-handedly serving the purpose of his sublimation, woman still needs a companionship to achieve her multiple orgasms. In the above lines, the poet vibrantly confirms the inner urgent need of woman in the companionship. Herein probably lies the naturalistic difference between man and woman. While man's need is acquired sublimation through the feminine counterpart, woman's need is that Platonic complexity called 'love' for want of any better verbal equivalent. By stating 'When you leave, I drive my blue battered car / Along the bluer sea. I run up the forty / Noisy steps to knock at another's door,' the poet wants to make it clear that a mere sublimation through ejaculation as it happens it in man is not at all the end or goal of love-play for woman. Simon de Beauvoir's observation in this context is worth quoting:

> . . . there is no doubt that for man coition has a definite biological conclusion: ejaculation. In woman, on the contrary, the goal is uncertain from the start, and more psychological in nature than physiological; she desires sex excitement and pleasure in general, but her body promises no precise conclusion to the act of love; and that is why coition is never quite terminated for her; it admits of no end . . . . even when overwhelmed, exhausted, she may never find full deliverance . . . (134-135)

Such being the true nature of the difference in the attainment of sexual pleasure between man and woman personalities, the ultimate requisite satisfaction comes to woman in keeping herself entangled with the companionship even after man exhausted himself. Here it is just possible that the exhausted man keep the companionship intact if only he realizes the naturalistic variances in the award of pleasure through multiple orgasms in woman. However, insofar as it is a state of nature, man, even as a vibrant and sympathetic partner cannot really help his woman in being a consistent partner until woman comes to a total satisfaction of companionship. This is all the more the reason that man is required to be a seasoned artist as a lover and not a mere male-animal that serves his own purpose and cold-shoulders his partner after. The whole fight of Kamala Das against men aims at coaxing the men-folk to become the necessary artists in love rather than relegating themselves to the mere male animal status. Behind the whole poetic fury and rebellion, the essential purpose of Das is to affect in men-folk a right co-ordination of their sense and sensibility in relation to woman with a particular reference to love-act, as well as in reference to the general social and cultural attitudes and disposition towards women. What she wants to imply is that in the naturalistic state of experience, love for woman is an inexhaustible and interminable course of activity. Thus, in the love-play both woman and man are equally active partners, but in their own ways. The lines, 'they watch me come / And go like rain' indicate the shortness of her stay, and the frustration she has at the end of the whole affair. The concluding lines: "Ask me why life is short and love is / Shorter still, ask me what is bliss and what its price . . . " (OP 51) are ironic and in fact imply that these are the questions to which even she could not find any answers.

This sort of imaginary wish-fulfilment of having freedom from familial bondage appears also in "I Shall Some Day" where she, in a challenging tone, addresses her partner in love:

> I shall some day leave, leave the cocoon
> You built around me with morning tea,
> Love words flung from doorways and of course
> Your tired lust. I shall some day take
> Wings, fly around, as often petals
> Do when free in air. . . . (OP 48)

Here we have a very interesting feminine confession put forth as a grudging reaction to what men usually compound in themselves as a phenomenon of doubting the fidelities of their women; woman might go to somebody else is a haunting doubt in man's psyche stuffed in the most conservative dimension of patriarchal traditions. Such wavering thoughts of man being given a confessional shape by his woman is only a matter of expression of the immensity of personal freedoms being vibrant in an assured ground of understanding.

But the source of her pain and violence within is the awareness of the impending failure at the end of each endeavour to free herself out of the 'webs of bewilderment.' However hard she tries to run away from the snare of domesticity she knows that some day she would have to

> . . . return, losing
> Nearly all, hurt by wind, sun and rain,
> Too hurt by fierce happiness to want
> A further jaunt or a further spell
> Of freedom, and I shall some day see
> My world, de-fleshed, de-veined, de-blooded,
> Just a skeletal thing, then shut my
> Eyes and take refuge, if nowhere else,
> Here in your nest of familiar scorn. . . . (OP 48)

Nair finds in the above lines "a sense of incurable ambivalence in the woman's strange urge to flee and to return and then again to 'jaunt' for a further spell of freedom. This paradox illustrates the freakishness of desire" (15). Nair misses the point, for what the woman persona says is a negative fact, that is, she would be 'Too hurt' to 'want / A further jaunt or a further spell / Of freedom.' Rather than the 'freakishness of desire,' it is her knowledge of the hurting nature of the 'fierce happiness' outside her husband's 'nest of familiar scorn' that compels a return. The point to be borne in mind is the fact that whenever she talks about the extra-marital relationships and the 'freedom' of the outside world, it is a product of her imagination, and these lines suggest that the world of imagination is short-lived, and ultimately she has to return and shrink into her man's 'nest of familiar scorn.' We have such famous lines of John Keats as: "Adieu ! the fancy cannot cheat so well / As she is fam'd to do, deceiving elf" ("Nightingale," L. 73-74). In both the cases it is the loneliness of the self that induces the mind to wander in imagination, and at the same time, it is the self's awareness of the inevitability to return to the stark realities of life that becomes the source of agony and violence. So far as her freedom of fancy is concerned, the younger Romanticists like Keats and Shelley greatly influence Kamala Das. The profound flights of imagination are quite fanciful and only real to the interior authentic modalities of poetic imagination asserting itself as a free and precise voice of personal freedoms shared in the imagined intimacies of male-female involvements. This kind of imaginary flight can be traced in another love poem called "Ghanashyam":

> In love when the snow slowly began to fall
> Like a bird I migrated to warmer climes
> That was my only method of survival
> In this tragic game the unwise, like children, play
> And often lose in. (CP 94)

The escape motive is obvious. The poet wants a childlike sojourn into the imaginary world, as the practical world is a cruel, coercive phenomenon. No doubt, for the poet life has been a losing game. Nevertheless, she would like to play this 'tragic game' indefatigably.

These extra-marital poetic stipulations that Kamala Das makes are purely fallouts of her autistic poetic imagination. Autism is a very interesting psychological phenomenon that shows in children beset at home resorting to impossible daydreams. Das's poetically vibrant escape modalities through flirting are such autistic imaginative poetic artefacts. They are in the nature of that of a daydreaming child who ultimately knows the contingent impossibility of really making his daydreams true. However, these fantastic imaginative flights have their own purpose for the poet. As Irshad Ahmed rightly observes,

> Trapped in a loveless relationship with an insentiate husband, the poetic persona escapes into fantasy and myth. What is denied to her in the real world is attainable in the shadowy world. The two worlds, as is clear, complement each other. Thus, a major aspect of her creativity can be called wish-fulfilment . . . . Thus, in her poems and her autobiography *My Story* the descriptions of and references to extra-marital love-

> affairs are nothing but fantastic adventures of the searching self during its sojourn in that 'shadowy world'. (131)

She knows that her flirtatious authentic poetic flights of imagination cannot really be achieved. They are not even really meant to be achieved; they are just there to be imaginatively engrossed and absorbed in a poetic moment. Therefore, she comes back to her partner's 'nest of familiar scorn.' The spacious imaginative freedom that she shares in her poetic flights is a mere chimera, but it is a threatening chimera for her as well as for her man. This is what Ahmed observes in the above lines while talking about her aggressive poetic efforts to conquer in imagination what has been denied to her in reality.

Thus, woman as a being, particularly in the Indian familial context, is almost a non-entity, a thing to be used and forgotten like any other tool. In the patriarchal mode of familial relations, she has always been like a tamed 'swallow' or a 'granite dove' whence her self always longs to fly away, but eventually it has to come back helplessly, sliding "pegs of sanity into / A bed made soft with tears" as is suggested in the poem "The Sunshine Cat" (OSK 54). Das's aggressive feminine sensibility is not ready to compromise on these social and familial parameters, and in the real world when she meets with non-recognition, personality crisis, and deprivation of the natural feminine experience both physical and metaphysical, her poems become violent outcries of the occasions. Her poetic world is a world of equality, freedom, love, and recognition of her feminine demands, as woman being the most important creative agent in the naturalistic context. The underlying principle of her ideal feminine world, as is portrayed in her poetry, is the quest for freedom from the vortex of social and familial tie-ups without being detrimental to the naturalistic feminine prerogatives and sensibilities. In that world both the sexes have equal significance. It has no norms for dominations or subordinations by any side. The freedom should come from within. The achieved or bestowed freedom can only deceive, and finally become "a dancing shoe" ("Composition," D 30). On the other hand, the real freedom should emerge from the bedrock of human existence itself without strings attached to it. Freedom should be inherent in the life processes, should be as indispensable as birth and growth, as natural as 'leaves on a tree', and as inevitable as death itself. Kamala Das aspires to achieve this unhindered freedom for herself knowing fully well that such atmosphere of freedom and choice is not at all available for her in the caged context of the woman's psyche. The more she feels the external constraints that cage her being, the more rebellious she becomes in her poetic imagery and rhetoric. While the imagery is quite uninhibited, quite fearlessly, the rhetoric of her poetry takes upon itself an irrepressible tone of agony and pain.

Alienation and the Ensuing Frustration

Another essential source of violence that gives its immense vibrancy to Kamala Das's poetry can be traced to the alienation syndrome. Since alienation syndrome is a pervasive phenomenon in the modern literature in general, and in the modern women's literature in particular, a brief discussion on the cause of this alienation syndrome in general instantly becomes pertinent before its particular effect on Kamala Das's poetry is taken up.

We have innumerable traditional cultural, social, ethical, and moral institutions, which contributed for the well being of humanity from time to time in the course of the historical past. These traditional institutions assume upon themselves certain broad, rigid formal parameters. With the growth and development of understanding in the intellectual dimensions, these rigid laws and conventions become quite nonadjustable to all the individuals at a time and to some individuals at various times. Thus, there is always a sort of tie and tension between individuals and the institutions in spite of the fact that these institutions are originally supposed to be protective, life-giving forms. Alienation, as such, is mostly a psychological context, which emerges as a potential reactionary force in a personality, particularly when the personality becomes incapable of adjusting harmoniously with the existing stringent laws of the institutions. Needless to say, the dawn of individualism coupled with a sense of unrestrained freedom of man that had become a mode of individual disposition after the Renaissance, probably contributed for a kind of unbridgeable cleavage between man with his strong determination to assert his freedom of mind, and the traditional social institutions which are more or less equally unbending in its rigid structural parameters. Somehow, instead of a free, frank, and transparent give and take between man and these institutions in which he prevails, there emerged a sort of irresolvable strife and tension between the members. As a result, the institutions started alienating the individual gradually; and the individual too started wilfully distancing himself from the rigid pursuit of the institutions. When the institutions kick at the individual it is called alienation, but when the individual starts kicking at the institutions it becomes a matter of resignation and renunciation. In both the cases, the individual suffers a great agony and strife.

1. *The Psychic Origins*

The poetic sparkles of women being alienated can be originally traced to the songs and anecdotes which are available in almost all the Indian languages. In the songs of the tribal people, we find glaring examples of the alienation syndrome verging upon out and out pornographic dimensions. Kamala Das inherited these two strains–alienation and pornographic imagery—from the songs of women and tribal folks of the past, in principle. But then, she is quite ingenious in coordinating and comprehending the feminine anxieties and tribal furies with the par excellence modern feminist literary fundaments of the West. In fact, Kamala Das made a profound innovation of the Indian feminine psyche being associated with the modern Western feminist literature.

P.K.J. Kurup feels that the feeling of alienation in Kamala Das emerges from a conflict between her individualism and the democratic upsurge in the country because, according to him, her individualism "prevents her from identifying herself with the larger democratic upsurge in the country and feels herself alienated from the society which expects women to be modest, submissive, unobtrusive and destined to be buried beneath a man's six-foot frame" (283). The so-called democratic upsurge in the country stooping to annihilate and destroy the democratic rights of Kamala Das as an individual is quite ironical. This also confirms the fact that India had adopted the 'democratic upsurge' in a half-hearted manner. So long as Das is not absolutely transgressing the fundamental laws of rhetoric, her democratic rights as an individual should not be questioned. While her conflict with the society can be chiefly attributed to her 'self-conscious individualism,' one cannot overlook her biographical particulars that have played a very important role in developing this aggressive individualism in her, and moulding her rebellious creative mind. If so, in Das's case, the character of alienation is not only of a historical nature but is an amalgam of various factors viz., social, familial, intellectual, and above all of the man-woman intimate relations, all of which came together to weave the "webs of bewilderment" (OP 51) around her. Her rebellion is also due to the biographical constraints that she suffered even as a child in the school, in the house, and in the society. In this context, her *My Story* is an autobiographical sketch of her own rebellious personality. When the family and other social institutions had shown no proper concern at all for women, she felt a compulsive need to present and represent the agony and pain of women being sidelined, alienated, and declared unworthy of human dignities and understandings. If so, it is a sort of psychological trauma that she undergoes, and the tone and tenor of her poetry vibrantly expresses her excessively traumatized self in its condition of privation, disownment, and more particularly dishonour. In the words of Arlene Zide, "She [Kamala Das] refuses the mold [sic] others would have her fit; her alienation from all such molds [sic], be they 'proper' language to write in, or 'proper' female role, are at the heart of what she is saying about being free, to be the 'I' she is" (240). So rather than freedom to be, what she experiences is a sort of distancing from the group, which leads to insufferable loneliness. Thus, different types of forces operate around the poet's life in varying degrees, which are instrumental in constructing a sort of absolute alienation syndrome that recurrently echoes in her poetry. These are mainly patriarchal literary traditions, institutional maladjustments, and interpersonal conflicts arising out of lack of proper understanding in between the life partners concerning their naturalistic, social, and psychological demands and capacities.

2. *Literary Traditions and Alienation*

The most characteristic feature of modern feminist literature is the pervading sense of alienation, an estrangement from the mainstream of history and civilization. This sense of alienation is certainly not a product of feminist imagination, but rather the result of a historical, cultural, and literary abandonment of women and their activities. The absence of active participation of women in the evolution of history made it exclusively a male dominion in almost all the modern cultural contexts, be it social, intellectual, moral, or ethical. Even the most aggressive modern feminist poets and novelists dreadfully feel the absence of predecessors on the one hand, and on the other the need for an empathetic audience to fully comprehend and appreciate the real meaning and import of feminist writings. Theirs is a continual struggle to free themselves from the male-centred literature, and attain a self-determined state of existence in the world of literature. Sandra Gilbert and Susan Gubar rightly comment on "the woman writer's artistic self-definition":

> . . . the loneliness of the female artist, her feelings of alienation from male predecessors coupled with her need for sisterly precursors and successors, her urgent sense of her need for a female audience, together with her fear of the antagonism of male readers, her culturally conditioned timidity about self-dramatization, her dread of the patriarchal authority of female invention – all these phenomena of 'inferiorization' mark the woman writer's struggle for artistic self-definition and differentiate her efforts at self-creation from those of her male counterpart. (qtd. in Showalter 468)

All the above cultural complexities are relevant for Kamala Das's creative upsurge. In the Indian context, this problem is even more significant as compared to the West owing to the unrelenting traditional roots in the field of women's writings.

In the case of Das, the most orthodox and conservative society of the sort we have in India absolutely cold-shouldered her formal poetic innovations. As a result, a kind of negativism emerged as a critical tradition against her. The fact is that in her poems she is vibrantly transparent concerning her grievances against the patriarchal authoritarianism of man as a class apart. Her aggressive manner not only irritated but also disgusted the male-readers as it had dared the very intellectual capacity/incapacity of men in establishing a proper understanding of the naturalistic uniqueness of woman as a person and also as an equally responsible agent in nature, as well as in the social counters. Quite naturally, the male readers turned out to be critical, oppositional, and sceptical about her creative preponderance. Sometimes the freedom of her poetic imagination overstretches themselves into images and acts of transgressing the moral and ethical propensities of social systems. But then, as she contends, women are emancipated from all the patriarchal moral laws insofar as they are instrumental in annihilating the feminine freedoms, harmonious happiness at all being the ultimate purpose of her poetry. The critics and reviewers including women have very often condemned this kind of attitude of Kamala Das. They even went to the extent of charging her with all sorts of personal insinuations. Referring to the first three volumes of Poetry by Kamala Das, what Eunice De Souza comments is pertinent here:

> Obsessive, confessional writing can be a source of power. It can also be tedious if it gets out of control, and then no amount of mere honesty will save the poem. Mrs Das's main problem is not knowing when to stop. . . . Too often there is scarcely a trace of grit or resilience to shape and control the emotions. (46)

The orthodox manner in which even Das's women critics respond to her poetic expressions speaks for what Gilbert and Gubar say above as the woman writer's 'need for sisterly precursors and successors,' and her 'urgent sense of her need for a female audience.' However, critics like Shirley Goelkin Lim aptly react to this negative response to Das's poetry even from women's quarters. In Lim's opinion,

> The negative responses of Indian women critics such as Monika Varma, Vimala Rao, and Eunice de Souza to Das's work and to the work of other candid Indian women writers such as Gauri Deshpande and Mamta Kalia demonstrate that perceived transgressions of social decorum and traditional behavior [sic] still affect literary evaluation. (86)

It is evident from this statement that Indian criticism has not grown enough to perform an in-depth, impartial evaluation of confessional writers like Kamala Das. This fact makes the women poets like Kamala Das feel an estrangement, an alienation from the literary mainstream.

3. *Social Institutions and Alienation*

a. *Familial Alienation*

The seeds of the feeling of alienation and frustration were first sown in Kamala Das in the alienated atmosphere of her own home spent with the unfeeling parents who, as she mentions in her autobiography, brought up their children without according them the love and care they deserved. She writes, "Gradually our instincts told us to keep away from the limelight" (MS 5). Thus, she was made to feel that her own parents considered their children "mere puppets, moving our limbs according to the tugs they gave us" (MS 77). Even the poet's poet-mother appears to have forgotten to bestow any motherly affection on her children. In an interview with Iqbal Kaur, Das says: "My mother has never been able to give me the love and security that I needed. She has always been indifferent" (161). Since a child is helplessly dependent on its parents, if denied proper nurturing, it becomes reflective and introspective, and sometimes even schizophrenic. This is what happens to Kamala in her childhood. So the feeling of a neglected entity as yet a child established in her mind an everlasting wound that played a dominant part in moulding her rebellious poetic personality. When her tender aspirations went unattended, she turned into an archetypal rebel. Even after she had grown up as an adult she looked everywhere for parental love, be it in her husband's arms. The following statement in *My Story* point towards the fact that she was looking for a sort of parental protective love and care even from her husband:

> I had expected him [the husband] to take me in his arms and stroke my face, my hair, my hands and whisper loving words. I had expected him to be all that I wanted my father to be, and my mother. I wanted conversation, companionship and warmth. Sex was far from my thoughts, I had hoped that he would remove with one sweep of his benign arms, the loneliness of my life. (87)

The confession in the above lines is vibrant enough to suggest that she had never got any sympathetic protective treatment from her own people. Her grievances against her husband as a partner are understandable. The grievances are not at all born out of self-pity or a need for a self-elation. It is a literal fact that the husbands usually do not establish any objective correlative in their female-counterpart probably because of their patriarchal authoritarian predilections. In the above lines, like an orphaned child even when the parents are virtually living, she pleads for love and care to be awarded to her. Her confessional manner of expecting these niceties from her husband devolves upon her from the autistic, archetypal imaginative counters of a child denied of all such fond necessities. Sometimes these expectations go beyond the domestic frame, and they take the shape of an ever-haunting psychic phenomenon; here the poet looks for such fondling from any male entity she comes in contact with. There is an ironic expression of such a longing in the poem "Glass." Even when the poetic persona offers her body to different men and "make of / every trap of lust a temporary home," she painfully confesses:

> I do not
>
> ever bother to tell, I have misplaced a father
>
> somewhere...
>
> and I look for him now everywhere. (BK 103).

Where the patriarchal dominations are vibrantly present, psychologists had pinpointed that Oedipus complex for male and Electra complex for female are inevitable archetypal properties that take strong inroads into their contingent personalities. The poetic sensibility invoking all sorts of fondling from her husband virtually emerges out of her inbred Electra complex. On the same analogy, the father figure in the fond child's psychic personality grows into that archetypal giant or traditional villain in the imaginary counters of women as creative writers.

Kamala Das always perceived her father in a fearsome light. In her poem "Next to Indira Gandhi" she writes:

> Next to Indira Gandhi my father I feared the most.
>
> He was the one who told me when I was five

That dark children should wear only white.
He was the one who had no time for me
When I was growing up. (OSK 118)

She, however, does not clarify as to why she feared Indira Gandhi the most. In putting Indira Gandhi and the poet's father in their own gradations as dreaded characters, Kamala Das probably wants to suggest that they both had contributed for the spoilage of domestic atmosphere. Instead of love and compassion towards other members of the family, they only catered a typical authoritarianism that ultimately resulted into an irresolvable conflict. It is just possible that Kamala Das implies a little bit of satiric humour in characterizing her father as a fearful person only next to Indira Gandhi. For the purpose of her family, it is her father as a strong autocrat that created a sense of dread and hatred among the children. As a child, she probably aspired for a fond petting from her father, which she always missed.

We have innumerable examples of autocratic parents contributing for overt and covert phobias, particularly in the young children within the family encirclements. Emile Bronte too nurtured in herself a sort of inexplicable dread in relation to her father; and the result is the character of that psychotic abnormal called 'Heathcliff' as the chief protagonist in her novel *Wuthering Heights*. Kamala Das, however, denounces and decimates the father figure in a very straightforward and vibrant manner by transparent confessions filled with anger and violence. Again, by delineating her father in such fearful dimensions, she is striking at the ominous generation gap and generation conflict, which, according to her, is the initiator of all kinds of disruptions in the otherwise harmonious family environment. It may not be an exaggeration to suggest that the father figure ultimately created the infante-terrible in the psychological nuances of young Kamala. In her grown up state, she vehemently resented everything that prevailed upon her as an oppressive insufferable exploitative phenomenon. Elsewhere in a poem called "My Father's Death" she betrays all her pent up suffocative emotions and longings as a neglected child:

You should have hugged me, father, just
Once, held me to your breast, you should
Have asked me who I was, in truth. (OSK 117)

Here she is obviously referring to the intellectual distance between her father and herself, which in years had widened to such a proportion that interactions almost became impossible. The most important figure in the family avoiding her and keeping her at distance becomes a cause of an everlasting feeling of alienation in her young mind.

b. *Racial Alienation*

Another factor that has contributed to the feeling of alienation in Kamala is the racial discrimination she faced in the missionary school in Calcutta, which might have worked as a catalysing agent to her already hurt sensibility and the inherent rebellious spirit in her. In the school she had the most unpleasant experience of discriminations, and the consequent atrocities committed by the wanton White students on the native children, both physiologically and psychologically. In *My Story* she narrates many incidents of such tortures her brother and she had to undergo only for the reason that they were brown children of Indian origin. The White children used to mock at her brother, saying: "Blackie, your blood is red" (MS 2). Once the principal asked Shirley, a White student, to read a poem that Kamala had composed. But when the visitor asked who wrote it, the principal said, "Shirley of course, she is a combination of beauty and brains, and then there was from the Governor's wife a special kiss" (MS 3). Also whenever there was a special occasion in the school like important visits, "the brown children were always discreetly hidden away, swept under the carpet, told to wait in the corridor behind the lavatories where the school ayahs kept them company." And she adds: "None of us looked too pretty in those days" (MS 3). Such unpleasant incidents became a serious point of personal grievance in Kamala's sensibility, as yet a child, and a matter of a lifetime trauma conforming in her a sort of emotionally irrepressible hatred towards all those who she considers are opposed to her as a being. It is interesting to note that she carries the essence of this trauma in her mind all through her life. The native children being discriminated and tortured was not something new in those days in India, but in all probability, the packed animus that she compounds in her poetry has its fictional source in the writings of Charles Dickens and Mark Twain in their novels *David Copperfield* and *Huckleberry Fin* respectively. The child-time experience had been a haunting archetype that takes innumerable hallucinatory dimensions in her poetry. As she grew in age and matured, there emerged in her an attitude of oppression and dissent, and she cries a cry of protest wherever she perceives differential treatment towards women in social and domestic environments. It is notable here that the very title of the first chapter of her autobiography *My Story* is: "The humiliation of a brown child in a European school" (MS 1).

c. *Collapse of Matriarchy*

The so-called modern middle class culture of India brought forth a sort of interpersonal segregation instead of a cohesive harmony. This middle class culture had evolved out of the cross-cultural rapports between the East and the West. The resultant middle class familial structure sustained irreparable damages in the sense that it could not remain Eastern in its essence, nor could it adopt for itself the Western familial ethos. The original Eastern familial system is the joint family system with an extended familial relational pattern in which the members constitute themselves as a harmonious whole. But the Western family system as it might be traced in the twentieth century context is altogether of a nuclear character where man, woman, and their minor children constitute themselves as a single family. The unified dimensions of Western and Eastern family systems contributed for a typical note of withdrawal and inhibition, particularly on the part of women as partners in the family unit. There occurred a strong erosion of woman's importance both in the structural and in the psychological dimensions of the modern middle class family institutions in India. Kamala Das takes up the onerous task of giving poetic expression to the intense stricken feminine feelings emerging out of the restrained circumstances in which the Indian family system found itself in our times. Poverty on the one hand and illiteracy on the other complexly contributed for a cultural context which provided no place of honour or dignity for woman as exclusively dependent individual within the society and in the family. It is this dependence ultimately that brought forth all kinds of constrictions on woman's freedom of expression by way of turning her choice-less. Therefore, woman finds herself in the crumbling structural dimensions of the family systems in the context of which almost all her freedoms are colossally eroded. The result is her alienation, which becomes an insufferable sore on her heart. It is with this sore that Kamala Das conducts her poetic activity whereby she fervently appeals for a kind of honourable and decent understanding of the Indian woman's problems.

A typical traditional family system from which Kamala Das descends adds to the feeling of alienation in her. This situation is associated with her racial particulars. She comes from a community (the Nayar [or Nair] community of Kerala) that remained out and out matrilineal for a long time in the past. In that system women enjoyed much more freedom and authority as compared to men, particularly in their marriages as well as in vital family matters. In this context, F. Fawcett makes the following observation: "The chief immediate interest attached to them [the Nayars] lies in the fact of their being the best, that is the fullest, the most complete existing example of matriarchy, or, to be more strictly accurate, of inheritance through females" (186). Although matrilineal system of family became extinct in the poet's family a generation before her birth, she appears to have an ardent longing for going back to the old system. Her frequent poetic indictments of the patriarchy are not individual charges against men, but they are impassioned urges of a conscious mind to do away with all such systems that are not humane and just in their operations. In a speech she voices her emotional attachment to the old tradition of her community:

> I come from another kind of community; we were matrilineal, matriarchal. So when I seek my roots, I find women used to run households, women owned property, the matriarch ruled. So it is sometimes very difficult for me to comprehend when people come and tell me this is what happens to women. You know only patriarchy. ("My Instinct" 160)

Her strong belief in the virtues of matriarchy makes her nostalgic about her past, and creates in her a sort of turmoil as is manifested in her violent poetic outcries. She uses two poetic symbols to convey her feelings of alienation from a traditional family system that offered love, warmth, and care. These two symbols are her 'grandmother' and her ancestral home, the 'Nalapat' house. In most of Das's writings these two symbols (one dead and the other on the verge of collapse) frequently appear one after the other to suggest her emotional attachment to the past. In this context, Nair rightly comments: "Often the images of the grandmother, great grandmother and the family house coalesce into each other to form an enormous memory-symbol that ballasts the tottering edifice of the poet's emotional existence" (86). This emotional attachment to the pedigree on the woman's side vibrantly speaks about her heart and its natural bias towards women. Even in the patriarchal contexts also, grandmothers and great grandmothers are usually held high in the Indian context. But as far as her nostalgic poetic plunges into the past are concerned, it is not regret but rather the violence against the elements that worked behind this separation stands as the prominent note of her poetry. In the poem "Composition" she suggests how the edifices of past innocence crumbled. Here she is reminded of the warmth and care she had enjoyed and the promise of love and life she had felt while "lying beside" her "grandmother" under the roof of Nalapat house. But gone are those days; now,

> . . . the red house that had
> stood for innocence
> crumbled
> and the old woman died,
> lying for three months,
> paralyzed,
> while the thieving ants climbed her hands
> and ate the cuticle. (D 29)

In a wider perspective these lines carry beyond its literal

meaning a melancholy in the poet's heart, born out of her having witnessed the extinction of a cultural structure that was unique in many respects. The grandmother is symbolic of an age that might have awarded a much better life for the poet than that of the present day. The lines 'the red house that had / stood for innocence / crumbled' suggestively point to the inherent goodness of a tradition that is no more. The expression 'old woman' is a reference to her grandmother who becomes an archetype in the poem. The slow and painful dying of the grandmother after having lain 'paralyzed / while thieving ants climbed her hands / and ate the cuticle' is a requiem for a now extinct tradition, and a lamentation for her inability to revert to the system 'that was long ago,' which was more sympathetic to her feminine demands. As she grew in age, the sound of the sea becomes as inaudible as the dead voice of her grandmother. Later in the same poem she confesses:

> The only secrets I always
> withhold
> are that I am so alone
> and that I miss my grandmother. (D 31)

Her passion for familial warmth and love is evident here. Even if she is partial and biased towards the 'grandmother' (here symbolic of matriarchal joint family system), what all she hoped to have within the familial context is a mere fistful of love and compassion, which probably would be available more in the maternal instinct than in the paternal enclaves.

Again, in the poem "Blood" there is a very pathetic picture of the old Nalappat house that stands as the last monument of matrilineal lineage in her family. Her great grandmother's words:

> You see this house of ours
> Now three hundred years old,
> It's falling to little bits
> Before our very eyes.
> . . . .

For I love this house, it hurts me much
To watch it die (OP 16)

and the poet's consoling words to the great grandmother,

When I grow old, I said,
And very very rich
I shall rebuild the fallen walls
And make new this ancient house (OP 16),

establish her ardent longing for associating herself with the past. Metaphorically, as Vrinda Nabar says, "The death of the house need not be interpreted literally in terms of its physical decay. It could also refer to the corruption of the old bond, of traditional values, and the erosion of the moral fabric on which the house/ family-circle had been built" (67). However, the poet fails to keep the promise given to her great grandmother to rejuvenate the 'house,' and makes a very passionate confession of her failure:

I have let you down
Old house, I seek forgiveness
O mother's mother's mother
I have plucked your soul
Like a pip from a fruit
And have flung it into your pyre. (OP 18-19)

In fact, in the poet's family the great grandmother and grandmother stand as the last living evidences of the matriarchal lineage that professed much more freedom to its women than any other system did in the known cultures in history. It is highly likely that Kamala Das's nostalgic attachment to the grandmother and the ancestral home (Nalapat house) grows from a defeated subconscious which, in her childhood, had asserted herself to be the next Matriarch.

There are many poems in which the poet nostalgically recalls her ancestral home and its inmates and environments. In "A Hot Noon in Malabar" she passionately thinks about the "wild men, wild thoughts, wild love" (BK 18) of her home and its environs.

Again in the poem "My Grandmother's House" she takes the readers back to that place where "There is a house now far away where once / I received love" (CP 120). Time has taken away much from her life, but the memories of her house are still afresh in her, the environs of which contrast with the present life situations of the poet. This prompts her to put a sudden question:

> You cannot believe, darling
> Can you, that I lived in such a house and
> Was proud, and loved... I who have lost
> My way and beg now at strangers' doors to
> Receive love, at least in small change? (CP 120)

The idyllic contentment that she had in her ancestral home (Nalapat House) when she was a child is lost forever. The angst of de-homing is obvious. Moreover, the sobbing manner in which she expresses her loss of inner containment and contentment is vibrant in the lines: 'I who have lost / My way and beg now at strangers' doors to / Receive love, at least in small change?'

The crumbling Nalapat house again appears in the poem "No Noon at My Village Home." The old pride of the house is now no more. It now presents her a pathetic picture:

> On the dust of
> Windowsills I spot the signatures of
> The patient ghosts the trees have thatched a darker
> Roof; the moon of cities, the moon of vast
> Rice fields sprinting past the trains, is nowhere
> To be seen. Only the fireflies light up
> Our porch, only the silence tells me that I must
> Stay... (CP 31)

This feeling that 'I must stay' is a desperate longing not only for arrest of time, but also to journey back in time to a past that was much better. If so, nostalgia in Kamala Das is not an individual's homesickness owing to a temporary spatial alienation, but it is a grown up individual's fear and frustration in the unfortunate state of being uprooted from a promising cultural heritage, and the anger against the wide gulf between the self's aspirations and the crude realities of everyday life. The poet here stands on the debris of a crumbled tradition, and what lies beneath is its innocence and meaningful associations. Her awareness of this irretrievable loss of a unique familial tradition makes her feminine psyche feel deceived. Her subsequent experiences in life confirm this deception. Her feeling of alienation is born out of her experiences as a neglected daughter, uncared wife, and probably even as an unloved mother in the modern familial context.

d. *Interpersonal Alienation*

The protagonists of Das's poems, with manifold manifestations of woman in her essence, perennially suffer on the anvil of patriarchal moulding, and struggle to free themselves from the roles of conventional womanhood in which they get only a negligible part to play. This subservient place of woman in the nuclear family presents a pathetic picture as is expressed in "A Widows Lament":

> This has always been
> someone else's world, not mine.
> My man, my sons, forming the axis,
> while I, wife and mother,
> insignificant as a fly
> climbed the glasspanes of their eyes. (OSK 125)

The longing as expressed in the poem "I Shall Some Day," "I shall some day take / Wings, fly around" (OP 48) like a free bird, gets shattered as she could only become a small insect 'insignificant as a fly' that cannot fly high in the heavens but only can get stuck to the 'glass panes of their eyes,' and wriggle. This shrinking of personality, this dissolution of the self is the horrid face of patriarchy where:

> There wasn't a thing
> that I could do to make myself grow
> to reach their ordained height
> although I loved shyly and from afar. (OSK 125)

The emotional distance between the woman persona and the male figures as husband and sons in the domestic environments, which relegate the woman to almost a non-entity, is unambiguously hinted at in the expression 'some one else's world' in the earlier lines and 'I loved shyly and from afar' in the later part. However, as far as the summation of this wretched existence of woman within the family is concerned, the poem "Gino" has the final word: "Perhaps some womb in that / Darker world shall convulse when I finally enter / A legitimate entrant, marked by discontent" (OP 13). It is this collective 'discontent' of women in being in 'some one else's world' that Das infuses into each of the protagonists in her numerous poems, giving a feel of her own life-experiences, invariably agonizing, from childhood to womanhood through adolescence.

For Kamala Das, the male-counterpart should be an understanding agent rather than a powerful and authoritarian entity that asserts his will on her. To her it is high time man shed his ego of a self-sanctioned autocrat looked towards woman as an essential part of his existence as a gregarious entity, particularly in the social and familial contexts. To know and understand each other should be the prime objective of their togetherness. To know oneself by knowing the other is the end of being each other. The poet clarifies this in the following lines of the poem "The Old Playhouse":

> It was not to gather knowledge
> of yet another man that I came to you but to learn
> what I was and by learning, to learn to grow, but every
> Lesson you gave was about yourself. . . . (OP 1)

As the woman persona as portrayed in her poems invariably undergoes a sort of psychic disintegration, she not only fails to learn what she was, but also, instead of learning 'to grow': "Cowering / beneath your monstrous ego I ate the magic loaf and / became a dwarf" (OP 1). This sheer contradiction between the desire to 'grow' and the reality of becoming 'a dwarf' compounds in her a sort of suffocating agony. It is this failure to come near each other psychologically that Kamala Das resents to the full length of her poetic life and products (poems). There is always a need for arriving at such compromises through a wilful effort of mutually compounding the said happiness in a free and frank atmosphere of total transparency. Therefore, 'I came to you, but to learn / What I was, and by learning, to learn to grow.' Her ultimate grievance in this context lies in the utter lack of such transparency and readiness in man to share the sublime experiences with equanimity. If so, man must maintain such temper or temperament of understanding his woman in the same manner as she aspires to understand her man. But her experiences in life have been otherwise, which have taught her to perceive woman's life from a subjective angle. When she finds that the modern life-giving institutions like family, society, which are meant to safeguard the interests of its individual members, are out to annihilate them and the personality of the individual, particularly woman, has never been given any significance, she becomes determined to take it up with the society on her own.

The poetry for Kamala Das, thus, is a potential form of appraising and intimating her male-counterpart, of course through taunting tonalities, about the so-called non-conspicuous features of woman as an intimate partner with her man. These non-conspicuous features are both psychological and physiological. The psychological fury in her poetry is intended to make bare and transparent the physiological uniqueness of woman as a woman. The physiological non-conspicuous features always remain unavailable for man for they emanate from her unique feminine personality. So what all that Kamala Das intends to suggest at is about the need for recognizing this physiological uniqueness of woman. For generations on end, it is man that alienated woman. Therefore she feels the compulsion of clarifying the feminine point of view. Alienation and ostracism that inevitably follows it are the structural ground realities of her poetry. Alienation, as such, is the spinal force of her poetic tract; and she comprehends the smothering man-woman relations from this alienated angle, like a caged bird, fluttering her poetic wings in order to seek the necessary freedoms of survival and existence.

Thus, the poetry of Kamala Das is a profound conversational

manner of grievously inflating the stricken causes of femininity in the context of male predomination and autonomy. At the same time, she is proudly conscious of the extra-ordinary importance of being a woman as a basic medium of entire creativity. This is the prerogative extended to woman through maternity by nature. Kamala Das's poetic violence springs from the realization that the institutional pattern of the process of civilization has interfered in this naturalistic archetype of evolution and progress. Patriarchal civilization, in the course of time, atrociously enslaved woman for its purposeless pursuits of supremacies and superiorities, thereby annihilating her personality and abandoning her as a non-entity. As a father, as a husband, and as a monitoring agent of the family affairs, man had always potentially undermined the very personality and psyche of woman in a sort of unfeeling, and out and out irresponsible disposition towards her. The tone of rivalry in her poetry emerges out of her strong psychological bias that wrenches in her personality a typical irresolvable alienation and disownment by the male counterpart in the family in a particular manner. As a feminist poet, these are the grievances of Kamala Das against man, and hence the sources of violence in her poetry.

However, it is not only towards man she looks with grievance. For that matter she indicts even nature for its pretence to be a well-wisher of human beings. Her rebellion often turns against the whole macrocosmic complexities in which human beings are destined to have a feeble existence, always extending their hands for the unfathomable, perennially striving towards the summit that is non-existent. If so, Kamala Das's poetic violence is directed not only towards the unfeeling fellowmen and the society that breeds them, but also towards the metaphysical aspects of nature and its complexities. In the following chapter an attempt has been made to examine the working of this exclusive feminist violence in her poetry towards nature and fellowmen.

3

Violence against Nature and Fellowmen

Kamala Das as a poet continually and constantly aims at comprehending the feminine interior potentialities in order to flash the focal length of her poetic vision into a sort of search for the very meaning of being a woman in the nature as well as in the society. The whole purpose of her poetry in concentrating upon the inner potentialities of being woman appears to be associated with analytically revealing the collective feminine psyche in its responses to the external realities in which it is nurtured. As Anne Brewster rightly comments:

> While investigating that chimerical creature, the female consciousness, in all its paradox and complexity, the poetry [of Kamala Das] further assumes a more primal function as a vital tool for the interpretation of the interaction of the consciousness and the external world of phenomena that surrounds, shapes and delimits it. (137)

Therefore, her poetry turns out to be a kind of tract in the act of liberating woman's entire being from the overpowering and subjugating powers of nature both external and internal. For the purpose of her poetic feud, to a great extent, the external nature is compounded in man who always apparently stands in opposition with woman in all the possible dimensions of life. Thus, the entire poetic property of Kamala Das turns out to be an incessant and interminable fight between man and woman. This does not mean that she is pleading for feminine dominations. On the other hand, she is just advancing a poetic proposal for man to come for an equal consideration of the earnest naturalistic, social, and interpersonal needs for companionship of each for each other. But then, since this fight is in between the inevitable and ens reale halves of the very human set, the fight itself takes a very interesting poetic manner of vociferously bargaining for recognitions and understanding of the needs and dignities in being woman on one side, and the unrelenting patriarchal authoritarian onslaughts on the other.

Somehow, other than the partners involved in this fight, there is a third powerful and mysterious entity to propose and dispose, to construct and dismantle the aspirations of the partners for sublimation in the man-woman intimate involvements. This entity, called nature, plays a vital role in constantly and continuously discarding the requisite level of sublime heights to the mutually incompatible entities called man and woman. While examining the property of violence in Kamala Das's poetry, therefore, there can be traced two rival camps in operation as far as the poet's notion of being a woman is concerned: one, the continual autocratic offending nature of the fellowmen, and the other, the very creaturely dimensions bestowed upon human life by nature itself leaving them no leeway for attaining true sublime experience. So in order to understand the treatment of violence in her poetry, it is necessary to examine its course both towards nature and fellowmen.

Violence Against Nature

Kamala Das as a poet has nurtured in herself a special grievance against nature. At the outset, she could never tolerate the idea of nature awarding distinctly different and antagonistic physiological and psychological structures to man and woman. She thinks that it is these variations that give an opportunity for man to subjugate and enslave her, more or less in the same listless manner as he conducted against nature itself. In her poetry, however, it is difficult to come across direct attacks against nature in the sense of the external natural world of our habitation. She loves nature as a vivid and life-giving property in all its wildness, primitiveness, and purity. Even as a grown up woman, she looked at nature in its myriad colours, shapes, and movements with childlike awe and dread. But her strong conviction that she being a grown up woman nature is not available to her in the same fascinating manner as it was available to her when she was a child makes her aggrieved and aggressive towards the natural process of growth itself. When this growth further pushes her into a situation where she, as a woman, has to encounter many a social dictate, formalities, and role-playings, she turns violent against nature for its pretence as a well wisher of humans. Two major symbolic gestures that present themselves in her poetry against this macrocosmic inscrutability and inconsistency are her revulsion against growth, and her agony of not achieving due fulfilment of being a woman.

1. *The Inscrutability of Nature*

On a close scrutiny of the ways of nature, it appears that it never had a programme of ultimate happiness or the highest pleasure for beings by way of sexual or spiritual fulfilment in the context of male-female union. All the sublimations and satisfactions are mysteriously held by nature as the possible formulas of irresolvable and interminable temptations. Such temptations are practically and particularly true in the case of Homo sapiens who are gifted with a rare felicity of imagination and a capacity to formulate projects for themselves in accordance with this extended imagination. While this imagination is considered as a gift of nature to man as a being, it functions in actuality as a never-ending agony for him. In the union of male and female this imagination works towards aspiring a conceptual sublime experience. Nature implants in all the living beings only an intuitive apprehension of sublime heights. But the reality of survival in its creaturely status as well as in its existential heights awards no such sublime complements in the real life. In other words, nature does not seem to offer total and complete satisfaction to either man or woman; it only gives a passionate desire and temptation through the instinctive properties of beings. This temptation as a well-founded property of nature has its own mysterious purpose in the context of evolution. So the sublime height that the humans aspire is not at all a factual felt reality in the present. But a passionate desire to attain for themselves this height is a perennially haunting dream for them. It is under this compulsive dream impetuosity that Kamala Das becomes counter-aggressive as against her man. As a matter of fact, reason and analysis, which are the attending intellectual properties in understanding the available reality, is a mere infinitesimal ignited portion or particle of intuition. Kamala Das has a profound intuitive apprehension concerning the human relations. So the painful manner in which Kamala Das pines for a unified and harmonious sublime experience simultaneously by the love-partners is a mere romantic wish fulfilment. Needless to say, she is attributing on herself a sort of representative capacity of every woman and all women into her personality, and poetically asserts herself as a prominent and dominant mouthpiece of the feminine frustrations and failures. To the extent that these frustrations and failures are purposely-implanted characteristic features by nature, there seems to be no real and realistically comprehensible solution for the feminine anxieties as represented in her poetry. If so, it is inevitable that failure in the sense of not coming to mutual sublimation simultaneously and the conscious psychological trauma of the possible failure invariably enter into the very neurons of the partners, and actively contribute for the frustrations. Therefore, the fundamental poetic structural fabric of Das maintains in itself a never-ending and ever-brewing frustration and failure. But for this infelt failure and frustration of women, she always finds a cause of revenge on the men-folk whom she always considers exclusively selfish and abnormally self-satisfying in being the life-partners of their women. So man's failure as a partner breeding in woman an irreconcilable revenge and grievance becomes the ultimate theme of her poetry.

Everybody admits that love-making is not a mere animal-like avidity; over and above the creaturely formula of the blue print of nature there is a secular and aesthetic height that has to be aspired by active partners in love. If so, Das has a quaint romantic view of ecstasy and exquisiteness to be shared equally by both the partners. But this is only a matter of her desire and aspiration. She is exclusively concerned with the feminine needs and feminine purposes, and she rebels against nature for the incompatibilities between the masculine and feminine entities. These incompatibilities, as she suggests in the poem "An Introduction," arise out of the fact that there is "In him the hungry haste / Of rivers, in me the ocean's tireless / Waiting" (OP 26). The 'river' metaphor indicates the aggressive manner of male approach towards female in his thoughtless urgency, whereas the 'ocean' metaphor speaks for the profound manner in which the female partner patiently awaits the arrival of the 'river.' Beauvoir arrives at a similar conclusion regarding the incompatibilities of male and female entities in being partners in love:

> Feminine sex desire is the soft throbbing of a mollusc . . . her expectation can become ardent without ceasing to be passive; man dives upon his prey like the eagle and the hawk; woman lies in wait like the carnivorous plant . . . . Hence it is that there is in her not only resistance to the subjugating intentions of the male, but also conflict within herself. (125)

All Beauvoir wants to prove is the fact that nature has created male and female as two totally incongruous entities both physiologically and psychologically craving and contending for physical and spiritual fulfilments by way of love play, which are never available to them in their optimum dimensions.

Happiness in the male-female union is a matter of both psychological and physiological compromises and adjustments. But the psychological and physiological needs of both man and woman are variant, and in this variance lies the very mystery of nature in its processes of evolution. If at all there is a possibility of achieving equal mutual sublimations simultaneously, the very urge to aspire for more and more comes to stagnation, which in itself is a property of self-denial of nature itself. Such self-denial through repression and annihilation does not seem to be the programme of nature. Thus, the aspiring partners after happiness must constantly and continually re-cycle their mutual efforts at contending for pleasure. Kamala Das's poetry insists upon the urgency of continual and interminable processes of such re-cycling with an added enthusiasm of mutual give and take. As a feminine partner she realizes the physiological and psychological limitations of male partner as the necessary stumbling block in woman's gaining of ultimate happiness as a definite property. Since this ultimate happiness is cut short and denied by the male partner, her poetry becomes a furious tirade against man. Her poetic fury is not against any man as such. It is more or less against the very withdrawing and sinking nature of man in his capacity as a partner in life. In effect, her poetry turns out to be incessant charges of fury against the very nature in general and the nature of man in particular.

2. *The Apocalypse of Growth*

Nature is available to the living organisms on Earth as a ground for primary activity, which is the same for all the species including human beings. The primary activity i.e. self-preservation, and preservation of the race is, again, the most important principle and purpose of nature in its scheme of things based on creation, reproduction, and progressive evolution. In this process of evolution human beings cannot definitely conclude that nature considers them different from other creatures, or sees the living distinct from the dead. In her poem "Daughter of the Century," Kamala Das hints at this indiscriminate behaviour of nature in its programme of evolution:

> At times, a storm sinks some ships with men in them
> Or a typhoon devastates a town.
> But nature, aware of life's intent,
> Does not care to seek anyone's pardon.
> It sees no great difference
> Between the living and the dead. (BK 140)

But nature's awareness of 'life's intent' that is birth, growth, decay, and rebirth becomes for man psychologically a leap from bad to worse. With the passing of each stage of man's organic development, in him is created a sense of loss; and he becomes nostalgic and melancholic owing to his own psychophysical experience that whatever is past was better for him. Kamala Das's poetry deals with this "tragedy of life" from a feminine angle of perception. As she clarifies in the poem "Composition,"

The tragedy of life is not death, but growth,
the child growing into adult,
and growing out of needs (D 30).

The 'tragedy' of the ultimate death is not as potential as the continually haunting death of the being in the sense that metaphorically it accompanies life from one stage to the other stage of 'growth': the death of the childhood in the youth, that of the youth in manhood, and ultimately that of the manhood itself in the threatening old age. Even in the strict Indian traditions of thought, death is not an event resigned and relegated to a future moment of operation. It is a perennial secret agent that constantly and continually attends life in all its continuing moments with an inevitable ultimate trump card in its custody to overpower, defeat, and destroy life in a certain future moment. The mysterious secret agency of death continually subsisting along with the moments of life is in itself a prominent property that affects the very growth and development of man from childhood to maturity. For Kamala Das, as she says in the poem "Life's Obscure Parallel,"

Life's obscure parallel is death. Quite often
I wonder if what I seem to do is living
Or dying. A little of each is in every
Gesture, both my mind's and my body's. (CP 54)

Thus, death is a constant and continual phenomenon that invariably attends life in its various stages of growth and development. Quite naturally, the last stages of the life of childhood, of youth, and of adulthood complexly create in the poet a poetic agony and melancholy compounding in her a fervent state of loss and frustration. This is suggested at in the poem "Daughter of the Century":

We are aided by death in our careers,
We ought to learn to take in each sight
Filtered through its eye.
At night the hunter and the hunted often lie asleep

In an innocence shared unwittingly
And all the hatreds seem fancied
All the prejudices unreal. (BK 140)

The expression 'the hunter and the hunted often lie asleep' suggests at the continuous and interminable company of death in the life of man, which makes all his attempts of flights from death a mere fancy; and all his self-pride a mockery. If so, for the poet death is not a future event staring and challenging life to be itself; metaphorically it is always attending man as his alter ego destined to inevitable destruction. This inevitable destruction of life's vitality through the process of growth is metaphysically rebelled at by Kamala Das in her inconsolable confessions.

Even for bringing forth a generalized picture about the exclusive predicament of woman in being a lesser social entity than man, Das uses an autobiographical formula in her poetry; and time and again plunges into her own childhood. She falls into loneliness, and the introspection thereby turns out to be a painful confession of her concerns with life, particularly as a grown-up woman in the Indian situation. In her poems the frequent reference to her grandmother's protective love and affection and the later agony of loneliness that she feels is also a concerned reflection at the loss of the childhood innocence with growth in age. When she was still a child, lying beside the grandmother at her ancestral (Nalapat) home, she "could hear at night / the surf breaking on the shore. / The sea was only two miles away" ("Composition," D 29). The vastness of the sea symbolizes the extent of freedom that the poet longs for, which was well within her reach both in its physical and metaphoric forms under the warmth and care of the grandmother. But

That was long ago
Before the skin
intent on survival
learnt lessons of self-betrayal. (D 29)

Here is a clear indication that with the growth in age woman also develops a sense of growth in the instinctive demands. The expression 'skin intent on survival' is very significant. It is inevitable that the growth in age automatically brings forth certain instinctive desires. These desires were not prominent so long as the grandmother took care of her. Ceasing of such a protective shade is the starting point of the skin's secret cherishing of new freedoms. The way she uses the expression 'survival' and not existence confirms the force of creaturely demands in growth and development. There is no alternative freedom left for the creature in growth. The almost coercive manner in which the child gets distanced from its childhood's warmth and care is beautifully expressed in the lines: "I was busy growing / I had then / No time for the sea" (D 30). Here the nursery rhyme's gusto is poetically reflected. The sea symbolizes the magnificent 'other' as against the self. The suggestion here is that when the self is totally pre-occupied with its own being it does not have a relative vision of the 'other,' as it usually happens in reciting the nursery rhymes. The 'sea' also symbolizes the sea of life in the sense of the grand panoramic problematic nature of existence in the world. The self, in its total pre-occupation with the concomitance of its own growth and growing demands, cannot concentrate on the 'other' as an entity available for its perusal. It precisely suggests the simple idea that when the instinctive urge predominates the self the inevitable 'other' as a presence ceases to be operative. This irreversible course of alteration resulting in the irretrievable loss of a much better time is the most agonizing experience in her.

Every passing phase of ageing has its own pains and pleasures inseparably grounded. This imaginative escape into the childhood as cherished by Kamala Das is just her own manner of poetically suggesting at the implicated agony of being-in-the present. It is not at all a 'Romantic' escape. It is just a way of telling that the present is insufferable. In fact all these moorings on the part of the poet verge on the unspeakable agony of being-in-the world. The very property of being-in-the world has to be complimented with the height of feeling of becoming or acquiring for oneself a sort of preciousness. If so, self-importance is the central point of her poetic ego. Both nature and the fellowmen somehow fall into a conspiracy of eroding her self-importance of being-in-the world attended by the necessary courage to be an individual. The causes are both physical and metaphysical, and to a great extent incontrovertible.

If so, it is rather the temporal departure than the spatial separation that is the cause of the nostalgic sentiments in Kamala Das's poetry. The root of every problem for her is the distinct phases of alteration and change from childhood to adolescence, and then to womanhood. The growth in age, particularly for women, becomes a confusing phenomenon as they cannot cope with the external environment compounded in the society and fellowmen. As Beauvoir rightly says about woman in general, "Oscillating between desire and disgust, between hope and fear, declining what she calls for, she lingers in suspense between the time of childish independence and that of womanly submission" (77). The relative manner in which Das presents the various facets of growth in life ultimately contributes to one simple summation that is life in its overall presentation of growth and development offers no relative comfort or ease. In all probability life has to be lived, and for the poet it has to be lived with all contingent regrets and distinct agonies from time to time. The manner in which she presents the agony of living ultimately matches with that of the Greek poets and philosophers who untiringly depicted life as a grim ironic presentation having no ease or respite from the pains of living. In her poem "An Introduction" Das expresses this agony of growth with an ironic tone: "I was child, and they / Told me I grew, for I became tall, my limbs / Swelled and one or two places sprouted hair" (OP 26). The expression 'they / Told me I grew' and further details of physical growth clearly suggest at the society's disregard for the development of a girl child's interior personality. Society measures her growth by the swell of body parts and sprout of hairs at new places. This physical change is no ecstatic experience for her but is only a prelude to the onset of social and cultural complexities of adjustments. This alteration or growth is typically nonadjustable because of its chaotic novelty conditioned to the pathetic reflection imposed by fellowmen and the family members. Beauvoir observes this sort of quandary and shame of being woman in the initial stage of adulthood: "When the breasts and the body hair are developing, a sentiment is born which sometimes becomes pride but which is originally shame" (47). The uneasiness and delicacy of the visible development in certain exclusive female organs on the one hand, and the onset of social and familial dictates on the other make a young woman vulnerable. To quote Beauvoir again, "Her inferiority was sensed at first merely as a deprivation, but the lack of a penis has now become defilement and transgression. So she goes onward towards the future, wounded, shameful, culpable" (68). This situation coupled with unfeeling fellowmen makes her introspective and sometimes even schizophrenic. Because what awaits her in society is a pre-determined and biased social order that makes her a timid daughter, an enslaved life-partner, a toiling mother, and so on. At the initial stage itself she becomes aware of her predicament, and "she feels in these changes the presentiment of a finality which sweeps her away from self-hood: she sees herself thrown into a vital cycle that overflows the course of her private existence, she divines a dependence that dooms her to man, to children, and to death" (Beauvoir 48). Voicing against such pre-determined 'finality' becomes a compulsion to such an aggressive poetic sensibility as that of Kamala Das because the whole process of changes that take place in a girl is seen by her as a preamble to a social categorization, a make-up to fit into a certain social pattern. She remains under constant threat of loss of the given; life appears to be slipping out of the grips, like a fish that constantly slips out of the clutches of the fisher in the sea of living. The dilemma that the poet projects is like that of a child eating sweetmeat that wants to relish it and hold it back too; hence her resolution, 'The tragedy of life is not death, but growth, / the child growing into adult, / and growing out of needs.'

Thus, her poems become the outbreaks of a never-ending violence against the Natural order of growth and decay. The naturalistic decay is something more than physical; it ultimately becomes a restraining formula of metaphysical yearnings as well. It is the degeneration of the delicate aspects of life into the 'lessons of self-betrayal' through interpersonal machinations of evil amongst the sexes. And she believes that this predicament is consequential to the process of growth. Her rebellion against the social formalities emerges out of this infelt betrayal because the repercussions of this naturalistic alteration and growth take her to a situation where all around her, the "categorizers" scream dictates like:

> Dress in sarees, be girl,
> Be wife. . . . Be embroiderer, be cook,
> Be a quarreller with servants. Fit in. Oh,
> Belong. . . . ("An Introduction," OP 26)

The 'presentiment of a finality' of status, roles, and functions of women, 'which sweeps her away from self-hood,' as observed by Beauvoir above, is sharply attacked in these lines. The dictates of the 'categorizers' to 'Fit in. Oh / Belong' imply a desperate attempt on the part of the society to fix the female entity into a pre-moulded groove.

In another poem called "Maturity" Das is still more vibrant and emotive in exposing the repercussions of growth:

> Growth is the stoicism of sewers
> beneath great cities, accepting the rush
> of putrid waste, the abstract pulling down
> of shades, the switch-off of curiosity,
> the closure of apertures that allow
> the river of unhappiness to flow in
> towards the heart's restive ocean. . . . (CP 48)

The metaphoric complexities of the 'sewers' symbol clarify the manner in which the nastiness of creaturely survival compounds in one, more or less a misanthropic agony of being-in-the world. The expression 'putrid waste' with its nauseating presence compounds this agony of being-in-the world. The expression 'switch off of curiosity' ultimately fulfils the poetic intensity of loss when the total darkness dawns on life and its precious treasures. The essential pain and misery of growth and its attendant devastations are well brought out in the immense metaphoric manner of the above lines. The very pain of growth in life cannot be expressed in any other manner. The 'river of unhappiness' flowing 'towards the heart's restive ocean' completes the miserable apocalypse.

3. *The Agony of Unfulfilment*

A person, either as a man or as a woman, is always unique and uniquely undivinable. As partners, the very depths of their personalities always remain arrestingly mutual mysteries to each other. One way of facing these mysteries is poetically comprehending and advancing the very tenets of their mutual personalities in an atmosphere of fearless freedom, joy, and transparency. The profound purpose of Kamala Das's poetry lies in the fact of capturing this freedom, joy, and transparency. It is not pessimism of any kind that lends a sort of tragic dimension to her poetry. She is full of life and it is this passion and fervour for life that give her poetry its vibrancy. Life is very precious for her, and she does not want to give up her thirst for living at any cost. The tragic tone of her poetry owes much to the frustration of not fulfilling life's longings and aspirations. In the kind of environments that she lives in, granting free flow to her desires would mean risking an existential conflict with the conventional social and familial codes. This is suggested at in her poem "A Souvenir of Bone":

> My desires
>
> Were many, if granted freedom I knew they would burn
>
> Down like tongues of flame, the monastic peace of my home.
>
> . . . .
>
> Rob me, destiny, if you must,
>
> Rob me of my sustenance, but do not, I beg
>
> Of you, do not take away my thirst... (CP 32-33)

The poetic content of her violent personality compels her to make such instant, instinctive, and emotional outpourings coupled with a stricken feminine psyche on to the face of the world. This compulsion arises not from a tragic vision of life but from dejection owing to her unfulfilled desires and the frequent set backs she has had in the process of seeking pleasures in life. Thus, for her the story of life is one of emotional and spiritual unfulfilment, and this spiritual vacuum gradually gets filled up with frustration and violence towards the very formula of nature as an agent with malevolent and insidious plans of its own. She makes a categorical comparison of the spiritual and the secular heights of being-in-the world with the naturalistic creaturely evocations that go with woman as a matrilineal agent. These creaturely evocations are awfully disgusting for her as they should be for any creature.

The agony of unfulfilment coupled with the fear of time slipping away functions as a catalyst to stir up a sort of urgency in Das's poetry. This urgency and fear give the poem "The Fear of the Year" its vibrancy, wherein she feels, "no smile, however fond, can / Settle time like a paper weight" (CP 108). The sum total of human life was deemed by T.S. Eliot in *The Waste Land* as only "fear in a handful of dust" (L. 30). Das suggestively elaborates on this aspect:

> . . . fear has warped us all; even
> In the freedom of our dreams, it
> Thrusts its paws to incarnadine
> The virgin whiteness, so that we
> Perceive the flying steel hands sow
> Over mellow cities those dark,
> Malevolent seeds and the red,
> Red mushrooms hotly sprout and grow
> On an earth illogically
> Stilled, and silenced, and dead, dead, dead. (CP 108)

Categorical suggestive references to T.S. Eliot are vibrant here. T.S. Eliot initiates *The Waste Land* with the words: "April is the cruellest month / Breeding lilacs out of dead land" (L. 1-2). The 'flying steel hands sow(ing) / Over mellow cities those dark, / Malevolent seeds and the red, / Red mushrooms hotly sprout(ing)' is her poetic parallel to Eliot's 'Breeding lilacs out of dead land.'

The imagery and its symbolic notations in Kamala Das are very vibrant in being uncontrollably more elaborate than in T.S. Eliot. Both are suggesting about the all-purveying deadness of earth around them. While Eliot is talking about the dead land (wasteland), Kamala Das is speaking of 'an earth illogically / Stilled, and silenced.' The very title of the poem "The Fear of the Year" substantiates the idea of the passing phenomenon of time in the modules of year after year, and confirms the invariable deadening process that mercilessly descends on human destiny. Every moment of time is invariably fated to death and relegated to the past in the very next moment. Thus the precious present is always 'dead, dead, dead.' If so, this is an expression of the inevitable loss that she perceives in every moment of her life, and which hangs on her as an insufferable phenomenon of time. In this context, Devindra Kohli rightly says:

> The "flying steel hands" of time sow the seeds for mushroom-like moments, which sprout quickly and die quickly, on desires which are "illogically/Stilled, and silenced and dead." Thus, with slow dead desires and moments coming and going, the poet is faced with the 'malevolent' challenge of unfulfilment. (Virgin 8-9)

This 'malevolent challenge of unfulfilment,' in its final analysis, is in the all embracing waste of life itself in that continually and uncontrollably wasted processes of time. This 'malevolent challenge' becomes more disquieting particularly when her conscious mind is wakeful to the fact that the waste is not only an eternal process in the game of being-in-the world but it is the only finale. This view of life being pervaded by the agony of 'unfulfilment' finds expression also in the poem "A Cask of Nothing":

> If I close my eyes I see nothing
> If I close my ears I hear nothing
> Nothing but nothing
> inside or outside
> the nothing that resides
> as an ache within

the only content
the human cask can contain. (BK 108)

It is this awareness of the finality of the 'nothing / inside or outside' that creates in her sensibility a sort of restlessness. From this angle, life for all the practical purposes is a mere matter of immense activity without any achievement or satiation. It is this conscious concern in her for the inevitable passage of time without ever awarding any substantial satisfaction of being-in-the present that is the ultimate metaphysical concern of Kamala Das.

Kamala Das's violence against nature has this metaphysical disposition of arguing out the cause of her feminine grievances against the backdrop of imperfections in the microcosmic existence of humans in the macrocosmic arrangement. She poetically implies that it is these imperfections that provoke man to fall into a mad race in the name of civilization and progress. In this race nature gives rise to material prosperities for man (of course 'by unequal laws'), but at the same time it also brings forth a sort of spiritual defeatism, thus making human life as low as that of any other creature on earth.

Violence Against Fellowmen

In the primeval circumstances of prehistoric context women prevailed as the centralized forces of power and prowess even in the domestic environments. Matriarchy ruled the roost; and man quite willingly served her more or less as a bondsman. This opinion gets validated by the following observation made by F. Fawcett: "This system [Matriarchy], obtaining at one time amongst the Celts and other races of Europe, was probably universal in the sense that it existed at some period in the life history of every race of mankind, and is now to be found here and there in the world" (186). But in course of time the man-made social and cultural systems perennially sidelined the importance of woman by way of adopting only for themselves a programme of enlightenment and progress. In this programme of enlightenment and progress the due share and prerogative of woman had always been neglected. Virginia Woolf in her book *"A Room of One's Own"* rightly comments on this sidelining of woman by history in all its practical counters:

Imaginatively she is of the highest importance; practically she is completely insignificant. She pervades poetry from cover to cover; she is all but absent from history. She dominates the lives of kings and conquerors in fiction; in fact she was the slave of any boy whose parents forced a ring upon her finger. Some of the most inspired words, some of the most profound thoughts in literature fall from her lips; in real life she could hardly read, could hardly spell, and was the property of husband. (qtd. in Singh 64)

Under the thundering shell of man's superiority it is but natural that woman self-negated herself to such an extent that she 'could hardly read, could hardly spell, and was the property of husband.' Such is the stupefying effect that man had imposed on woman. Just as he enslaved and used many of the lower species as domestic hands to facilitate his comforts, he looked at women also as mere enslavable products of nature. The surrealistic avidity of man abolished the natural as well as the real concrete worth of being-in-the world in callously sidelining woman and her real naturalistic prerogatives. It is not only a matter of neglecting woman's all important place of honour in the naturalistic counters but also a stringent suppression of the feminine faculty itself with a great strategic control almost as a matter of privilege extended to man by the anonymous, unwritten, and incredible laws of self-supposed superiority.

In effect, the relationship of man and woman is not that of master and slave. Kamala Das fervently clarifies that she as a woman has greater place and purpose in the scheme of nature. From this angle, she does not bargain for a mere equality of sexes; she wants that there should be a wide and proper recognition of the superiority of woman in the state of nature. In the name of morals, ethics, and religion, this naturalistic phenomenal property of woman should not be sabotaged. It is a naturalistic fact that nature depends primarily on woman as a creative base in its formula of evolution. So far as the genetic standards are concerned, man is merely a provider of seed. It is woman who receives the seed and synthesises it with egg in her, and contributes for the formation, growth, and fulfilment of the living human agent. The following very striking lines of Das's poem "Jaisurya" would illustrate how precious is this motherhood for her:

> Love is not important, that makes the blood
> Carouse, nor the man who brands you with his
> Lust, but is shed as slough at end of each
> Embrace. Only that matters which forms as
> Toadstool under lightning and rain, the soft
> Stir in womb, the foetus growing, for,
> Only the treasures matter that were washed
> Ashore, not the long blue tides that washed them
> In. . . . (D 27)

Even the present day naturalists admit the primacy of woman as a creative agent. But then, the very purpose of nature in its evolutionary phenomena is a permanent secret of nature itself. In spite of Darwin's theory of evolution and that of natural selection, the ultimate purpose of nature in evolution is still a mystery. On the same analogy Kamala Das contends that woman as the primary creative base of nature should be regarded with a sense of mystical adulation.

There are two polarizing grounds on which woman transacts with her man: in the social context and in the feminine physiological context. In the social context man always tried to subjugate and enslave woman by way of dictating the very terms and conditions of her survival; and in the feminine physiological context, which includes her psychological personality also, man had never shown a reasonable understanding of woman as an equal individual personality nor awarded her due share of opportunity to enhance her inner being and its significance for herself. In the companionship of man, there are again two levels of operation at which woman struggles to establish her identity: one is at the inevitable creaturely level of survival in the context of nature; and the other refers to the existential height and honour that she deserves in accordance with the social laws of equality, fraternity, and love. Kamala Das perceived that both at the creaturely level of survival and the existential level of heights there is a gross unsympathetic man prevailing upon woman, as a malignant force to reckon with. In the present context, more particularly in the Indian situation, there is a great and deplorable lack of mutual understandings between man and woman, as a result of which the whole communal life suffers a sort of atrophy. Ultimately, the whole poetic argument of Kamala Das turns out to be a fervent appeal for the men-folk to co-ordinate their senses and sensibilities in an equal plane of mutual understanding. Her poetry becomes a clarion call on behalf of woman making a serious and violent threat probably of the very extinction of human content from humanity, if man would not make proper coordination of his senses and sensibilities, more particularly in relation to woman and quite generally in relation to nature itself. She never hesitates in charging that men never come to the requisite and expected levels in being equal partners of their women companions as understanding and loving friends. In the poem "A Losing Battle" she evaluates men's worth, "Men are worthless, to trap them / Use the cheapest bait cf all, but never / Love . . ." (OSK 48). Here 'the cheapest bait of all' is the same as the "grand flamboyant lust" of the poem "The Freaks" (OP 11). The use of the word 'trap' itself is an indication of the snare of lust from which man can never redeem himself in his relationship with woman.

Therefore, what Kamala Das traces in the male entity is a macho-syndrome in all the cultural counters of interaction: linguistic, social and familial, and psychological. Each of the personae of her poems portrays the quintessential woman who always asserts herself against the patriarchal prejudices and hypocrisies ingrained in the social and cultural counters. If so, the ultimate purpose of her poetic arguments is to denounce and demolish the culturally sanctioned structure of patriarchal authoritarianism, its linguistic parameters, and above all, the inauthentic macho-syndrome embedded in the male consciousness.

1. *The Crusade against Patriarchy*

It is a fact that the naturalistic prerogative of woman was ruthlessly suppressed by way of imposing upon her all sorts of psychological and physiological abstractions in the way of her freedom of thought and action. Further, as far as the differentiation between man and woman in the context of social and familial interactions is concerned, again, it is a strategically contrived malady by the patriarchal civilization with the intriguing purpose of carving a superior place and status for men in the society. In this context, the following findings of Beauvoir are very important:

> One is not born, but rather becomes, a woman. No biological, psychological, or economic fate determines the figure that the human female presents in society; it is civilization as a whole that produces this creature, intermediate between male and eunuch, which is described as feminine. (9)

The fury of Beauvoir at the patriarchal bias in our existing system is understandable. The place apportioned to woman by the existing conventions is well brought out in the expression 'between male and eunuch,' and is quite vibrant. In addition to the fact that such exploitation is absolutely humiliating, it is also a matter of deriding the fundamental human dignities of being-in-the world. The central experience in Kamala Das's poetry is the feminine fury directed towards this 'civilization as a whole that produces this creature, intermediate between male and eunuch, which is described as feminine.' In her poem "Ode to a Lynx" she says:

> Civilization irks me with its cunning ways
>
> I connect only with candour. (CP 88)

Civilization is particularly a human property. The process of civilization invariably transcends the parameters of the blue print of nature. In the name of civilization the social, cultural, ethical, and moral institutions very often prescribe some rigid codes of conduct which are likely to crumble and annihilate the naturalistic potentialities of men and women. Very often the naturalistic necessities of women are mercilessly crushed and crumbled. The whole poetic purpose of Kamala Das is to reaffirm the most needful clarification concerning the naturalistic demands of woman in a growing civilization. She intensely feels that the civilized man should not neglect the freedoms and choices of woman. It is with a kind of courage to be a woman-in-the world that she writes her poetry. She certainly does not accept the idea of woman and her faculties being neglected in the civilized social system of the sort that we have in the world today.

Apparently the naturalistic exploitation of woman is simultaneously linked with the breadwinner-ego in men. At the outset, the male-world deprived woman any access to self-dependable economic prerogatives. In many of the traditional cultures women are deprived of their inheritance facilities in the family properties. Even the educational polarities also are awfully variant and different in the man-woman ratio. This is another extraneous manner in which man held all the choices and freedoms of woman tight in his hand in the name of traditions, moralities, religions, and last but not the least, the most unfounded concept of purity of the race. It is this ruthless and meaningless manner of man that ultimately contributed for a furious revulsion and rivalry that all women commonly share in their hearts of hearts. But interestingly, they would not come to open challenges for fear of losing the minimal survival facilities and protections offered by man in the context of the social and cultural systems. However, these minimal survival facilities are mocked at by Das in her poem "A Feminist's Lament":

> An ideal woman, they said, was but
> a masochist. Trained from infancy
> to wear the flannels of cowardice
> next to her skin, trained to lie inert
> under a male, committed by vows
> to feed her, clothe her and buy for her
> the 1000 sq. ft. flat with a loft
> for storing the debris of passing years. (OSK 127)

The suggestion that woman is not innately inert is notable in the expression 'trained to lie inert.' The life force in man and woman is naturally of the same measure, but it is her 'training' that makes the passive woman that she is in the social and familial environments. As soon as she becomes the property of a single man, the fire of her essential feminine faculty is put out and she is made to 'lie inert / under a male.' Also in another poem called "Love," she talks about how the intellectual faculty of woman is shattered by male company:

Until I found you
I wrote verse, drew pictures
and went out with friends
for walks.
Now that I love you,
curled like an old mongrel
my life lies, content
in you.... (OP 23)

Again, this 'Now that I love you' situation is something feigned and hollow, and this hollowness is born out of the dismal state of the woman persona. Instead of a heartening and comforting bestowal of love and care of equal measure from her man the woman lies 'curled like an old mongrel' at his feet. Since the literal meaning of the word 'mongrel' is an animal, particularly a dog of a mixed breed, for the woman it is again the minimal survival necessity i.e. food, clothe, and 'the 1000 sq. ft. flat with a loft / for storing the debris of passing years' that compels her life to lie 'content' in him.

Precisely speaking, the poet considers that men are definitely aware of the superiority and importance of the female genetic system; but in their pursuit of selfishness and self-aggrandisement they prefer to suppress and marginalize this naturalistic superiority of women by way of neglecting and sidelining her existential privileges, choices, and freedoms in the context of the institutional strictures. It is not a matter of exaggeration if a conclusion is made that man virtually fear woman and her naturalistic superiority. Therefore, he invents all sorts of myths for the purpose of exploiting and subjugating woman under his iron clutches. This social and cultural phenomenon is worth denouncing according to the modern civilized contexts of life, where equalities and equal dignities are constantly and consistently being bargained in the name of social justice. As a matter of fact, so far as the naturalistic genetic variations are concerned, there is an urgent need for a reasonable perception of the nature's need in conceiving man and woman as different entities. Nature does not appear to approve of the naturalistic variations and differences being taken as a ground for opposition and strife. Therefore, in the strict metaphysical comprehension, life, its preservation, and its propagation in the name of race enhancement and enlargement still remain a mystery even after innumerable analytical academic studies through Sociology, Psychology, Prehistory, Phenomenology, Anthropology, and the Logistics of the politics of sex. Through her poetry Kamala Das makes a threatening challenge to men by way of forcibly inviting them to consider the pros and cons of their ham-handed autocratic behaviour towards woman.

2. *The Logo-Centric Anomalies*

It is important to note that all personal experiences, both of men and women, are unique in being their exclusive personal affairs. If so, the deficiency in the traditional language in evaluating male-female personal experiences in an equal manner of understanding became a casualty. Needless to say, woman as a person has her own personal comprehensions and apprehensions of herself; and these comprehensions and apprehensions are required to be attended to prominently by way of lending a sympathetic and judicious ear to her voice. So far as women's writings are concerned, they are not exposed to the full resources of the available theories of language because women as writers have been traditionally constrained to conceal the most intimate details of feminine experiences. In this context, Elaine Showalter's remarks are pertinent. In her opinion, "Women's literature is still haunted by the ghosts of repressed language, and until we have exorcised those ghosts, it ought not to be in language that we base our theory of difference" (467). This truth about language has prompted the modern women writers to altogether reject the traditionally prescribed language formula in their writings. They had to invent new idioms, new phrases, and a new language that is efficient and capable of expressing their experiences, their agonies, and their anxieties. Therefore, as Shoshana Felman puts it, "The challenge facing the woman today is nothing less than to 'reinvent' language . . . to speak not only against, but outside of the specular phallogocentric structure, to establish a discourse the status of which would no longer be defined by the fallacy of masculine meaning" (qtd. in Showalter 465). In the Western feminist poetry, however, this 'challenge' to 'reinvent language' was first taken up by American confessional poets like Anne Sexton, Sylvia Plath, and Adrienne Rich. While making their own rules and ideology of social existence, these women poets have also discovered new dominions and vistas of language that can poetically express the exclusive feminine concerns and experiences. The language they have invented is so potent that it has disturbed the complacent siesta of the masculine world, and upset the applecart of male hegemony.

In Indian English poetry, Kamala Das pioneers the experiment with the creation of a new poetic language suitable to spell out the agonies and aspirations of the collective Indian feminine psyche. She felt the need to redefine the 'specular phallogocentric structure' that is unsuitable and insufficient to catch up with her emotions, feelings, and volitions as a woman. She realized the impotency of the male-oriented traditional language, and for the first time in Indian poetry, she has successfully created a new and powerful language of fury, and expressed it in full blatancy. In the unprecedented poetic revolt unleashed by Kamala Das in the Indian poetic milieu she had no native predecessors to fall back on. She had to experiment with a new style of writing and use of a fresh language and idiom, one suitable for the expression of her exclusive feminine problems. The traditional women poetry in India obviously did not help her as it was too plastic to suit her rebellious temperament. In fact no physical language seemed to have been fit enough to catch up with her stream of consciousness. In this regard Das herself admits:

> I don't find it easy to write either in English or in Malayalam. Language has been very difficult for me. . . .Thoughts were there, but to cover them up, to wrap them up in decent language is very difficult. I am discovering a new language, trying to make a new language, create it, which will suit me. Because I have yet to find a language which can keep pace with thinking. (My Instinct 161)

This kind of logo-centric lacuna is endemic with the male-centred social and cultural activities. The special and unique interior components of woman's experiences as conformed by the male-generations are absolutely lacking in the needful depths of understanding the feminine psychology as well as physiology. The extra-romantic poetic eulogies confectioned by man about woman are substantially defective, for they are born of male-personal apprehensions without any corroborative consent or approval from the feminine angle. If so, all this argumentation by the poet about the parameters of language here suggests at one simple point that her inner experiences of agony cannot be translated into the available logo-centric formulas. As Anne Brewster rightly comments: "She [Kamala Das] craves the total freedom that language can give, to express herself fully in all her paradoxical and complex ramifications, without being bound by reason, reputation, morality or other limiting codes" (142).

In order to 'express fully in all her paradoxical and complex ramifications,' Kamala Das makes vibrant poetic innovations of inventing a verbal medium by way of introducing unique gestures, suggestions, and movements through a sort of symbolic idiom. Her poetry in a way is her unique body-cross against any male-attempt at destroying her feminine worth. In effect, it is this vibrant body language that she invented for her poetic purpose that becomes absolutely inflated with the prominent gestures. This is one of the reasons for the emergence of obscurity in the sense that there is a profound divergence between what the poet offers and what the reader comprehends. One of the many types of ambiguities in poetry occurs, says Empson, "when a statement says nothing, by tautology, by contradiction, or by irrelevant statements; so that the reader is forced to invent statements of his own and they are liable to conflict with one another" (207). This is what can be called the poetic reasons as to how obscurity or strategically implanted defect in the particulars of the poems ultimately turns out to be an exquisite poetic formula of experience acquired by the reader. In this poetic transaction of what exactly happens to the reader as poetic experience in the act of reading, may be distinctly different. This is to say that in the lyric poetry particularly, there is no possibly of insisting upon what T. S. Eliot called 'objective correlative.' The subjective or the personal experience being unique and non-repeatable even for a poet, compounds in itself certain emotive properties whose nature eludes verbal communication. Therefore, in an imaginative poet like Kamala Das what all that perspires in her revolting experience very often remains as a subjective non-correlatable. This non-correlatable, instead of taking a verbal form, comes out in the form of delicate gestures. Whenever the fury becomes uncontrollable and reaches a high pitch, she resolves the problem through tenuous gestures whose performance very often remains ironic both in tone and meaning.

All said and done, with all the initial reactions of opposition and criticism towards Kamala Das and her poetry, the male generation has been profoundly compelled to her voice and to her urgency of clarifying the feminine point of view. Rightly speaking, Das is a love poet and not a poet of hatred as she has wrongly been comprehended. The strong and vibrant phenomenon of hatred poured upon the ignorant manners of man in all its dimensions of strife and fury is only a matter of her own stylistic mode of expression. If so, it is the new idiom and language of Das that becomes a thing to be aesthetically appraised and comprehended not through opposition and criticism but by way of assuming upon oneself the actor's trunk of interior paramour in being one with her subtle and vibrant exposition of feminine concerns.

In creating her own poetic language, Kamala Das surpasses all the possible linguistic conventions. However, while inventing a language, like in the case of any other new inventions, the inventor will have to deal with the 'saviours' of traditions. Helen Cixous very aptly clarifies the reason for this confrontation. In her own words,

> . . . as soon as we exist, we are born into language and language speaks (to) us, dictates its law, a law of death: it lays down its familial model, lays down its conjugal model, and even at the moment of uttering a sentence, admitting a notion of "being". . . . we are already seized by a certain kind of masculine desire, the desire that mobilizes philosophical discourse. (482)

All this confirms that we are stringently ensituationalized by language, as a result of which the very inborn freedom of being-in-the world gets smashed. In order to shake off this seizure of 'a certain kind of masculine desire,' one needs extra energy and audacity. One is in a vicious circle and getting out of this circle becomes a daredevil act. The situation becomes graver particularly when the traditional roots are embedded in the logo-centric stylistics. For Kamala Das the traditional language, insofar as it restricts her poetic imaginative freedom, becomes absolutely of no use as a medium for self-expression. For a poet of her sensibility and sensitivity language should effectively reflect her interiority and the turmoil it goes through in a social milieu where she finds herself a misfit. She is not a painter of the plasticity of the outer panorama; but she is a scriptwriter on her deep and turbulent interiority. As this interiority is a state that is almost inconceivable, the spontaneous outflow of emotions born out of this state is not fully comprehensible by any available language formulas. But the urgency of expression in her is so potent that she would not falter; and she takes up the task of creating her own language. In the poem "An Introduction" Kamala Das spells out her rebellion in clear terms against any criticism on her poetic language; like a critics' critic she asks:

> Why not leave
> Me alone, critics, friends, visiting cousins,
> Every one of you? Why not let me speak in
> Any language I like? The language I speak
> Becomes mine, its distortions, its queernesses,
> All mine, mine alone. It is half English, half
> Indian, funny perhaps, but it is honest,
> It is human as I am human, don't
> You see? (OP 26)

The exhortation of the poet to her 'critics, friends, and visiting cousins' speaks for itself that the ground realities of general public in India and their attitudes towards the women's movement are not at all worthy of decent rhetoric. In pleading that she as well as her language be left to herself, she indicates her prerogatives as a creative artist in handling her ideas as well as her language almost in an exclusive manner of her own. This is one more way of suggesting at the uniqueness of her poetry, which she is consciously aware of. Also she is aware that she would incur the personal displeasure of her readers because of the simple fact that they would not approve on their own authority the freedom of expression for a woman in a male oriented society. In effect, her 'All mine, mine alone' language is a violent formula of expressing the very heat and dust of her humiliation in being a sabotaged and relegated being in the world. It is interesting to note that all this heat and dust is directed towards the trenchant sexual politics ingrained in our social and domestic conventions.

The naturalness of her language is confirmed in the subsequent lines of the poem by asserting that her poems are spontaneous outcries of the occasions: ". . . it is useful to me as cawing / Is to crows or roaring to the lions, it / Is human speech" (OP 26). 'Cawing' of crows, and 'roaring' of lions are involuntary and instantaneous outcries of the occasions. Likewise, the human occasions in the volatile circumstances prompt such involuntary outcries in order to give vent to the pent-up repressed feelings and emotions. What the poet implies here is the fact that her poems are the proper outcries of the occasions. The pleasure and the pain of these 'cries' are inseparably involved. The love of expression on the one hand and the agony of the inexpressibility on the other ultimately contribute for the sad outcries, i.e. her poems. In this context, her poetry takes its life-blood from the British Romanticists and the modern confessional poets who always insisted upon pain as the necessary springboard of human expressions. Kamala Das's 'outcries' are on the central ground of the painful experience of being a woman. The spiralling self rages within against the lack of recognition. The articulation of this anger becomes impossible in any socially recognized traditional language formulas. It has to be honest, and, therefore, as she says in the poem "Loud Posters," it necessitates stretching of her

> two dimensional
>
> Nudity on sheets of weeklies, monthlies
>
> Quarterlies, a sad sacrifice" (OP 47).

The active world of experience as we have it is always three dimensional, but the world of poetic imagination, like a cinematographic picture present on its screen, is just two dimensional like a mirror image when we are face to face with the mirror. In her poetry, Kamala Das is always face to face with her poetic imagination, and renders the felt image in the possible language, which instantly provokes her to 'cry' out. And in doing so, her poems become unique and vibrant articulations of the suffocative experiences that lay hidden for centuries in the interiorities of the women's psyche. She is aware of this uniqueness, and asserts that her poems are:

> . . . the speech of the mind
> That is here and not there, a mind that sees and hears and
> Is aware. Not the deaf, blind speech
> Of trees in storm or of monsoon clouds or rain or the
> Incoherent mutterings of the blazing
> Funeral pyre. ("An Introduction," OP 26)

The use of antithesis and paradox is vibrant here. The demonstrative complexity of phrases like 'here' and 'not there' really does not need any further clarification to what they express on the occasion. However, Vrinda Nabar complains of ambiguity in these lines, and asks: "What precisely do phrases like 'here and there' mean? . . . All this sounds suspiciously like raving, an extravagance" (31). If the content of 'ambiguity' is present, it is there with the poetic purpose of suggestively pointing at the poetic target. However, a closer look at the context as brought out in these lines would reveal that there is no place for ambiguity or verbosity here. The 'mind / That is here and not there' is a confident pronouncement of the originality of her poetic revolt. This originality is asserted through suggesting at the spatial variation of the mind, the mind that is not to be found elsewhere ('That is here and not there'). It is a hint at her resolution to override the traditional limits prescribed for the expositions of the feminine psyche. Further, 'the deaf, blind speech / Of trees,' the 'monsoon clouds,' 'the rain,' and the 'mutterings' of the 'funeral pyre' are basically meaningless sound productions. These elements of nature may have the ability of expression, but they are free from suffocating experience of inexpressibility. Also, since the dead do not know who died, the funeral pyres cannot subjectively lament the death. Here the condition of her poetic mind is in contrast to that of these elements. It has to find relief by ventilating the agonies and suffocations. It is through poetic expressions that it fulfils this purpose. In fact the above lines have the effect of a sudden waking from a hallucinatory state of inexpressibility and suffocation, and bursting out; and at the background of this outburst is a rebellious spirit against centuries of oppression undergone by women.

Das's awareness of her powerful language makes her place a warning, though ironically, before the 'critics' and 'friends':

> But I tell myself, words
>
> Are a nuisance, beware of them, they
>
> Can be so many things, a
>
> Chasm, where running feet must pause. ("Words," OSK 36)

Such are the dangers of words "growing / From within" (OSK 36). And also she is aware of the isolation she may have to face owing to her curt language because words sometimes become "A knife most willing to cut your best / Friend's throat" (OSK 36). But she cannot help their coming 'From within.' They come quite effortlessly and naturally, "like leaves on a tree, / They never seem to stop their coming / From a silence, somewhere deep within" (OSK 36). Nissim Ezekiel in his poem "Poet, Lover, Birdwatcher" insists, "The best poets wait for words," and then alone "the poet finds his moral proved" (L. 3), whereas for Kamala Das, waiting for words might lead to camouflaging truth. In her poem "Write Without a Pause" she exhorts the poets to:

> Write without
>
> A pause, don't search for pretty words,
>
> Dilute truth, but write in haste, of
>
> Everything perceived, and known and loved . . . . (qtd. in Radha 24)

While writing 'in haste, of / Everything perceived, and known and loved,' Kamala Das's poetic vocabulary defies all conventional norms. The 'All mine, mine alone' language grows in her naturally 'like leaves on a tree,' which is charged with powerful emotions, and is invariably targeted at the patriarchal bias. The honorific tradition of women poetry might also be abounding in descriptions of love, frustration, marriage etc; but it had never endeavoured to display its creator's "two dimensional nudity" (OP 47), or give an account of how they played "Naked in the pond" (D 3), or "the jerky way he / Urinates" (D 25). They never gave the reader "The warm shock of menstrual blood" (D 25). Writing about "pubis" (OP 51), "the musk of sweat between the breasts" (D 25) or about the "chests where / New hair sprouted like great-winged moths" (OSK 54) was a wild dream for the traditional women poets. As Nabar rightly points out in the context of Das's powerful poetic vocabulary, "One of her chief strengths is her ability to write of love honestly, not in order to romanticize or soften, but to describe even what had conventionally been hardly mentioned – the smell of the body, sprouting hair on chests and elsewhere, menstrual blood, uneven teeth etc." (63). For a poet who incessantly writes about the most intimate relationships and experiences, their elations and frustrations, use of such vocabulary becomes quite natural in order to express their complexities in the most passionate and subtlest manner. Kamala Das, however, uses such expressions in her poetry not for their cheap erotic or rhetorical effects, but she does it with a vengeance in order to mock at the hypocrisy ingrained in the hollow social prejudices of nice feminine concealments and sacrosanctities. Thus in her poetic language we find a 'different kind of beauty' that is not present in the plasticity of the language used by the Indian Romantic poets.

3. *The Denouncement of the Inauthentic Macho in Man*

Coming to the practical experiences, the formulas of male and female dominations are categorically institutional, and differ from person to person. What the modern feminist thinkers suggest is that there is but a gross imbalance and insufficiency in the man-woman relationship. In reality, the man-woman relationship always hangs on the central beam of petty male ego. Kamala Das as a feminist poet is conducting a poetic feud against men. Since 'everything is right in love and war,' it can be squarely understood that she has some strong point of view in writing her revolutionary and aggressive poetry. In the case of Das the concept of society and fellowmen is compounded in the volatile familial relations. The poetic manner in which she taunts and exposes the incapacitated nature of man in understanding his woman projects her almost a feminist virago challenging the very potential and intention of man in considering himself as an equal loving partner. In a way she rebels at the inhuman tendencies of a self-engrossed and self-elating society in perpetuating what the modern psychologists call 'macho' as a ruling passion in the male progeny. So the ultimate tenet that Das wanted to demolish is the proneness of men towards macho compounded with a strident egoism born of their exclusive, self-emanated, and self-sanctioned temperamental superiority as the intended trend-benders of the social systems. She is absolutely convinced with the idea that it is the macho-egoism of man that had blinkered and blinded his naturalistic potentialities in properly coordinating his senses and sensibilities in a harmonious manner in relation to women and their naturalistic rights of being-in-the world as persons endowed with all human dignities.

In the poem "In Love," the brutal and self-centred approach of the male partner is revealed by the woman persona as unbearable as "the burning mouth / Of sun" (OP 15); looking at the 'sun,' she is reminded of

> . . . his
> mouth... and his limbs like pale and
> carnivorous plants reaching
> out for me, and the sad lie
> of my unending lust. . . . (OP 15).

The expression, 'the sad lie / of my unending lust,' is in fact poignantly revealing, which suggest at the indifference of the female partner to a shallow physical transaction between them. The female persona avenges the male self-centredness with a deceitful show of 'the sad lie' of her 'unending lust.' Here the love play becomes a mere mechanical act only involving the bodies of the partners in love. In such an outward togetherness,

> Where
> Is room, excuse or even
> Need for love, for, isn't each
> Embrace a complete thing, a
> Finished jigsaw, when mouth on
> mouth, I lie ignoring my poor
> moody mind, while pleasure
> with deliberate gaiety
> trumpets harshly into
> the silence of the room. ("In Love," OP 15)

The moment 'mouth' sets on (my) 'mouth,' 'I' becomes absolutely unmindful of the 'poor moody mind.' The expression 'poor moody mind' is important here. The very 'moodiness' of the mind confirms the need of intended desire for absolute freedom of mind to be itself. But the 'mouth on mouth' deliberately marginalizes the essential freedom of the mind and declares it as a non-entity. This state of the mind is insufferable because 'pleasure' harshly trumpets 'into the silence of the room' with a 'deliberate gaiety.' The most requisite sublime ecstatic state of mind, which is otherwise desiring silence i.e. freedom, becomes disturbed. Thus, the love-play is a momentary 'deliberate gaiety' into the mind and crushes mercilessly the calm and quietude of the mind ('silence of the room'). The anticipated delicacy and softness of the situation is contrasted by the expression 'pleasure / With deliberate gaiety / Trumpets harshly into the room.' When 'Each embrace' turns out to be as mechanical as a 'Finished jigsaw,' each painful 'Finished jigsaw' reverberates in her senses through horrid images like:

> . . .the sleek crows flying
> like poison on wings and at
> night from behind the Burdwan Road

the corpse-bearers cry 'Bol
Hari Bol'. . . . ("In Love," OP 15)

The images of 'poison on wings' and 'the corpse-bearers' suggest at the deadening effect of each interpersonal entanglement on the senses and sensibilities, and the ultimate outcome of life-in-death.

The woman persona's frustration with the partner's attitude towards mutual intimacy, is vibrantly expressed also in the poem "The Freaks":

Can this man with
Nimble finger tips unleash
Nothing more alive than the
Skin's lazy hungers? (OP 11)

The entire verbal fury of such lines in her poetry is in its reality a sobbing appeal to her male counterpart to be more and more concerned in being a partner. It is all a plea for a sort of equally shared sublimation. Man being a proud self-serving agent (due to his false ego) often leaves his woman in a lurch and vacuum. He never gives himself a chance to understand his female-partner other than 'unleash(ing)' 'Skin's lazy hungers.' Thus, her real hatred is against the vituperative manner of man as a performer; she expects him to be a seasoned artist in performance just like women by nature are artists. The artistic finesse of woman as arrogantly claimed by Kamala Das may not be real; but one thing is certain, and that is, nature exclusively endowed woman with the creator's prerogative as a mother, as a wife, as a daughter, and even as a situational partner in life. In the naturalistic context male principle is a mediate phenomenon, and the female principle is the immediate base. It is her umbilical association and relation with the created beings that makes woman comparatively superior to man.

The stigmatic manner of the masculine entity showing a sort of gross unconcern and irresponsibility is more or less common for all women; and, to that extent, Das violently represents the frustrated feminine concerns in the man-woman relations. In her fight against man and his self-supposed superiority, she goes to the extent of exposing man's abject ignorance about the feminine psyche and the naturalistic physiological demands of woman as woman. As a matter of fact, the poet, in this particular poetic operation, charges and rails against the most probable lack of the needful vigour and vitality in the men-folk to come to the expectations of women in general. This is more or less the stand taken by Simone de Beauvoir in *The Second Sex,* and Virginia Woolf in *A Room of One's Own.* For instance, one can trace the trumpets of a new awareness in the modern feminine sensibility when in the said book Woolf comments, "Women have served all these centuries as looking glass possessing the magic and delicious power of reflecting the figure of a man twice its natural size" (qtd. in Woolf, "Quotations," *Hutchinson*).

However, whereas Woolf sees in women all the properties of a 'looking glass,' for Das the 'looking glass' is a third device against which the male figure wants to juxtapose himself and his woman only to see himself reflected bigger and stronger. In the poem "The Looking Glass," she ironically suggests at these male expectations:

> Getting a man to love you is easy
> Only be honest about your wants as
> Woman. Stand nude before the glass with him
> So that he sees himself the stronger one
> And believes it so, and you so much more
> Softer, younger, lovelier . . . . (D 25)

The ludicrous manner of male demands from his female partner is pornographically exposed here. Man is such a daft creature that he would be complacently happy with a mere two-dimensional image of himself and his beloved reflected in the mirror. His image of relative superiority of himself gets a boost here. But then he is absolutely oblivious of the three dimensional literal woman available for him in his hands. In effect it is the mirror image of egocentric male superiority that makes him the necessary fool of himself without ever ranging his vision to the reality of things. The irony in the initial line 'Getting a man to love is easy' suggests that a lover who gloats on his own male-superiority image is very easy to find, as more or less every man is stuffed with this ego and superiority complex. Contrary to the above condition, getting a real man to love is not at all easy, particularly in a world where only mirror images make everything and the reality on hand is nothing. The ironic suggestion at the need to inflate the male ego in the lines, 'Stand nude before the glass with him / So that he sees himself the stronger one / And believes it so, and you so much more / Softer, younger, lovelier...' suggest at a vicious and clandestine agenda tacitly operating within the social system to see woman as a weaker entity than man. What is expected of woman, not by man alone but by the society as a whole, is a total surrender of her personality before 'her man.' She should customarily

> Gift him all,
> Gift him what makes you woman, the scent of
> Long hair, the musk of sweat between the breasts
> The warm shock of menstrual blood, and all your
> Endless female hungers. ("The Looking Glass," D 25)

The expression in the last line 'all your / Endless female hungers' is very important. Virtually speaking, the 'endless female hungers' do not come under the category of giftable items. In fact the poet means to imply that she is required to mercilessly sacrifice all her desires just to be a plaything in the hands of her male partner. In the above lines Das is at the height of her piercingly potent language that prima facie appears distasteful and pornographic. Here S.C. Harrex rightly comments on the effectiveness of the poem: "We notice in "The Looking Glass" how she confidently speaks in tones of dramatic irony, portraying the expectations of Indian male egoism, while being ironically bitter about the sexual politics of female submissiveness" (163). In the poem "Composition" she mocks at such 'expectations of Indian male egoism' in the familial context:

> Husbands and wives,
> here is my advice to you.

Obey each other's crazy commands,
ignore the sane.
Turn your home into a merry
dog-house,
marriage is meant to be all this
any way,
being arranged in
most humorous heaven. (D 33-34)

The new poetic definition that she gives to marriage is quite ironic and quite mind- harrowing simultaneously. The marriage institution itself needs to be radically emancipated from its traditional structural rigidities. Since it is a personal matter of wives and husbands, she draws the attention of Indian 'Husbands and wives' to the burning problem on hand by way of looking at the marriage institution itself in a vibrantly transparent manner instead of taking a traditional parameter for granted as they are. In a sense Kamala Das implores husbands and wives to become human personalities at the outset, without ever relegating themselves to the traditional typifications of 'husbands and wives.' Therefore, the above lines vibrantly speak about the manner in which traditional marriage norms make the family institution into a 'merry / dog-house.' Elsewhere in an article she says, "In twenty years marriage might become unfashionable. Already I hear the rumblings of revolt among the upper middle classes" (*Path* 137).

As a matter of fact, the poetic outcry of Kamala Das is a persuasive appeal to the fellowmen to free themselves from the dogmatic forces that have been fiercely in operation in the social and familial environments throughout history. She invites the men-folk for an introspective understanding of women's needs, and implores them to initiate a process to better the future of human race by correcting the cultural mistake. The mother-woman dichotomy that rocked the imagination and chiselled the personality of D.H. Lawrence is plentifully recognized by Kamala Das in railing against the ambivalent self-serving manner of man as an agent. The traditional manner of attributing sacrosanct phenomenal features to womanhood and the simultaneous manner of attributing a sort of hateful disposition towards femininity ultimately contributes for an overall nerve-lock in men in their equivocal transactions with women. If so, the poetry of Kamala Das is a concerned invitation for an analytical outlook as to how best the fruits of life can be shared to the satisfaction of all. It is an invitation for consideration and discussion. Hers is a transparent confessional formula of pouring forth the feminine desires and emotions. For generations together, man, brought up in the chauvinistic, autocratic traditions within the patriarchy, really metamorphosed himself into an egocentric and authoritarian patriarch. Das's grievance is against this exclusive patriarch syndrome in fellowmen. It goes without saying that man should humble himself by way of relinquishing his false ego, and start functioning as a real creative and progressive agent along with woman, and as a perennial cherisher of happiness and not misery.

In Kamala Das, thus, the phenomenon of nature and phenomenon of fellowmen get turned into a curious admixture or synthesis. The synthetic effect of fellowmen and nature in their togetherness contributes for her experiences coupled with emotions, feeling, volitions, and desires. The outward expression of these experiences in reaction performs themselves as violent products of intentions. One important aspect that comes with her attitude is with experience itself. For her, experience is not what all that happen to her in the formal and informal interactions. Experience for her is the way she receives it, she reacts to it, and she reconciles/irreconciles with it. Intention too is a subtle and evasive property of energy. It cannot be handled or concretised in the manner that we comprehend time, space, fellowmen etc. In a subjective sense, intention is an abstract that stands as a backbone for mutual affections as well as disruptions of it, and the consequent ironies and antitheses. The resultant poetic creation lands on a sort of irresolvable tension that in its term breeds a natural violence and retaliation towards the objects of her intentions. Very often the object of her intentions is conformed in the male counterpart who, according to her, callously and unconcernedly cold-shoulders her aspirations for consummation and sublimation of feminine self and feminine physical entity. The protest that reverberates through her poetry towards men takes the form of violent poetic reactions. However, her poetry of violence and anger towards man is not with the purpose of defeating him or throwing him out as a hateful entity. Behind this streak of poetic violence and retaliation, there is always a bleak and omniscient cry of persuasion in order to make the feminine demands transparent. Her poetry is vibrant with a tone of restlessness and grievance, with the help of which she tries poetically to plead for a glorious prospect of mutual understanding and enhancement of happiness.

The properties of violence against nature and fellowmen automatically directs the artist to evaluate the impressions on one's own self. Poetry for Kamala Das is a medium of her personal experience. It becomes imminent to take up a critical reflection and evaluation of the subjective self of the poet. And this aspect is taken up for discussion in the next chapter.

4

Violence and the Self

There is a way of understanding Kamala Das's practical immediate poetic fight with her male counterpart as a symbolic gesture of an eternal metaphysical phenomenon, as an unerasable ground of operation between the self and the other, between mind and matter, between spirit and substance, between essence and figuration. This mind-matter tug of war is constant, continual, irresolvable, and unending. In the mutual transactions of the self and the other, the other permanently remains a mystery, and the self indefatigably tries its own strength of falling into a war (of words) with the other. In this war, since it is a matter of nature's mystery itself, there are no victors or vanquished. In the true metaphysic of things in the world, mind and matter have to conduct their mutual transactions without any support from the third. The third does not exist at all in a rational sense. It is just like the relation of water and river where water is the self and the river the other. Kamala Das symbolizes this metaphysical fight that subsists in the woman-man relationship where woman is the self, and man is the other. The self is perennially, and fervently too, trying its own strength at exhausting the meaning of the other, but the other always eludes such a possibility of exhausting the essential mystery of being the other. Das is well aware of the fact that she would not gain any viable point of victory in the fight she conducts with man as the other. But then, the mystery of man as the other remaining perennially intact, what all she wants to assert for herself is the very strength of her freedom as a being in the world. As Jerry Aline Flieger confirms, this transaction between man and woman should be conducted with the help of language of the Unconscious itself. This point can be elaborated in Flieger's own words: "The paradigm of desiring intersubjectivity is written in the very language of the Unconscious itself" (358). What exactly is this 'language of the Unconscious'? In the context of Kamala Das we arrive at two contradictory formulas: one is that same old Wordsworthian formula of 'spontaneous overflow of powerful feelings,' and the other refers to the fundamental manner of decoding the body language into a perceivable poetic entity. In spite of the fact that there is a tilt towards the British Romanticism, she prominently addresses her poetry to the twentieth century readers, where Naturalism and Realism are the essential ruling poetic forces. The body language which converts into poetic symbols and metaphors, instead of being a rationalized clarification of the women's needs, awfully turns out to be a fervent invitation for men to probe and find for themselves the essential content of the women's needs, where man and woman are mutually desiring intersubjective entities.

Elaine Showalter draws our attention to "The Mad Woman in the Attic" by Sandra Gilbert and Susan Gubar wherein they had pinpointed "a feminist revision of Harold Bloom's Oedipal model of literary history as a conflict between fathers and sons and accept the essential psychoanalytic definition of the woman artist as displaced, disinherited, and excluded" (qtd. in Showalter 468). Needless to say, the 'psychoanalytic definition of the woman artist' as comprehended by Harold Bloom is biased and insufficient in the context of the generation of feminist writers. The possible alternative for the 'Oedipal model of literary history as a conflict between fathers and sons,' should be available in the conceivable Electra model of literary history where the conflict is between mothers and daughters. But, however, this Electra model is not to displace, disinherit, or exclude men as artists. On the other hand, Kamala Das starts a new poetic paradigm as suggested above. In this context, it is relevant to resort to the words of Adrienne Rich; says Rich: "In order to live a fully human life, we require not only control of our bodies . . . we must touch the unity and resonance of our physicality, the corporeal ground of our intelligence" (qtd. in Showalter 463). The expression 'control of our bodies' simultaneously refers to man and woman equally. Such a 'control' must invariably address to 'unity and resonance of our physicality.' Here comes the major problem of clearly and transparently knowing and understanding the mutual intersubjectivity. It is a fact that nature conceived man and woman as genetic opposites, and their personalities are absolutely held in the relative mysteries of uniqueness and ambiguity. If the biological needs of man and woman are held as nature's secret in this unique ambiguity there is specific difference between the needs of nature in its evolution, and the intersubjective fulfilments of man and woman in the living moments of experience.

The purpose of nature itself was prominently designated as evolution through natural selection as confirmed by Charles Darwin. If the 'natural selection' complexity of Charles Darwin is right, the mystery of intersubjectivity should permanently remain a mystery only. But unravelling this mystery, to the extent that it is a programme of Kamala Das, she just rails and rebels against the oppressions as resorted to by generations of men in their attitudes and disposition towards women. Her immediate poetic programme is just in evocatively denouncing the traditional contexts of oppressions. Man's psyche, which had inherited the oppression syndrome, must first be rationalized. Therefore, her poems are rebellious reverberations of the essential need of perceiving the 'unity of our physicality,' which is 'the corporeal ground of our intelligence.' In her poetry these reverberations manifest themselves through her self's expeditions along the precipices of life in its interactions with the 'other,' its passion for life, its futile jaunts through the labyrinths of love and lust, and the self's final comprehension of the sterile vacuum and darkness in which it has to grope, having no way out.

The Agony of Being-in-the Here-and-Now

As a matter of fact, the feminist violence as articulated in Das's poetry displays the tug-of-war between her inner self and the external realities that are compounded in the immediate social and familial situations. This violence springs from a perpetual struggle between the psychic aspirations and the social compulsions. The poetic self rebels against the strategically contrived imposition of a 'cultural unconscious' over the feminine 'natural unconscious' by the patriarchal autocratic civilization. In this context Helen Cixous' clarification about the 'unconscious' is quite relevant: "There is work to be done on female sexual pleasure and on the production of an unconscious that would no longer be the classic unconscious. The unconscious is always cultural and when it talks, it tells you your old stories" (488). It was Levi-Strauss who had pertinently drawn a distinction between nature and culture. According to Robert Con Davis and Ronald Schleifer, Strausse even goes to the extent of discussing "the great opposition between Nature and Culture" (Davis 450). Kamala Das insists upon the idea of erasing the cultural 'classic unconscious' from the minds of men and re-introducing the natural unconscious in its place. Precisely speaking, the basic cultural stands and standards rigidly determining the place of women in culture must be modified in such a manner that the natural unconscious goes to fill the gap. When this natural unconscious takes the poetic form, there emerges clarity of understanding woman in her naturalistic context. This kind of visualizing woman in the natural context through poetry is always a matter of effecting open insights instead of closed endings that are usually dictated by the cultural unconscious. The 'cultural unconscious' blinkers the vision of men by way of conforming to certain set situational responses. The ultimate purpose of Kamala Das in constantly and continuously speaking about her natural unconscious is to present it as a formula to be re-discovered by man in one form or the other. In turning against her own self she re-discovers for herself the feminine natural unconscious and poetically presents the same through innumerable poetic images and symbols.

For the authentic self of the poet being-in-the here-and now itself, to the extent that it is absolutely informed by the 'cultural unconscious,' turns out to be a trauma. The signals that the perceiving mind communicates from the external world to the inner self get rejected recurrently at the psychic level. Similarly when the outer world continually discards the gestures transmitted by the inner self, it becomes a persistent shuttling of incompatible signals to the self and back like sea waves, which eventually sparks off violence within resulting in rebellious poetic outrages.

The poet attributes her bitter personal experiences to the disorder of the so-called civilized world and its prejudices. The malaise thus created within flows out in the form of poetic confessions giving vent to the pent-up suffocative emotions which eventually brings about a relief in the poetic self. If so, her poetry is not a portrayal of the outer landscape; what is revealed is the vast, complex inner panorama and the existential pressures it confronts in its interactions with the outer world. There is always a conflict between within and without. The self seems to have a predilection to withdraw into the shell of solitude fearing defeat. This sense of impending defeat finds expression in the following lines of "Anamalai Poems VII":

> If someone would only remove the sun
> from my way I would not have to face
> another sorrowful day but I would
> lie then in kind night's embrace, soothed by its
> blinded compassion while its groping fingers
> would anaesthetize my private terrors... (BK 156)

Such lines emerge clearly from a self, defeated and fatigued by the external world of the 'other.' Whenever the poet touches upon the external world it is only to contrast it with her psychic demands emerging out of its yearnings in the early childhood. Hence, the frequent nostalgic reminiscences that appear in poem after poem are mere subterfuges to escape the present both in the spatial and the temporal contexts. In the poem "My Grandmother's House" she becomes reflective about her ancestral [grandmother's] house:

> How often I think of going
> There, to peer through blind eyes of windows or
> Just listen to the frozen air,
> Or in wild despair, pick an armful of
> Darkness to bring it here to lie
> Behind my bedroom door like a brooding
> Dog. (CP 120)

The expression 'armful of darkness' is in itself is an ironic suggestion. The initial enthusiasm of going back to the grandmother's house' ultimately turns into acquiring nothing ('armful of darkness'). This is so because of the simple fact that the grandmother's house itself is a symbol of 'cultural unconscious,' which in many ways compounds in her a sense of disgust and frustration. Yet here the awareness of the present malady is so intensely painful that the 'blind eyes of windows' or the 'frozen air' or even 'an armful of / Darkness' – all images of loneliness and isolation, can console the poet's self and take her away from being in the insufferable here-and-now.

In fact this kind of need for a regress into the childhood is a formal stylistic device in the Romanticists and their followers, the confessional poets. This relative escape through regress into the childhood is their potential manner of expressing the painful undecided nature of being-in-the here-and-now. Being-in-the here-and-now is a matter of inordinate crisis and indecisiveness. The imaginative stress on the need for escape from the arduous nature of being-in-the present into a childhood that might have been comparatively freer from constraints is a mere fib of poetic imagination.

Love of Life and Love for Life

Every person has experiences both agonizing and exhilarating. But only a passionate sensibility can concretise these experiences in the form of a vibrant poetic formula. In order to do this the artistic self has to undergo a traumatic process through which his artistic personality develops; and the predicament encountered by the poet invariably transcends the personal and assumes a generality. Thus, the poet's artistic personality develops into a collective poetic sensibility. Kamala Das has shaped her feminine poetic self on the anvil of her naturalistic experiences and visions, and her poems are the direct results of the psychic trial she underwent throughout her life on instances. Though in her poem "Forest Fire" Kamala Das gives a commitment "To take in with greed like a forest fire" (OP 39) all experiences to her creative dominion, yet her poetry gains both its charm and tension from her personal views on the most important aspect of life—

love. But these personal views of Kamala Das, to the extent that they are equally important in the life of any woman and every woman, maintain in themselves a typical poetic flavour of trying to comprehend the very feminine niceties insofar as they are required to be urgently attended to. Though study of many of her major poems will reveal ample proofs of a wider and more matured vision in the outlook of her poetic self, yet as T.N. Dhar rightly observes, "It is true that Das has lived up to her promise, but all through she has shown partiality towards the lovers; most of her poems deal with the theme of love" (21). It is important to note here that for her love has various connotations and manifestations. Beyond the physical and divine dimensions of love, for her it is the fundamental source of energy that gives life its vehemence and its contours. Love being the most vital of the primary instincts of man as a creature, naturally, the all-pervasive spirit of the whole poetic world of hers cannot be anything but love and its vigorous manifestations drawn from life-experiences, both exhilarating and agonizing.

In spite of the fact that Das's treatment of love takes innumerable dimensions—the love of a wife towards her husband; the love of a beloved towards her lover; the love of a fond mother; the love of a daughter towards a dictatorial father; and the love of a grand daughter towards her grandmother—, the very fundamental nature of her treatment of love substantially concerns itself with man-woman relations as lovers. This theme of man-woman relations as lovers had been attended to poetically from the time's immemorial past; but love as treated in the traditional lore maintains in itself a kind of romantic evocativeness, where it all turns out to be a kind of imaginative fire-play. In Das also there is a slight romantic tinge wherewith she very often attributes a kind of imaginative height to love as the most needful concretising force of unifying humanity into a happy social blend. But she very often looks at the natural context of man-woman relations from a creaturely angle; and thereby she demonstrates that man-woman love has to be attended in its naturalistic ground realities instead of making out a pleasant winning story out of it as an instinctive fundament. As such it needs the most needful libation, satiety, and satisfaction.

Love, in order to be real, must force itself as a typical naturalistic educative phenomenon, in the context of which man and woman have to learn something of their mutual personalities. In fact Das considers love as the fundamental manner of human-creaturely disposition of man and woman towards each other. She makes a clear-cut poetic analysis of the necessary expectations of the partners and equally necessary manner in which they practically respond to each other. The phenomenal nature of love-play starts in high hopes and ends in deep depressions. The expected magnificence versus the achieved nothingness is the manner in which she builds a kind of irresolvable poetic tension. All her love-poems end up in this atmosphere of tension instead of acquiring for themselves the most needful happiness through liberation. Reading Kamala Das's love poetry is not at all a pleasant exercise. It does not give any pleasing conclusions. On the other hand, she leaves most of her love poems with a big question mark. Insofar as they are structured within the stylistic devices of irony, paradox, antithesis, and ambiguity, they maintain in themselves a serious touch of modernity in its stylistic vibrancy. As a result, her love poems breed in themselves a kind of paradoxical tension between the love of life as we have it and the love for life as it is required to be. Many of her love poems, to the extent that they contain in themselves certain fantastic, even obscene episodes, can be interpreted as mere dreams and nightmares rather than the realities of life.

Thus the earnest creative urgency in Kamala Das is always with the expression of a stricken and frightened psyche deprived of the pleasure of love, helplessly raving for proper answers for her exclusive problems in being a woman. These problems are concerned with her search for an escape from the perpetual loneliness she undergoes in life. She is aware that such an escape can be attained only through engaging herself in an eternal search for true love. So with utmost honesty and without inhibition her poems express her infelt loneliness and her self's wanderings in search of an ideal lover in addition to searching for her own satisfaction of the self. In her own words: "Like alms looking for a begging bowl was my love which sought for it a receptacle" (MS 105). The same sentiment is expressed also in the poem "A Phantom

Lotus" where again the giver is the female who is saturated with love:

> The only truth that matters is
> That all this love is mine to give,
> It does not matter that I seek
> For it a container, as alms
> Seek a begging bowl, a human
> Shape to envelope its wealth. (OSK 93)

The expression 'alms / Seek a begging bowl' aptly depicts the pathetic and fallen state of woman in being a seeker of the most needful thrill in life, which is fated to be unavailable for her. Her instinct for search of true love is so aggressive that the male entity is placed at the receiving end and the female is the desperate hunter for the 'begging bowl.' This is the reason why all her poetic property is preoccupied with love in its various aspects. This preoccupation sometimes becomes an obsession, which only shows the self's desperate attempt to get hold of love and life at any cost, and of course the ensuing frustration. All this shows that the tone of her violence towards the very femininity, in all probability, is the sum and substance of herself as a lovelorn woman.

The Sea of Life : Love-Lust Tangle

1. *Love as a Phenomenon*

Love is an authentic phenomenon both conceptual and perceptual simultaneously. In the conceptual context it is Platonic and a chimera. In the perceptual context it dwindles into what can be called the creaturely evocative dimension. There is no possibility of reconciling both. They both are simultaneously felt experiences, hence the 'love-hate tangle' towards the very prospect of love in life. The essential dilemma in Kamala Das's poetry emerges out of this simultaneous predominance of love in its higher and lower dimensions. As Kurup rightly says:

> The confessional self in her [Das] is presented through her shifting moods where apparently contradictory images of

> the most sublime and the most mundane mingle with one another; the images of deep involvement in the physical act of love mingle with those of physical rotting and disgust (175).

This mingling of 'the most sublime and the most mundane' is an inexorable phenomenon in a poet who presents her experiences in all its genuine colours, smells, and sounds; a poet who attempts with all sincerity to portray life in its full blatancy. An equally vigorous pull of the self towards opposite directions i.e., the higher and lower aspects of being, amounts to what critics call the 'split self' of the poet. She is conscious of the heinous and hateful nature of the creaturely survival, but then, any humanistic elevation of ideas and ideologies must necessarily state this creaturely survival as the primal springboard of secular, existential, and aesthetic heights in being-in-the world. This is so because love, in the sense of passionate generic entanglement of the partners belonging to the opposite sexes, is only an honorific logo-centric coinage. As such it is an extended Euphemism for the same creaturely activity of entanglement for procreative activity. It is just the *elan vital* ("life force") whose ultimate purpose for nature is beyond the comprehension of human imagination.

Love in Kamala Das, then, connotes the visualization of man-woman relations through which the partners involved attain the ultimate goal of their being. For the poet love is on the one hand an end in itself, and on the other a means to attain a greater meaning to life. In being a means, it aims at achieving a kind of ultimate freedom that puts aside all kinds of secondary concerns of life; and, in being an end in itself, it goes to reveal her philosophy of life: a life full of love, warmth, and care from her partner. When in reality such love is denied in the present modes and modalities of living, her poems become the story of her self's itinerary in search of love and life even outside her home. In fact in her case it is love as an end that tilts the balance. Since the genesis of love is our being-in-the world, her concept of love does not reject the seat of it—the body. As Sunanda P Chavan says, "She believes love to be a fulfilment of soul realized through body—an experience of sex, beyond sex" (Unity 143). This belief in the reciprocity of the physical and the metaphysical aspects of love is clearly expressed in the opening lines of the poem "The Suicide":

> Bereft of soul
> My body shall be bare
> Bereft of body
> My soul shall be bare. (D 1)

The needs of the body for the soul and the soul for the body are absolutely important. Here the word 'soul' has to be taken as a verbal substitute for self in its physical state of being. Self in its metaphysical dimensions may not be having anything to do with the body. But in the actual world of physical survival both the body and the self are absolutely required to be inalienable partners of the being. In fact, the poet is asking for something which is not practically viable. This nonviability aspect becomes clear when the self and the body in the above context are taken as mind and senses inherent in the being. Needless to say, the mind is always attended by the ego and the senses are attended by the most needed satisfactions. The mind that is the self with its ego and the body that is the senses with their passion for satiety quite naturally come into a conflict. As a result, mind cannot control the senses and the senses cannot satisfactorily depend upon the mind for the purpose of acquiring for oneself the most needed satisfaction. Soul and body in the above context, if taken as mind and matter, are absolutely left for themselves to contend with each other. Here the mind has no alternative except to go through the matter. And the matter (body) has no other source of animating itself with the life-principle. If only there is a possibility for a third principle that could unite mind (self) and matter (body) equally, there is a scope for harmonious understanding. The necessity of soul for the body and body for the soul has to be clarified by some third principle. That third cementing principle, for Kamala Das, is pleasure through love. When that pleasure through love is not available for a concrete experience, both the mind (self) and matter (body) appear to rend asunder. Frustration is the inevitable result of all this mind-body distancing. In this desire for a harmonious unification of soul and body (or mind and matter) Das is quite romantically apprehending a Platonic state of being-in-the-world. Very often in her practical life self ferociously reverts upon the body almost as an interior critic bent upon controlling the freedom of the body. What she actually wants is a sort of hymnal cohabitation of self and body as interior paramour of each other.

2. *Creaturely Survival and Existential Heights*

There are two antithetical dimensions of life: existential heights and creaturely survival (aspiring for superior states of existential heights and crying and cringing for creaturely properties of survival). While one is the outcome of civilization and progress, the other is born of the primal animalistic urges that are inevitable and unavoidable. Human survival is ultimately rooted in these two dimensions more or less in the same measure. With the concept of sublime that man aspires to reach, it is also true that he has to practically remain tied up to his creaturely evocative dimensions. Totality in human life is reached only in a holistic and harmonious intermixture of both these dimensions. This contention goes in perfect agreement with the Hindu view of life, which advocates the gradual elevation to sublimation – *Dharma, Artha, Kama,* and *Moksha*. Thus, *Kama* or sexual instinct remains one important aspect of human life, which not only concerns itself with self-preservation and preservation of the race but also is a necessary ingredient in his progression towards attaining transcendence.

The art of success in life lies in properly co-ordinating the creaturely dimensions with the existential heights. Moreover, nature absolutely depends upon the creaturely avidities for the purpose of its evolution. So in the naturalistic context man cannot really distance himself from the creaturely survival modalities of life. From this angle the instinctive aberrations are not a matter of stigma. On the other hand, proper knowledgeable insight into their profundities adds for the human interest, not as a matter of progress but as a significant matter of containing the human entity with the needful completions of being-in-the world. Nevertheless, the need of conducting oneself towards existential heights compels one to look upon the creaturely survival dimensions as low, primitive, and worth renouncing. That they cannot really be renounced practically is the hitch.

However, in the historical process of progress through constant civilization and progress, there emerges a tendency to give excessive importance to the existential heights by way of ideologically downplaying the necessity of creaturely dimensions. It is in this tendency that the primal creative urges and faculties receive no proper attention and importance. On the other hand, they attract utter negligence in the name of civilities and decencies of life. Being-in-the world, as such, is a matter of surviving with a 'necessary courage to be' within the parameters of social, ethical, moral, and cultural conventions and traditions.

Kamala Das prominently tackles the problem of love quite antithetically from both the angles of creaturely survival and secular existential heights. In fact she arrives at a poetic conclusion that capturing the existential heights is not at all possible without an awareness and recognition of the inevitable creaturely dimensions of being-in-the world. Any act of aspiring for existential heights should necessarily suggest this creaturely dimension. In a small poem called "Winter," she suggests at the significance of these creaturely dimensions of being-in-the world:

> It smelt of new rains and of tender
> shoots of plants, and its warmth was the warmth
> of earth, groping for roots ... Even my soul,
> I thought, must send its roots somewhere,
> and, I loved his body without shame . . . (BK 92)

The analogy between the 'tender shoots of plants . . . groping for roots' and the 'soul' sending 'its roots somewhere' downward is expressive of the needful balance between the higher and lower aspects of life. The expressions 'its warmth was the warmth of earth' and 'I loved his body without shame' indicate the exclusivity of motherhood and the ecstasy of the creative process.

The creaturely dimensions in themselves are closely associated with the assertion of naturalistic freedom as against the social and cultural strictures. But in the name of social decencies as well as ethical and moral standards, the naturalistic freedoms of creaturely avidity are always invariably sabotaged and sacrificed by the so-called sophisticated conventions, moralities, and ethics. As a result, the very essence of naturalistic freedom of being-in-the world gets crumpled and even annihilated very often. Kamala Das as a poet absolutely resents the manner in which the very life-giving institutions directly go to the extent of crushing and annihilating the innate naturalistic freedoms and choices through extraneous formalities and conventions. Das continuously puts a positive and exulting insight into the so-called forbidden aspects of instinctive aberrations, more or less with a missionary purpose of exhorting and evocating the readers for proper co-ordination of their senses and sensibilities in the most requisite manner of surviving with laudable self-emanating sanctions emerging out of the implorations of the conscience, and not the exterior morals and ethics.

3. *The Love-Lust Labyrinth*

All said and done love-act between man and woman, rather than being confined to the creaturely dimensions, goes to involve both body and mind in equal proportion in attaining a greater satisfaction by the partners involved. The absence of such involvement of mind and body would pave way for frustration and agony in the partners. Kamala Das's concerns in the man-woman intimate relationships, as have been expressed in her poetry, have to be understood in this perspective. She is equally concerned for the physical and metaphysical aspects of love in order to attain a meaning for life. According to her, unity is achieved only through involving both body and mind in love relationships. Denying either of these would result in a sense of frustration and waste in the partners involved. In fact, it is this sense of frustration and waste that gets reflected in most of her love poems, as she is conscious of the fact that man as love partner very often shows no serious concern for the needs of his beloved in love-play. Each of the protagonists of Das's poems longs for a meaningful relationship with her lover, be it within or outside the marital life. But ironically, none of the male-lovers she comes across gives her the kind of emotional support and satisfaction she longs for. In any transaction between man and woman the independence and individuality of both the partners are absolutely required to be protected and safeguarded. The very manner in which she offers the facets of independence and individuality invariably becomes an arresting tale of the shattered and destroyed niceties of feminine aspirations. Therefore, it is an anxiety-ridden poetry in the uncontrollable and inexpressible contexts of personal agony at the deprivations of the naturalistic freedoms. At the same time the verbal violence of her poetry is only a potential poetic means of ventilating the feminine personal grievances.

Thus, the whole body of Kamala Das's poetry is the story of her self's search for true love. One may notice that the "tamed swallow" of "The Old Playhouse"(OP 1) could not remain 'tamed' for long, and flies away looking for "wild" freedoms and ecstasies "as often petals do when free in air" (OP 48). Very often life is infused into the "granite dove" of "The Stone Age," and it flies away from the husband's "webs of bewilderment" (OP 51) searching for new vistas for nesting. But ironically, every search and every flight eventually culminate in a denial of what has been aspired and the ensuing frustration. This sort of running away in search of true love and the resultant frustration is the theme of her poem "The Sunshine Cat" (OSK 54). Like in "The Old Playhouse" and in "The Stone Age," here also the husband is portrayed as a man "who neither loved nor / Used her, but was a ruthless watcher" (OSK 54). To escape the tyranny of the husband, the woman turns to a :

> . . . band
> Of cynics. . . . clinging to their chests where
> New hair sprouted like great-winged moths, burrowing her
> Face into their smells and their young lusts to forget,
> To forget, oh, to forget . . . (OSK 54)

Each of the men she turns to, tells her: "I do not love, I cannot love, it is not / In my nature to love, but I can be kind to you . . ." (OSK 54). The statement 'I do not love, I cannot love, it is not / In my nature to love' is a strategic indictment of the men-folk on their failure to love in the true sense of the term. One who shamelessly confesses that 'it is not / In my nature to love' must either be a psychopath or one lacking in virility. But in a superficial manner he says: 'I can be kind to you.' In a system where people are divided into superior (men) and inferior (women), kindness flowing from the benefactor towards the beneficiary is all the more humiliating and painful to the beneficiary, for it is more a gesture of ego-fulfilment than a real and earnest extension of love on an equal footing.

Further lines of the poem are a poignant confession of how a woman's personality dwindles in the world of men. Her search for a true relationship both with the husband and outside the domestic life bears no fruit. Moreover, "Her husband shut her / In, every morning; locked her in a room of books / With a streak of sunshine lying near the door" (OSK 54). These are the doings of a cold psychopath. The husband locks her every morning 'in a room of books' where there is no light ('With a streak of sunshine lying near the door' and not in the room). A dark room, if properly understood, stands for the heart of the husband symbolically. In the context of such an impenetrable dark scenario the drama that follows is not a mere tragedy but a melodrama of the sorts. On one evening when "He returned to take her out, she was a cold and / Half-dead woman, now of no use at all to men" (OSK 54). That is to say that her very feminine niceties and potentialities are crushed to the hilt. Vrinda Nabar's comment on this passage is worth quoting:

> The eerie image of the husband metaphorically locking the poet in, prisoner among a roomful of books, while she slowly aged, is startling. . . . We are not to take the lines literally, but they have a convincing authenticity because they hint at disturbing aspects of both the poet's relationship with her husband and of her own sense of inner collapse. (26)

The poem simply suggests at the fact that she can never withstand the loneliness thrust on her by the mindless husband. Love for woman is always a matter of transparent living companionship, in the absence of which she is as good as dead. Kamala Das here opens up a new area of woman's heart and interiors. What woman needs is not at all a boorish animal virility in her man. She only wants a free, frank, and transparent companionship with her man.

Another poem called "Herons" expresses the heinous approach from the husband figure. Here he prefers to make love after sedating the wife so that:

> My speech becomes a mistladen terrain
>
> The words emerge tinctured with sleep
>
> They rise from the still coves of dreams
>
> In unhurried flight like herons... (CP 105)

And the husband, before making love, "Sing lullabies to his wife's sleeping soul" in order to "thicken its swoon" so that "my ragdoll limbs adjust better / To his versatile lust" (CP 105). The modern day psychologists very often talk about masochistic abnormalities in the male partners in sexual congress. While psychological abnormality itself takes its origin, growth, and development in the conditioned manner of social institutions, in some quaint and queer cases masochism becomes a painful trait in males. In the abnormal psychology we have references to certain male-types who insist on their female partners remaining as silent and passive as dead bodies. This kind of insistence, psychologically speaking, is born of sexual diffidence and doubts in the male partner concerning his own strength and virility.

In all these poetically narrated instances, the orgasmic experiential dimensions of the female personae and that of the male partners are at great variance. While the sensibility of the female persona seeks ecstasy and exquisiteness in the oneness of the moment, the male persona refuses to comply because, as she says in the poem "The Old Playhouse," "You were pleased / With my body's response, its weather, its usual shallow / Convulsions" (OP 1). And the final result is, "I lost my will and reason, to all your / Questions I mumbled incoherent replies" (OP1). Here she is accusing her partner for throwing her into a state of incomprehensibility, in the context of which her response would be helpless mumblings. In a woman these 'convulsions' and 'incoherent replies' can mean more than mere sound productions. About such convulsive signs in woman, Beauvoir observes, "There are other than physiological reasons for her susceptibility to convulsive manifestations: a convulsion is an interiorization of energy which, when directed outward into the environment fails to act there on any object; it is an aimless discharge of all the negative forces set up by the situation" (340). In Das's poem the woman's mumbling of 'incoherent replies' is suggestive enough of what Beauvoir confirms in saying that 'it is an aimless discharge of all the negative forces set up by the situation.' Whereas her partner should have transparently and sublimely shared the occasion, he appears to be in an interrogative state of mind in the most intimate interactive moments, which is indicative of a pathological abnormality in him.

However, in Das's different poems, response to this abnormality has different manifestations. In the poem "The Stone Age," it changes into a revengeful attitude, where the female persona goes to "knock at another's door" (OP 51). In "The Sunshine Cat," again, the woman persona seeks love outside marriage but fails to have it; every lover she comes in contact with refuses to love her but only uses her to satisfy his 'young lusts,' and eventually:

> They let her slide from pegs of sanity into
> A bed made soft with tears and she lay there weeping,
> For sleep had lost its use, I shall build walls with tears,
> She said, walls to shut me in. . . . (OSK 54)

Here the 'shallow convulsions' of "The Old Playhouse" subside and transform into a passive but more pathetic state of schizophrenic frenzy. This is most pertinently the psychological negative response of a woman that flirts constantly and continuously in the hope of gaining for her self the most requisite sublimation and pleasure of companionship. Everywhere her experience comes to a drastic failure for the simple reason that all the male partners she came into contact are equally selfish and self-centred without any concern for the exact purpose of the woman. In stating that she 'shall build walls with tears,' she is creating such heavy poetic metaphors that go to aptly apprise her shattered state of mind, more particularly when a number of paramours also utterly failed in awarding her the needful pleasurable relief in the act of love. The stylistic dramatization of the events of failure culminating into 'walls' of 'tears' is something quite exasperating and damaging for the female personality.

However, it is important to note that the protagonist in the poem "The Sunshine Cat" is referred as 'she' wherewith the poet implies a sort of third person evaluation of her own subjective experience. So it is a profound stylistic dramatic device aimed at confirming the vicissitudes of women that always fail in acquiring the rightful pleasures of companionship. At the same time, as Kurup points out, "it may be wrong to consider these attempts as betrayal or infidelity of her personal lust. In fact it is her disgust in failure of achieving the ideal lover that leads her to a frantic search" (136). It is also important to note that, according to Kamala Das, such an ideal lover is impossible to find in the world of our survival. In a way she is targeting the very social system that always denies the rightful opportunities and privileges to woman in general.

In the poem "Substitute" one may notice that the poetic sensibility's 'disgust in the failure of achieving the ideal lover,' turns from the pathetic state to a sort of indifference. In poems like "A Hot Noon in Malabar" (BK 18), "Composition" (D 29), "My Grandmother's House" (CP 120), "No Noon at My Village Home" (CP 31), her self is seen trying to retreat into the past in order to flee the agony of being-in-the present. But in "Substitute," the self's desperate attempt to escape both the past and the future is obvious. Here she wants to keep away from the memory that intrudes her peace of mind:

Memory
Great moody sea,
Do not thump so
Against my shore. (D 6)

The 'sea' metaphor and the 'shore' metaphor are significant.

The 'Great moody sea' stands for the sea of life and 'my shore' suggests at her suffering mind and conscience incapable of standing the dashing 'thump(s)' of the sea. The moodiness of the 'sea' is implicative of unpredictability and unassuredness of the world which defeats and frustrates her mind and conscience that always cherish a calm and quiet state of survival. But the 'moody sea' strikes at it whimsically and mercilessly. The 'thump' of the 'sea' is unbearable for her simple peace-loving mind. Her fond desire is for peace of mind even if it were to be for a short while. Therefore, she says:

> Let me lie still
> Without thought or will.
> For a benign hour or two
> Dear night, be my tomb. (D 6)

John Keats once acclaimed, 'Oh for a life of sensation rather than of thought.' Almost all the romantics fervently cherished for a life of sensations, even when the sensations and the sublimations that they improvise are purely temporal and momentary. Life of thought, on the other hand, is the phenomenal manner of introspectively brooding over the bygone and dead sensations. The very deadness of the lively moments lived and lost invariably lands the protagonist into a state of despondency and frustration. To quote John Keats again, in the poem "Happy Insensibility" he says:

> In a drear night at December
> Too happy happy tree
> Thy branches ne'ver remember
> Their green felicity. (L. 1- 4)

In the above lines Keats is fervently pleading for a life of insensibility like the 'December tree' oblivious to the bygone vernal felicity of the month of May. This kind of fervent desire for a sublime life of senses in the immediate context should be a moment of permanence for both Keats and also for Das. To subsist in the exquisite excitations of senses and their pleasures is all that can be considered as happiness in life. Needless to say, this soul-filling involvement with the senses and their pleasurable moments is a matter of blissfully subsisting in the here-and-now. So the poet confirms for herself that a life 'without thought or will' provides for her the requisite abundance of being-in-the world.

Mainly with the Romantic poets, as with Das, the Western historicism based on the bifurcation of time into past, present, and future, duly studded with memories (referring to the past) and desires (referring to the future) automatically obviates the present, particularly in the contexts of past experiences and future hopes and desires colliding with each other. As a result, the complex of here-and-now, as a matter of confluence of the past and future, gives no sustainable availability of the present for a fullness of experience. The fundamental loss of this fullness of experience in life's living moments harrowingly contributes for a kind of melancholy and pathetic nostalgia. The loss of the very pleasurable nature of love through 'thought' and 'will' conforms to what T. S. Eliot classically initiated in his poem *The Waste Land*. Even on the point of repetition, Eliot's lines are worth quoting in this context: "April is the cruellest month, breeding / Lilacs out of the dead land, mixing / Memory and desire. . . ." (L.1-3). For Eliot 'April is the cruellest month' because of the simple fact that 'Memory' (referring to the past) and 'desire' (referring to the future), as for Das 'thought' (referring to the past) and 'will' (referring to the future), in their smothering togetherness contribute for a colossal loss of the present. Invoking the very 'night' to be her 'tomb' is plentifully expressive of the agony of her mind in the felt loss and death of the given moments of sense- excitations and exquisiteness. The poet is ready to cherish death, again like Keats, as a welcome alternative to a life of miserable thought and unfounded desires. She wants the 'night' to be a 'tomb' for her i.e., a state where all living sensibilities are colossally suspended. Put into a simple argumentation the very loss of sublimation of senses and the pleasures is a matter of death for her. This implies that she poetically measures the worth of life in the felt moments of sense-sublimations. This may appear to be an excessive hedonistic craze on the face of it. But in its reality the poet wants to suggest that life's worth should invariably mean a compacted simulation of felt excitations without which life will turn out to be a formula of nothingness and void.

The world now demands a cosmeticized show of life, and not a life with due naturalistic vitality and life force. This socially and culturally imposed show of life on women vexes and frustrates her. The following lines of "Substitute" clarify the the point:

It will be all right when I learn

To paint my mouth like a clown's.

It will be all right if I put up my hair,

Stand near my husband to make a proud pair.

It will be all right if I join clubs

And flirt a little over telephone.

It will be all right, it will be all right

I am the type that endures. (D 6)

In determining and deciding the man-woman roles, a kind of typicality was socially and culturally thrust on them, in the context of which the male 'type' always arrogated after having conceived and conformed the women-folk in the most passive and typical manner. This kind of socially inflicted typicality on women in the bygone centuries gradually contributed for a total negation of individuality and personality for women. Women are expected to conform themselves as mere pleasure-offering objects without any freedom and individuality of being-in-the world. She, however, does not like to be a mere pleasure-offering entity to the men-folk, particularly when such freedoms of acquiring pleasures for herself are potentially smashed and denied by the society.

Further, in painfully stating 'I am the type that endures,' it is clear that the individuality worth her personality was required to be mercilessly sacrificed on the threshold of modern day life, which is a mere pantomime. There is something quite chagrined in her grievance here. These lines seem to imply that it is inevitable for her as a woman to join the social group and start adopting all the mean tricks in order to endure in the society. However, "Substitute" concludes on a note of a self-created indifference and coldness towards such pantomimic performance of life. Here onwards a sort of revengefulness takes over the woman:

> We kissed and we loved, all in a fury,
> For another short hour or two
> We were all warm and wild and lovely.
> After that love became a swivel-door,
> When one went out, another came in.
> Then I lost count, for always in my arms
> Was a substitute for a substitute,
> Oh, what is the use, explaining—
> It was a nameless, faceless crowd. (D 7)

The very title, 'Substitute,' is important in the sense that human individual, instead of realizing his own natural worth of being-in-the world, always falls into the idea of relative and comparative introspection. Consequently, he starts evaluating his own worth by way of comparing and contrasting himself with others. In doing so, he obliviously forgets his own being and behaves himself as a metaphoric entity to somebody else, which he calls 'one like the other.' This 'one like the other' formula is a phenomenal insistence of any social and cultural system. But from the personal point of view of the being, he is none like the other. It is in this formula of none like the other lies all the worth of individuality and the height of personality. But a social system imposes on the individuals a kind of generality which becomes an average necessity to be a member in a group. According to the principle of sociability, everyone has to assess and access his worth to the generality and commonality. Therefore, in the intense moments of introspection, everybody ultimately appears to himself, from the social and cultural point of view, as his own 'substitute.' This is the result of social conformism and conventionality. In the context of one being a substitute, his originality gets lost. When this originality of being a woman gets smashed through conformism, conventions, and traditions, the poet becomes inconsolably restless. She hates the idea of herself being relegated to be a substitute of herself. Herein we have the implication that God gives us one face and we in the social and cultural contexts make many out of it. This multiplication of one into many and the resemblance of one with some or all is something that is thrust on the person in being-in-the world. But in the ultimate sense of being-in-the world, it is not this kind of evaluation that matters. But it is the very sense of being as 'none like the other' that ultimately creates the height of being-in-the world. Thus Kamala Das confirms the fact that in spite of the demands of the society and culture one should strive to live like oneself and not like the other or the 'substitute.' Hence, she herself is insisting upon the exclusivity of the existential choice and freedom of being-in-the world. The 'nameless faceless crowd' that she is talking about is the manifestation of her multiple existence according to the demands of the society and its conventions.

In the poem "The End of Spring" Das states more clearly this multiplication of one into many by saying, "I split each minute into strangers, a lot / of them, a sort of game to fill the void / In time" (BK 26). In "Substitute" such 'split' into a 'faceless crowd' becomes a compulsion with a kind of freedom that "was our last strange toy. / Like the hangman's robe, even while new / It could give no pride. Nor even joy" (D 7). This is the kind of agony that emerges out of existential fear where the purpose of the very existence is unknown and unperceivable. The ideas of Kamala Das here are cognate with what Jean Paul Sartre evaluates in the context of *Being and Nothing*.

In fact, "Substitute" is a great attempt to reach out to the dark interiors of the female psyche, and dig out the deep-rooted agony of the frustrated self. The outward indifference is only a mask to camouflage the overflowing anguish, which only heightens it. Unlike in the poem "The Sunshine Cat" (OSK 54), in "Substitute," she targets the male entity and the society not directly but by use of ridicule, irony, and repetition. The line 'It will be all right' is repeated thirteen times in the poem. Linda Hess, however, does not agree with the readability of such repetitions in Das's poems. As Hess puts it, "There are frequent repetitions of words and phrases, another quick solution to the problem of filling up a line, but one that has disastrous effects on intensity and precision" (40). But in "Substitute," these lines do not give the reader the impression of tedious repetition nor do they degenerate to the level of a poetic trick of 'filling up a line,' as complained by Hess. Instead, they do function as an effective device to communicate the mounting crisis in the poetic self. As Iyengar rightly says, "In 'Substitute,' the reiteration of the words 'it will be all right' has a telling effect" (680). In this context even a critic like Nabar, who otherwise is very critical of Das's extreme unconventionality in poetic structures, comments: "The lines ['It will be all right, it will be all right'] have a cantatory tone. This suggests a sort of self-hypnosis, as if the poet wills herself into believing that she can endure. There is also an element of irony, even mockery, in the mention of the roles it will be alright for her to play" (44). In the ultimate analysis, the poetic manner of repetitions of the line 'It will be all right' contributes for a rare poetic fulfilment.

The mocking indifference of "Substitute" again surfaces in the poem "Glass" where the woman is "pure misery / Fragile glass" which, under the rudeness of the "lover's haste," breaks into "an armful / of splinters, designed to hurt, and, / Pregnant with pain" (OP 21). The 'faceless crowd' of the "Substitute" is presented again with stern determination:

Why did not I tell him that

I no longer care

Whom I

Hurt with love and often without. ("Glass," OP 21)

Here the woman persona assumes the role of a parasite who tries to use men rather than being used by men. This is a sort of attempt to console the self by presuming that she hurts rather than being hurt, that she exploits rather than being exploited. The expression 'often without' [love] simultaneously refers to the contingent hatred she breeds in her towards the unfeeling male counterpart. And the expression 'with love' quite ironically substantiates the passive unfeeling manner in which she entangled herself with her partner. It is this passive unfeeling manner that ultimately contributes for 'an armful / of splinters.' The broken 'glass' image further compounds her infelt suffering and also a typical abnormal self-pity that she attributes for herself in her fallen and defeated state of being in the companionship. This self-pity quantum in Kamala Das is comparable to that of P. B. Shelley. In the poetic act of exhibiting her wounds, she comes very near to the British Romanticists. But then, the poetic manner of representing pain in Kamala Das is certainly not out of unfounded Romantic imagination; the hurt is real and it is this realistic dimension of Kamala Das that ultimately distinguishes her as an anti-romantic and as a neo-realist. The neo-realism of the sort that Das practices is a profound supplement for the early twentieth century realism.

In "Glass" her deep rooted frustration in the self's interiors springs from the fact that her initial offerings of her body as a 'bait' to men and her expectation of love in return meet with failure. None of the lovers could in any way exorcise the loneliness of her life. Gradually this turns into a revengeful determination, and now:

> With a cheap toy's indifference
>
> I enter others'
>
> Lives, and
>
> Make every trap of lust
>
> A temporary home. ("Glass," OP 21)

The expression 'temporary home' is important, poetically speaking. If 'home is the place where your have somebody to receive' with love and compassion, the temporary nature of man possessing woman ultimately produces in her a typical pain of the loss of the certainty of home.

The poem "Convicts" also falls in the category of poems that express the overpowering heat of lust as the only binding thread between the lovers. Love is delicate whereas lust is excessively forcible and exploiting. But in the poem the union is portrayed as a mere lustful physical labour that is tiring and fatiguing. After each encounter in love, the lovers lay on bed like "The toys dead children leave behind" (OP 25). With this expression the intensity of pathos is quite harrowing. It refers to her own enthusiastic self that maintained in itself innumerable dreamy ecstasies before the love act. And the lovers are thrown back to a heart-rending question: "what is / The use, what is the bloody use?" (OP 25). Further lines strengthen this question:

> There were no more
> Words left, all words lay imprisoned
> In the ageing arms of night. In
> Darkness we grew as in silence
> We sang, each note rising out of
> Sea, out of wind, out of earth and
> Out of each sad night like an ache. . . . (OP 25)

Growing 'in darkness,' and singing 'in silence' are inward and self-centred activities without visible or audible consequences and without a second agency being involved. While the bodies of the lovers are involved in the act of 'hacking at each other's parts,' their minds are meandering in the dark worlds of their own, singing songs 'in silence,' which are songs of not ecstasy but of incommunicable agony and tedium.

In the poem "The Millionaires at Marine Drive" which is intensely autobiographical like the poems "An Introduction" and "My Grandmother's House," the poet is aggrieved at the ultimate doom her life has come to after having lived for many years looking for an intimate relationship. But in that search she had to live her life as the "early rising doves" (CP 97) at Marine Drive, which feeds on the grains scattered by the millionaires. After fifteen years of her grandmother's death, she recalls,

> . . . no longer was
> There someone to put an arm around my
> Shoulders without a purpose, all the hands,
> The great brown thieving hands, groped beneath my
> Clothes, their fire was that of an arsonist's,
> Warmth was not their aim, they burnt my cities

Down. . . . (CP 97)

It is only in warm companionship of her grandmother that Kamala Das probably experienced the absolute gratuitousness in the human relationship. All the other companions in the name of lovers approached her for snatching away something from her, which in itself is an obnoxious selfish act. Now she feels sorry for the pleasure-hunt she has had throughout her youth: "Oh, why did I mix my / Pleasures like I mixed my drinks to pass out / So soon on the velvet couch of life?" (CP 97).

4. *The Torn Mask of Apathy*

"The Testing of the Sirens" is a poem where the poet finally betrays all her self's hitherto pent up agony. The poem depicts the events following two kinds of love-hate relationships. It is interesting to note that both the lovers are absolutely imaginary. While she is painfully aware of the last nights lovemaking with a man "speaking words of love / In some tender language I do not know," in the morning it was another man with "a pock-marked face, / a friendly smile and / a rolleiflex" (BK 58) camera, who took her for a drive. The "wail" of the "sirens" and his "mirthless laughter" (BK 58) weave together, which in fact become one with the 'wail' of the woman's own self. The poet evokes two repellent images—one, "a pregnant girl bared her dusky / breasts" and washed them sullenly," and the other, "crows bickered over a piece of lizard- meat" (BK 58)—, which suggest at the disgust and insensibility within the protagonist's mind towards the whole love affair. The triviality of the whole situation is further revealed in lines such as:

> I want your photo, lying down, he said,
> against those rusty nineteen-thirty-four guns,
> will you? Sure. Just arrange my limbs and tell
> me when to smile. (BK 58)

The negative dimensions of the lover himself in being a partner who wishes to have a static posture of the beloved confirms the fact that her personal freedoms are completely eroded. It is quite ironic that she suggests to him to 'arrange' her 'limbs.' The imposed passivity on her is quite disgusting, but then, what the lover wants is a static mechanical replica of her body for his purpose. The irony becomes all the more painful when she implores him with the words 'tell me when to smile.' This poem, like the poem "Substitute," reflects at the harrowing personal experiences of woman in being a passively dead or mechanical partner. It is imperative here to suggest that in both the poems the love-partners are imaginary characters subsuming in themselves the self-centred male-chauvinistic authoritarianism. As a matter of fact, Das is trying to make a poetic improvisation of the male-biased authoritarianism which is the widest spread phenomenal feature in the society. The 'rusty nineteen-thirty-four guns' metaphor implies the meaning that the male-chauvinism and authoritarianism in being the dictators of the social systems are absolutely old, useless, and outmoded features particularly in the context of women's exacting for their freedoms and choices during the feminist revolution of the modern times.

Though the female personae positively responds to the lover with the same inertia, yet towards the end, the poem is laden with the feeling of all love's labour lost, and of sheer frustration. In the concluding lines the mask of apathy is torn; and, behind all this veil of numbness and indifference, she betrays a feeling of unbearable agony of insatiate passion after such lustful encounters with the lovers day and night:

> Shut my eyes, but inside eye-lids, there was
> no more light, no more love, or peace, only
> the white, white sun burning, burning, burning...
> Ah, why does love come to me like pain
> again and again and again? (BK 58)

She becomes awfully pained at the contingent manner in which she shut her eyes in the close company of her man out of helpless shudder and not out of experiencing the ecstasy of love. The ecstasy-less mechanical experience of hers is further qualifying in the expression 'only the white.' With the closed 'eye-lids' all her visions of freedoms and choices are turned into a blind spot, where the black in her eyes, i.e. the lens mechanism of her eyes is totally eroded and the ghastly white abnormal shattering of sun obliterating any vision.

The image of 'the white, white sun burning, burning, burning' is something very powerful and all pervasive in Kamala Das's poetry. Therefore, Devindra Kohli rightly finds a thematic identity between her poems "The Dance of the Eunuchs" and "The Testing of the Sirens," which happen to be the first poem and the last one respectively, of her first volume of poems (*The Summer in Calcutta*). In Kohli's words: "The 'virgin whiteness' of the sun is the outward blaze of the irony of the 'virgin whiteness' of the heart which keeps on sulking, smouldering in the privacy of the poet's accursed loneliness, of the 'vacant ecstasy' of the dancing eunuchs" ("Virgin"14).

In fact, Das's poetry is a wild and violent cry of invitation for victimization. Self-pity and the contingent call for victimization (exaggerated scene making) is inherent in all Romantic poetry. Psychologically it is linked with self-pity born of inferiority complex. As Bruce King says,

Her poems are situated neither in the act of sex nor in feelings of love; they are instead involved with the self and its varied, often conflicting emotions, ranging from the desire for security and intimacy to the assertion of the ego, self-dramatization and feelings of shame and depression. (151)

In expression (poetry) these 'feelings of shame and depression' become a phenomenon of exhibiting superiority, which sometimes becomes a psychological abnormality. In Shelley we have this coupling of self-pity with cry of invitation for victimization in his "Ode to the West Wind" in lines such as: "Lift me like a leaf, a wave, a cloud, / I fall upon the thorns of life I bleed" (L. 53-54). While Shelley displays this self-pity with a tinge of romantic idealism, in Das it manifests itself as the fallout of the overall sterility and sham that her self experiences in its interaction with the outer world.

Many of Kamala Das's poems display an almost similar sentiment of her involvement with the body, 'the cheapest bait' and the subsequent dejections. In "Captive" the poetic persona narrates the painful story of her plunging herself into the world of lust, seeking love and warmth in return. But with each lover she was invariably falling into a mere snare of physical lust:

> What have
>
> we had, after all, between us but the
>
> womb's blinded hunger, the muted whisper
>
> at the core . . . for years I have run from one
>
> gossamer lane to another, I am
>
> now my own captive. (D 17)

The very phenomenon of love-act with abundant enthusiasm and desire for exquisiteness of experience ultimately comes to a slovenly disgusting end. Towards the end, the love-act turns out to be a mere physical out-loading of body's aggressions. For an introspective analysis, love-act is always enthusiastic to start with, and a disgust in the end. But the disgust of Kamala Das in the above context is altogether different. She rebelliously indicts her partner as the essential cause of imposing a disgusting experience on her, instead of giving an equal opportunity to feel the exquisiteness of the interpersonal experience. The expression 'womb's blinded hunger' and 'the muted whisper at the core' are poetically expressive of her inexorable grievance. Self-pity in the above lines becomes quite harrowing when she declares that she ran hither and thither ('from one / gossamer lane to another') fondly pursuing the instinctive pleasures and excitations of life. In an ultimate analysis all the desired pleasures eluded her, and what all that remains for her is a mere disgusting regret. At least in this poem Das is vibrantly clear that the feminine instinctive aspirations are invariably fated to defeat and failure simply because of the excessiveness of the aspirations and the contingent depression that befalls as an alternate reality. Therefore, she is a 'captive' because of her own personal exceeding dreams. The poem maintains in itself a typical melancholic nostalgia and such nostalgia is quite unbearable for her. The poem harrowingly complements the unbridgeable gulf between hopes and desires on the one hand, and the reality of personal experience on the other. Here the hope is for a permanent love relationship that she seeks in life, and the reality is the ever-elusiveness of such a relationship. But for the poet this permanent lover that she seeks could be her own creation out of frustration. The impending ultimate agony of knowing that the eternal lover would never be met is what she dreadfully longs to escape.

Being-in-the World and the Cognitive Self

The poetic self of Kamala Das journeys through many worlds of despair and unfulfilment, and violently expresses its feeling of loneliness, anxiety, and the futility of being-in-the world itself. This state further leads to dejection, depression and violence. The sense of nothingness and sterility sometimes are so extreme that it cannot be expressed in any usual logo-centric terminologies. There are many poems in which the poet has successfully tried to objectify her psychic distress through repellent images like 'funeral pyre,' 'womb's' darkness, 'menstrual blood,' 'low paid street girl,' 'maggots nipping the corpse,' 'crows bickering over a lizard-meat,' and the like. But it is in the poem "The Dance of the Eunuchs" that the objective world of the eunuchs most powerfully symbolizes her psychic struggle in terms of the barrenness of love-life experiences.

1. *Self's Convulsive Manifestations*

Like T.S. Eliot's *The Waste Land*, the world of eunuchs revives in the mind of the poet her own internal world of barrenness, frustration, and agony. "*The Waste Land*," says Manju Jain, "in fact, is haunted by memories of a failed erotic relationship, and by feelings of guilt and remorse which remain unresolved, as in the episode of the hyacinth garden" (*A Critical Reading 136*). To support her argument, Jain recalls Eliot's own observations about the thematic complexities of *The Waste Land*. In Eliot's words:

> Various critics have done me the honour to interpret the poem in terms of criticism of the contemporary world, have considered it, indeed, as an important bit of social criticism. To me it was only the relief of a personal and wholly insignificant grouse against life; it is just a piece of rhythmical grumbling.' (qtd. in Jain, *A Critical Reading* 145)

Likewise, Kamala Das's "The Dance of the Eunuchs"

outwardly depicts a particular Indian scene, but the poem definitely objectifies the poet's subjective wriggle through the sterility and sham of the eunuchs' dance. Here the poet feels that in the practical world of experiences she has the same vapid world of love-life as eunuchs have. In *The Waste Land* Eliot significantly celebrated quite deploringly some man-woman intimate relationship in the process of their utter failure. In the 'hyacinth girl' episode and the 'lady typist-carbuncular' affair, we have the disgusting poetic example where he reflectively apprised the interpersonal associations fated to inevitable failure. Kamala Das, as a modern feminine counterpart, prominently understands the intensity of agony created by the male-partner. As an extreme example of the expressions of her frustration, helplessness, and hopelessness in the love life, she visualizes the whole world in a synthetic metaphor of the eunuchs' dance:

> It was hot, so hot, before the eunuchs came
>
> To dance, wide skirts going round and round, cymbals
> Richly clashing, and anklets jingling, jingling,
> Jingling. Beneath the fiery gulmohur, with
> Long braids flying, dark eyes flashing, they danced and
> They danced, oh, they danced till they bled . . . (CP 106)

At the outset, to call the convulsive movements of the eunuchs a dance is in itself ironic and absurd. In the Indian traditional context, we have sacrosanct notions of *Sakti* and *Sakta* performing the dance in the form of *Siva* and *Parvati*. Quite ironically, Kamala Das celebrates the anti-life or negative life proponents of our times in the eunuchs' performing a restless revel which she calls a dance. The whole atmosphere is suggestive of the horrible barrenness in the life of the eunuchs. 'It was hot, so hot, before the eunuchs came / To dance.' The 'fiery gulmohur' with its red flowers intensifies the heat of the atmosphere. There is a tragic irony in the lines: 'They danced, they danced, oh, they danced till they bled' because it is not menstrual blood that the eunuchs bleed. In women menstrual bleeding is an exclusive phenomenon and the sign of the onset of fertility; but in the case of the eunuchs, it is a forced bleeding bereft of the exhilaration and ecstasy associated with the onset of motherhood. In answer to a questionnaire by S.C. Saha, Das says about the above lines: "I was probably thinking of the menstrual flow when I wrote of 'blood.' . . . I was hoping that these eunuchs would become real women by dancing till they bled" (qtd. in Saha 15). But it is a hope against hope, and the lines are movingly remindful of the contrast between hope and reality. Further, outwardly the eunuchs had all the embellishments of women:

> There were green
> Tattoos on their cheeks, jasmines in their hair, some
> Were dark and some were almost fair. Their voices
> Were harsh, their songs melancholy; they sang of
> Lovers dying and of children left unborn... (CP 106)

Women usually make themselves up with jasmines for attracting their lovers. The eunuchs outwardly looks like women with their make up, but their voices are 'harsh' and 'their songs melancholy; they sang of / Lovers dying and of children left unborn.' This is a poignant suggestion at the incapacity of the eunuchs to become real beloveds or real mothers. Further lines, "Some beat their drums, others beat their sorry breasts / And wailed, and writhed in vacant ecstasy" (CP 106), are suggestive of the convulsive nature of their movements which the poet ironically calls dance. The expression 'vacant ecstasy' very successfully functions as the objectification of the inexpressible frustration in the poet's own self through the barrenness of the eunuchs' situation.

Even the tiniest creature on earth has the capacity to procreate and multiply, but the eunuchs, in spite of the fact that they are human beings, feel themselves lower than any other creature because nature has denied them the prime creaturely activity. That might be the reason why "Even the crows were / Silent on the trees" (CP 106) feeling themselves greater in stature than the creatures dancing below. The concluding lines of the poem harrowingly intimate the sterility aspect:

> The sky crackled then, thunder came, and lightning

And rain, a meagre rain that smelt of dust in
Attics and the urine of lizards and mice..." (CP 106).

The first rain on dry earth usually produces a pleasant smell, but here the rain is not the usual rain that makes the earth fertile and tender. Its smell is repellent like that 'of dust in / Attics and the urine of lizards and mice... .'

The far-reaching influence of T.S. Eliot is obvious in the imagery of the poem. While the loss of naturalistic regeneration is the theme of *The Waste Land,* procreative capacity denied to humans are the central theme of "The Dance of the Eunuchs," at the outset. Again, like *The Waste Land,* all this is 'just a piece of rhythmical grumbling.' And this 'rhythmical grumbling' reaches very disgusting heights the poem visualizes a total world of impoverishment, as the eunuchs are supposed to be incapable of containing in themselves the usual physical instinctive sources of experiencing the sublime moments of life.

As a matter of fact, the poem is completely studded with Websterian melodramatic imagery. John Webster had a very great influence on T. S. Eliot, particularly in improvising melodramatic imagery. That way we do not find any direct parallelism to this poem in Eliot unless we resort to poetically comprehending with a sense of nausea the imagery in *The Waste Land*. The human agony concerning the potential infirmity created by the modern culture finds its echoes in *The Waste Land* and in "The Dance of the Eunuchs." The rhythmic manner of enhanced existential 'fear' or 'dread' is equally present in both the poems. While the 'fear' or 'dread' in *The Waste Land* concerns itself with the preternatural apprehensions, the same in the eunuch's dance is compounded by the naturalistic impoverishment. However, in both the poems it is the impoverished nature of human survival that becomes the centre. In a horrifying manner Das quite intriguingly comprehends the whole modern world scenario in the impoverished and exasperating 'dance' of the 'eunuchs,' whose urgency of purpose is involved in a proper naturalistic procreative felicity. The eunuchs are by nature denied the life force just like the inhabitants of *The Waste Land* are compositely turned to sterility. This sterility point of *The Waste Land* and the impotent nature of the 'eunuchs' are more or less the same. Ultimately both Das and Eliot find their source of influence in Webster's imagery. Expressions like "Pressing lidless eyes" (L.138) and "chuckle spread from ear to ear" (L.186) in *The Waste Land*, and the expressions such as "Lovers dying and of children left unborn," "wailed and writhed in vacant ecstasy," "half-burnt logs from / Funeral pyres," and "urine of lizards and mice" in Das's "The Dance of the Eunuchs" (CP 106) are some such fistful images that show "fear in a handful of dust" (*The Waste Land*, L. 30).

Towards the end of the poem, the poet calls the dance 'convulsions,' i.e. involuntary restless movements of limbs due to some sickness. The sickness of the eunuchs is understandable, and Das invents a vibrant poetical reflective prospect of presenting her concerned reactions to the eunuchs' dancing in a chorus. Even in the dance, whose movements are expected to be exulting, the total atmosphere of the poem is quite suffocating and unbearable. The imagery makes the necessary poetic trick. The overall effect of the poem is in the nature of black comedy or black humour (a sick joke) traditions of our time.

However, Vrinda Nabar gives a negative comment on the poem. For her

> . . . the poem ["The Dance of the Eunuchs"] is an example of how sensitivity to the world of sights and sounds, while providing its own vitality and authenticity, does not necessarily produce a good poem. The unusualness of the theme, the special response of superstitious fear and a degree of revulsion which the eunuchs evoke in the average Indian mind, the aggressive, socially accepted roles they play in the Indian context, all these appear to make the poem larger than it actually is" (21-22).

By a 'good poem,' Nabar hopes to have an aesthetically agreeable poetic improvisation of imagery. But in the classical Indian *Rasa* theory ("theory of aesthetic emotions"), *Beebhatsa rasa*, ("the repulsive emotion") has an equal place of dignity and honour along with all other emotions. Das is quite pertinently invoking the ultimate tenets of *Beebhatsa rasa* in the wild 'dance' of the 'eunuchs.' If we take the 'eunuchs' as a general symbolic expressive metaphor for the obnoxious and hateful manner of modern life, the ultimate meaning intended by the poet becomes more vibrant. Nabar's demands for 'a good poem' are difficult to understand. It is true that "The Dance of the Eunuchs" arouses disgust. But this arousal of disgust is a poetically intended phenomenon in the structural dimensions of the poem. In arriving at the conclusion that the poem is not 'a good poem,' Nabar is not at all convincing. In fact Nabar errs in viewing the whole situation as a mere outward poetic portrayal of the eunuchs' revelry. The poem is to be viewed as an objective correlative for the absolute barrenness of love-life the poet herself experiences. The poet comes to see the whole world as a wasteful phenomenon. Every act, every happening, for her, is devoid of its prime purpose. The vast inner landscape of the poet's self with all its heat and sterility finds objectification through the portrayal of the vapid, pathetic world of the eunuchs. In this context, what S.C. Saha writes is worth quoting. As he puts it: "The pathos, the helplessness, and the meanness of the situation are evoked and fused together into the superb lines that embody Kamala Das's exquisite identification with the barren spectacle of the spasm-shaken eunuchs" (24).

2. *The Inescapable Snare of Body*

The tragic dimension of Kamala Das's poetry emerges from the irredeemable contexts into which the human instincts thrust the entire body and soul into a sort of covetous exactions for achieving sublime pleasures. The tragedy in her poetry emerges out of the situational anomaly, in the context of which such sublimations are self-denied or forcibly denied by the others in a given social system. This ultimately refers to the naturalistic need of the creaturely survival. At times her self is passionately involved with the "body's wisdom" (OP 41), and at others it is in a desperate need for an escape from there. But whatever situation the self is in, it remains an inescapable condition. If it is the psychological vacuum that she objectively presents through the poem "The Dance of the Eunuchs," it is the hopelessness of life and the coldness of death that she reveals in the poem "The

Descendants." The poet's self cruises along many a turbulent sea of love-lust-frustration with the hope of ultimately finding an answer to its exclusive predicaments. But every trial eventually leads to the agony of unfulfilment, and no relief has ever been in sight. In the poem "The Descendants" she expresses this irredeemable nature of her preoccupation with love and lust. Here the lovers are involved in blind and inconsequential love without genuineness of emotions. The Biblical echo in the lines: "We have lain in every weather, no, not / To crosses, but to soft beds and against / Softer forms" (D 8), and the ironic comparison of 'beds' with 'crosses,' are suggestive of sin and the consequent punishment. The lovers surrender themselves to every trap of lust:

> We were the yielders
>
> Yielding ourselves to everything. It is
>
> Not for us to scrape the walls of wombs for
>
> Memories, not for us even to
>
> Question death. . . . (D 8)

In a metaphysical manner the poet comprehends the inescapability from the two naturalistic conditions thrust on human existence: one is the life instinct, and the other is the death instinct. In an agonising manner she proposes that these two properties do not yield any feasible answers for human questionings to the extent that the beings are encompassed between birth and death, whose purposes are not known. The unforgettable nature of 'the walls of wombs' and the unquestionable state of 'death' itself as a certain inevitability are the two bedevilling features that destroy the human balances of thought and action. The Biblical echo is clear in the following lines which indicate a tormenting state of hopelessness:

> None will step off his cross
>
> Or show his wounds to us, no god lost in
>
> Silence shall begin to speak, no lost love
>
> Claim us, no, we are not going to be

Ever redeemed, or made new. (D 8)

The unavailability of Jesus 'step(ping) off his cross' compounds the female persona's spiritual agony or explicates her physical thirst for redeeming water, i.e. the spiritual ablution. Her self's attempt to elevate the love-relationships to a sublime level by transcending the 'body's wisdom' ultimately draws a blank. The self is interminably entangled in the vacuum between the tormenting but inexorable state of being-in-the world and the elusive heights of transcendence.

Thus, all through her poetic journey Kamala Das talks chiefly about her search for an ideal relationship that she eventually fails to find, and the ensuing psychic violence. But she never comes in contact with this ideal lover because the right man has not yet been evolved in nature. Here the following observation of Sunanda P. Chavan is right in the practical context:

> Kamala Das's search for ideal love and the resultant disappointment seem to involve the psychological phenomenon of 'the animus' struggling to project the masculine imprint as interpreted by Jung. The attempt to seek in every lover the perfection of masculine being is destined to end in failure because of the impossibility of realizing the ideal in human form. (Fair Voice 64)

But then, the incessant creative urge in the consciousness invariably stimulates the poetic sensibility to an eternal search for the immortal ideal. As Camus points out on the authority of Nietzsche, "No artist tolerates reality.... " and further adds, "Artistic creation is a demand for unity and a rejection of the world. But it rejects the world on account of what it lacks and in the name of what it sometimes is. Rebellion can be observed here in its pure state and in its original complexities" (222). It is this intolerance for reality and the ensuing urgency of the mind to create an ideal world with all that is lacking in this world, a world lacking all that is superfluous in this world that we see in the poet's search for the ideal. When the creative self rejects all that is unreasonable, it inevitably goes to replace in imagination the unreasonable with the reasonable. Thus the poet's search for an ideal lover with his ideal love in an ideal world is the psychological necessity of her own creative self.

All this automatically leads to and points at the essential philosophical counters of the phenomenon of love and the human survival. In the following chapter it is proposed to make a critical study of the broad philosophical counters, particularly in the context of the emergence of violence in the poetry of Kamala Das.

5

Metaphysics of Violence

The leftist upsurge and the feminist liberation movement, both of the nineteenth century origin, took up their massive popular assent and confirmation in the Twentieth Century. Karl Marx and Simone de Beauvoir formulated the profound theoretical bases through *Das Kapital* and *The Second Sex* respectively. Both these sociological developments are the proper landmarks in the Western Historicism which stipulates and envisages a continual human progress attended by the ultimate human perfection at the end in course of time. Both the feminist and the leftist movements respectively and ideologically stipulate that the right of instinctive happiness must be through equal manner of sharing the exquisiteness and ecstasy of intimate relations between men and women, and that the material comforts in a way must accrue first to those who produce those material effect (say, labour), in a given social system. Both the movements are partially physical and rational, as well as metaphysical and irrational; and, at the same time, they both finally address themselves to the ultimate manner of acquiring happiness for individual members, and their happiness in all probability is a state of mind and a personal prerogative.

"Metaphysics," according to F. H. Bradley, "is the finding of bad reasons for what we believe on instinct." As happiness or otherwise is basically dependent on our instinctive capacity to apprehend and comprehend the knowledge of experience, Bradley hastens to add to the above: "the finding of these reasons is nonetheless on instinct" (qtd. in W.E. Hocking 5-6). All admit that language as such is an insufficient and insubstantial medium in the act of expressing what all abundance we feel on the instinctive base; and the metaphysical course of violence has its origin in this insufficiency and insubstantiality of language, at the outset. Therefore, Blaise Pascal in one of his Pensees says, "Ask not, lest I would be forced to tell you a lie" (qtd. in Pascal, "Quotations." *Hutchinson*). Pascal's *Pensees* squarely asserts that what all that can be expressed through language is bound to be a tentative lie, for the ultimate Truth like Immortality invariably eludes the human grasp through intelligence of language. As all the human aspirations of happiness are in one form or the other equivocally cognate with ultimate Immortality of Truth, the contingent manner of Kamala Das constantly and continually exacting for such happiness in her poetry approximates itself to a broad metaphysical sphere of understanding life in its true intuitive dimensions. Whereas all the sweetness of life is in doing away with formalities, Das aims at comprehending life itself in its vibrant instinctive flares of operation, which she confirms by saying, "I am always guided by one guru, that is my instinct" ("My Instinct" 161).

The pursuit of happiness and the pursuit of Immortality and Truth or Immortality as Truth are more or less aetiologically the same in the metaphysical manner of pursuit. Both are subtle and evasive of any concrete illustration and example, for they do not find apt metaphors in any given language. Both are equally instinctive, and are available for intuitive apprehensions. Where reason fails, intention helps. Thus, metaphysical rebellion or violence has an instinctive conviction and thrust of its own because, to invoke Blaise Pascal again, "The heart has its reasons which reason knows nothing of" (qtd. in Pascal, "Quotations." *Hutchinson*). The concluding lines of Kamala Das's poem "The Suicide" are worth quoting here, where she appeals to the sea:

> Take in my naked soul
> That he knew how to hurt.
> Only the soul knows how to sing

At the vortex of the sea. (D 2)

The very idea of 'soul sing(ing)' is somewhat antithetical. In fact soul is a silent presence within the self. If the poet says that it sings, that too at the vortex of the sea, it is all her heart's reasons which probably the reason itself does not know. All this implies that there are many things in the world of the heart where reason cannot penetrate. This is one nice example of giving 'bad reasons' for what she immensely felt as true in her heart of hearts, probably through intuition.

What all Kamala Das apprehends as the exclusive feminine province and property of happiness eludes a rational grasp. Therefore, it cannot be distinguished, defined, and designated in any specific terms of a language. The urgency to tell it and the lack of means to tell, compound in her a typical metaphysical fury that operates poetically as a strong and vehement argumentation for a square recognition and understanding of women's problems in the course of achieving for herself the most requisite pleasures and happiness. She poetically affirms and analyses the feminine aspirations and prospects of happiness. Thereby she wants to bridge the gulf between the manners in which men and women thought and comprehended differently about the content and quanta of happiness they derive in their relations. But insofar as it refers to happiness, even when it is interpersonal, it has its own metaphysical distinctions. Happiness and pleasure in its fullest measure always elude both men and women. The contingent unbearable nature of this state of affairs of women turns into a verbal charge and expression of frustration in Kamala Das. For her poetic purpose, she targets men as the immediate cause of violation of the rightful tenets of happiness for women. Thus, her verbal feud in all probability can be defined as sexual metaphysics.

Metaphysical rebellion is always a fission that reverts on itself. Therefore, the rebellious content of Das's poetry turns against herself in exposing her fever and fret as unbecoming of a decent woman in the honorific social traditions. Moreover, in her poetry there is no specific or reasonable clarification as to what the exact requisites and demands of a woman are, and to what extent they could be fulfilled by man even as perfect sympathetic partner. As had already been observed, nature does not provide all such pleasures and happiness as free gifts. Nature's purpose in implanting hopes and desires for pleasures and happiness both in men and women is inscrutable. Since it is inscrutable, Das's outcry is a mere metaphysical 'sound and fury signifying nothing'. However, insofar as it is an expression of these metaphysical concerns—these concerns themselves are half-truths—her poetry profoundly substantiates the emotional extent of her fury and rebellion. This is what takes an ultimate shape in tone and tenor in the poems like "The Dance of the Eunuchs." The vibrant manner in which she implants far-reaching procreative desires in the eunuchs is in itself a matter of a critical controversy. Likewise, most of her poetry takes its sum and substance out of some controversial point of determining the sexual relations of men and women as equal partners with equal mutual responsibilities.

Violence in art and literature is fundamentally metaphysical to the extent that it emerges out of heart's unattainable aspirations and inordinate desires for happiness and Immortality. It does not mean to imply that the heart is an impoverished agent. It just suggests that its empowerment is not as potential as it could substantially achieve happiness in its fullest measure. The automatic outcome of all this is frustration. The sort of great frustration that one finds in the poetry of Kamala Das mostly emerges out of her own infelt incapaciated state—a sort of inferiority complex. When this inferiority complex takes a superiority posture in all its outward appearances, it takes the form of a hectic rebellion. Thereby she resorts to charge her poetry with immense accusations against her co-sharing partner as is found in expressions such as "Can this man with / nimble fingertips unleash nothing more / alive than the skin's lazy hungers?" A few lines after, she says, "I am / a freak. It is only to save my face / I flaunt at times. . ." (The Freaks, OP 3). Read together, the above statements clarify her inferiority complex taking a superiority posture, which may be classified as an example of her metaphysical violence.

So far as the metaphysical nature of the feminine concerns

of Kamala Das, the specific causes can be elucidated from what Albert Camus says as the ground of metaphysical rebellion. In Camus' words,

> Metaphysical rebellion is the means by which a man protests against his condition and against the whole of creation. It is metaphysical because it disputes the ends of man and of creation. The slave protests against the condition of his state of slavery; the metaphysical rebel protests against the human condition in general. . . . In fact in both the cases we find an assessment of values in the name of which the rebel refuses to accept the condition in which he finds himself. (29)

If so, the drive behind metaphysical rebellion and violence is an urgency to change 'the condition in which he finds himself,' and 'an assessment of values' that have been the sources of development of all consciousness and consciences. Metaphysical violence as such erupts inevitably from the newly enlightened self of the one who rebels, and it emerges from a realization that something better exists beneath the available, beneath the given, which has been practically denied to him. Thus, rebellious or violent art emerges from polarities and conflicts in personal impulses and worldly values. Worldly values, ironically, has a mask of the ingredients for human progress, but they never do offer a strategy for naturalistic creative development to the individual's self, and would rather insist on the perpetuation of society's rigid notions on the myth of enlightenment and progress. We are travelling in time on the wheels of a civilization that has always endeavoured to impose a sort of discriminative value systems on its subjects. These values have two contradistinctive faces: at the conceptual level they prevail as the vital ingredients for an ideal human world, and at the practical operational level they function as a sort of deceitful, discriminative, and double-edged set of laws tacitly operating within a given social set up, which invariably make ominous inroads into the domain of personal freedoms and choices. But in most cases the affected remain mute sufferers of their own destiny because in their case, as Camus very pertinently observes, "the problem of revolt never arises, because for them it has been solved by tradition before they had time to raise it–the answer being that tradition is sacrosanct.

. . . Metaphysics is replaced by myth" (26). The following ironic lines of Das's poem "Nani" will further illustrate Camus' point:

> They are lucky
> Who ask questions and move on before
> The answers come, those wise ones who reside
> In a blue silent zone, unscratched by doubts
> For theirs is the clotted peace embedded
> In life, like music in the koel's egg,
> Like lust in blood, or like the sap in a tree. (OSK 76)

'Music in koel's egg,' 'lust in blood,' and 'sap in a tree' are synonymous non-thetic properties that are being thought of as the real propellers of self's aspirations. It is true that in its embryonic state koel's egg does not contain any 'music'; that the blood alone is not the accelerator of lust; that the sap in a tree is only a catalyst contributing for the tree's growth. These properties, unless activated by a second agency, are not fully capable of bringing forth their respective effects. According to the poet, the 'clotted peace' that the 'wise ones' enjoy is like that of latent things such as 'koel's egg,' 'blood,' and 'sap in a tree.' As Nabar observes, "Perhaps, the logical interpretation would be that the music in the koel's egg, the lust in the blood, the sap in the tree, if not allowed to manifest themselves, are really not symbols of vitality but of life-in-death. Hence the peace the 'wise ones' experience is 'clotted,' not smooth or unblemished" (71).

However, for those who 'ask questions' and "do not" 'move on before / The answers come,' it invariably leads to conflicts within and without. By the expression 'without' is meant that for more passionate and less creative minds, these conflicts get manifested in violent actions or physical violence. But in a creative and highly imaginative psyche, the drive for physical violence is replaced by metaphysical violence and a passion for creative imagination. If so, metaphysical violence is the refusal of the artistic self to yield to the present order of things; and this penchant to refuse to yield eventually propels an artistic creation that may be violent in its operations—emotions, feelings, and volitions.

Rebellious works of literature are such products of conflicts within the creative minds. Camus has further clarified this by saying that creation "presumes uninterrupted tension between form and matter, between evolution and the mind, and between history and values" (238). Here, by 'values' what Camus means is the archetypal values theoretically sanctioned to the dignity of being human. However, in the poetry of Kamala Das, more aggressively than in any other contemporary Indian poetry, is manifested this 'uninterrupted tension' in between the primary and secondary concerns of human life.

The tension that Camus speaks of in between 'form and matter' and 'evolution and mind' is evident in the above quoted lines of Kamala Das. When there is no scope to resolve the tension itself even in poetry, as well as in life, the inevitable outcome is a kind of mad fury. But this mad fury becomes poetically convincing and aesthetically relieving. Thus the irresolvable nature of the tension itself becomes an aesthetic particular that enthuses the reader's attention. All questions do not have answers, and the answerless postulates invariably contribute for a tension. Therefore, the very tension here is a poetic particular and it gets resolved through the irrational metaphors. This is so because of the fact that the very tension, thus created, is in itself irrational. It is a tension clashing with another tension and providing a momentary release through a startled reaction that they go to create. Any tension, whether poetical or real, has to be released and relieved through proper sublimation. This kind of sublimation need not be pleasant or agreeable in operation. It can as well be in its own unacknowledgeable dimensions like active war or a street fight between two neighbours. As a result the sublime relief offered by Kamala Das's antithetical metaphors certainly contribute for a release through a sudden surprise or a wonder. The very unacknowledgeable nature of the rationale of certain expressions in her poetry contributes for a release of charge or tension through a sudden wonder as a matter of reaction. Thus in the reader's mind the wonder itself has its own 'bad' or absurd reasons emerging out of instinctive reaction. In such contexts the meaning of the poem reaches the reader's heart long before the poem reaches his analytical attention. Such is the cryptic manner of metaphysical reaction through instinctive operations.

On a close analysis it perspires that Das's poetry is a categorical documentation of the personal grievances that emerge in a woman from the tension between 'history and values' because of her rigorous conditioned nature of life as lived and practised in the male-chauvinistic world. Her poetry being a potential expression of personal grievance as a woman, it attributes for itself an unabashed tone of violence. This violence is born out of her extraneously constrained freedom of herself. This violence is inborn in her personality because of its transparent awareness of the need of such freedoms as a necessary prerequisite for happy living. It is a matter of her personal experience that such freedoms which should have been enhanced and accelerated in the context of human survival, have invariably become incidental casualties. The feminine clarifications that she offers through her poetry are awfully vibrant with the very needful nature of the feminine contentment. But the impossibility of gaining such contentment by way of freedoms and choices is a fact, for in the practical context the unyielding traditions leave no leeway for her to demand such freedoms. The consequence of her interrogative temper is certainly known to her as the following lines of the poem "Tomorrow" suggest:

> Tomorrow they may bind me with chains stronger than
> Those of my cowardice, rape me with bayonets and
> Hang me for my doubts.

Further lines have tragic but challenging tone:

> Resident Gods,
> Seal the high notes of pain, still the faltering will's
> Ultimate grown, grant
> Me silence below the gallows . . . (CP 28)

The expression 'Hang me for my doubts' is very important. The 'doubts' always manifest themselves as questions that invariably carry the seeds of resentment and rebellion. This resentment and rebellion against the 'Resident Gods' always deserved 'silence below the gallows' in the rigid traditional environment.

But Kamala Das's resentment and rebellion is the natural fallout of the instinctive flares in operation owing to her primary concerns and, therefore, cannot be contained by any secondary agencies. The caged and conditioned manner in which women survive in the present context compels her self unleash a violent and vociferous poetic campaign against 'form,' against 'evolution,' and against 'history' by way of transparently clarifying the need of naturalistic freedom of woman as prime movers of the very creative process. If so, the balance in which she weighs her concerns of freedom tilts towards primary concerns based on the primitive animistic lawless and flawless atmosphere of human interactions.

Freedoms – Primary and Secondary Concerns

Northrop Frye talks of two types of "concerns" in human life:

> There is a primary concern and there is a secondary concern. Primary concern is based on the most primitive of the platitudes, the conviction that life is better than death, happiness is better than misery, and freedom is better than bondage. Secondary concerns include loyalty to one's own society, to one's religion, or political belief, to one's place in the class structure, and in short to everything that comes under the general heading of ideology. All through history, secondary concerns have had the greater prestige and power. (21)

Thus the 'primary concerns' are naturalistic acquirements of men, whereas the 'secondary concerns' emerge out of the emotional attachments to the man-made traditional institutions and their conventions. Needless to say, the naturalistic acquirements are invariably superior to the man-made institutional traditions. Man-made institutional parameters invariably alter and change in course of time, and these alterations and changes in themselves are likely to become nonadjustable constraints at a later stage of life in the historical process. Therefore, these man-made conventions very often require reformations and revisions in accordance with the immediate temporal demands. However, the response of a person to his surroundings is dependent on how strongly or less strongly he receives these conditions into his inner self. If and when the secondary concerns get overstretched beyond their necessity in operation by nature, the response of the individual to them is most likely to be negative. This creates a conflict between the individual and his surroundings. Humanity in its abstraction is permanent and the institutions are temporal. This provokes the cognitive self to take a rebellious stance against all the forces of culture and civilization, which have menacingly interfered in the primary individual freedoms by way of awarding exclusive importance to institutional prerogatives.

A close study of Kamala Das's poems would reveal that she is all for the primary concerns and permanent aspects of human existence, for her ultimate poetic concern is feminine happiness or for that matter denial of happiness, particularly in the counters of man-woman relationships. The very manner of attributing a defeatist tone and tenor to her poetry completely explains the horrifying manner in which the feminine primary concerns are subjugated, exploited, and declared as non-entities. The feminine self that suffered for centuries the muted silences which are mercilessly imposed upon it suddenly opens up the floodgates. And the confessions that she makes become highly important for a humanistic discernment, if not for an aesthetic establishment of the feminine primary concerns and freedoms. Her poetry invariably reflects her demand for this naturalistic, primitive freedom of existence.

This demand time and again takes her back to the rare moments of past experiences and ecstasies related to her childhood. In the poem "A Hot Noon in Malabar," she journeys back in space and time to the simple unadulterated wild experiences of the childhood. She is now sitting in a farther and modern city like Calcutta. She thinks that had it been her childhood home atmosphere, she would have been having a lot of wild ecstasies and experiences. In her ancestral Nalapat house:

> This is a noon for beggars with whining
> voices, a noon for men who come from hills
> with parrots in a cage and fortune-cards,
> all stained with time, for brown Kurava girls

> with old eyes, who read palms in light singsong
> voices, for bangle-sellers. . . . (BK 18)

It is just like coming back to her childhood home, imaginatively of course, from her place of living which, in the present context, is no home at all. Home is not a mere structure; it is where you have someone to receive you with all familial warmth and love. But for the poet, the present "home" is "where the dream awaits us / and the knife sharpened for the kill. / Home is where the god who failed us stands awaiting" ("The Word is Sin," BK 145). Gradually towards the end of the poem, "A Hoot Noon in Malabar," she betrays all her pent up agony in being plucked away from this 'wild' atmosphere: "Yes, this is / A Noon for wild men, wild thoughts, wild love" (BK 18), but contrasts it with the absence of such wild ecstasies in her present life:

> To
> Be here, far away, is torture. Wild feet
> Stirring up the dust, this hot noon, at my
> Home in Malabar, and I so far away ... (BK 18)

This affection and need for primary freedoms of life makes her always long for the 'wild men, wild thoughts, wild love.' When these 'wild' freedoms are sabotaged, particularly when the feminine aspect gets atrociously conditioned to an awful state of passivity with growth in age, condescending it to non-entity, such over-doings by the patriarchal culture flare her rebellious temper or temperament, and she feels that 'To / Be here far away (from what is aspired) is torture.'

Looking from this angle, the feelings expressed in "A Hot Noon in Malabar" are not a mere nostalgic craving of a commonplace sentimental mind. But it is a retreat into the past in space and time, and a keyhole peep into the tender psychic aspirations of her childhood innocence. The images of wilderness, which follow one by one with a cinematographic effect, such as 'beggars with whining voices,' 'men who come from hills / with parrots in a cage and fortune-cards / all stained with time,' 'brown Kurava girls / with old eyes,' 'bangle sellers,' whose "voices / run wild, like jungle voices" (BK 18) clearly indicate the longing of a throbbing mind for the primitive animistic pleasure. The more she realizes the arduous nature of her physical and metaphysical limitations in aspiring for such primary pleasures of life in the present modalities of social intercourses, the more violent and rebellious she becomes in her poetical tone and tenor.

The East-West encounter played a very positive role in the life and poetry of Kamala Das. The Western culture and historicism which is predominantly linear in its approach with a faith in the possibility of real enlightenment and progress inducts into man a sort of aggressive approach to life with achievement-mindedness. Since materialistic achievements are detestable for the Hindu mind, he always preferred a sort of primitive animism in tune with the rhythms of nature as against the Western man's idea of ultimate perfection of humans. For Kamala Das personal prerogatives and personal satisfactions are inevitable necessities for acquiring real happiness in life, in spite of the fact that she believes in the possibility of enlightenment and progress. Since her prominent personal demands are concerned with happiness, she poetically insists upon a sort of needful personal adjustment between man and woman as partners in life. This insistence of Das on the needed adjustment is akin to the ancient primitive animism wherein men and women were well adjusted with the profundities of nature, and their intimate relations were attuned to the rhythms of nature and the spiritual demands of liberation. Because liberation in its totality becomes possible for humans in the naturalistic gregarious performance, in the exercise of which lies their fullest realm of experience. The entire plea for 'wild ecstasies' spread over her poetry, as expressed in "A Hot Noon in Malabar" as 'wild men,' 'wild thoughts,' 'wild love,' could, therefore, be taken as a longing for the primitive animistic freedoms in the naturalistic primary essences of human existence. Almost all her nostalgic poems that talk of unlimited love and uninhibited freedoms as well as certain passages of her "My Story" point towards this yearning for a 'lawless' and 'flawless' peaceful co-existence against the backdrop of naturalistic prerogatives rather than a feeble animal existence reeling under the burden of institutional predominance in the context of civilized life. As it is, the peripheral reasons are the 'bad reasons' that she gives, for what all she believes instinctively as true ultimately conforms her poetry to a kind of metaphysical operation. Her real need is the necessary warmth of being possessed and comforted by her partner in love. This needful possessive instinct gets a shattering blow when she realizes the fact that all the prospects for happiness and happy living have gone into the historical past; and, in the present, the only feeling that emerges as a violent outcry is the essential feeling of the loss of all the life-giving and instinctively enthusing phenomenal particulars. If so, the loss she sustained is awfully a regrettable one, and that she does through vivacious evocative introspections.

Romantic Love and Primitive Animism

Romantic love, to the extent that it is fallout of plastic imagination, does not vitally and vigorously fulfil the primitive animistic demands. Moreover, Romantic love is a mere echo of the extended personal desires for a 'cloud cuckoo land.' To that extent, they are not well founded in the reality of human existence. They only emerge exclusively out of the desiring dreams. The primitive animistic evocations are not like that. The instinctive polarisation of the gregarious needs of humans subsisting in groups demands a clear understanding as to 'how it looks like being the other' in all the interpersonal transactions. This kind of mutual transaction in an atmosphere of absolute freedom of mind gives the needful gregarious fulfilments. In the absence of such free, frank, and transparent atmosphere, there is only a colossal denial of all that is instinctively derived as good for man as well as for woman. While the desiring self constantly makes certain fulfilling approximations, the denying self blindfolds itself to the fervent needs of the other. There emerges a sort of insufferable emotions, and these emotions have to be evacuated on instances. The entire corpus of Kamala Das's poetry, in a way, is a kind of evacuation of the pent-up grievance that reaches the metaphysical excesses as a feminist rebellion. As a poet, in spite of the fact that she emulates the structural probity of the British Romanticists, she can be considered as an anti-Romantic in the context of her treatment of creaturely avidity of love. There are no Platonic extensions here. There are stringent critical scoops concerning the relative responsibility/irresponsibility of men and women as partners in love. It is this fundamental manner of evaluating these man-woman relations that acquired for herself the status of a naked realist without any romantic orgies and circumlocutory extensions. It is her fearless uninhibited poetic spirit that ultimately becomes an arresting performance in her poetry.

Thus, the development of Kamala Das's poetic self gradually reveals her concern for human beings as a species rather than for man and woman as opposite genders. It is interesting to note that even here she takes along with her themes a touch of love-relationships in humans. In the poem "A Relationship" she says:

> This love older than I by myriad
> Saddened centuries was once a prayer
> In his bones that made them grow in years of
> Adolescence to this favoured height. (OP 41)

If love is 'older than I by myriad / Saddened centuries,' this relationship between man and woman is not of here-and-now, but it is much older than what it appears to be. The word 'I' goes beyond its semantic connotation and stands here as a sort of agent travelling down 'myriad / Saddened centuries' to the present. By this expression she is clarifying her stance that love is a gregarious instinct informed by the primitive animistic forces. So it is a not a mere personal prerogative to be in love. It is the very essence that established the family institution itself in the 'myriad / Saddened centuries.' They are 'saddened' because of the simple reason that the primacy of love as a foundation stone was plentifully overlooked during all these centuries. Long ago, i.e. in the beginning of the family system, it used to be 'a prayer' that nurtured a strong passion to take inroads in the 'Adolescence,' which ultimately brought them to 'this favoured height.' In stating that love is bone-deep in being a passion, she suggests at the inevitability of true love for all the human felicities. If so, what helps man and woman exist here is each other's desire for the opposite: "Yes, / It was my desire that made him male / And beautiful" (OP 41), and this desire is as old as human life itself.

Here-and-now is the meeting place of two principles rather than two physical entities, hence the lines: "Betray me? / Yes, he can, but never physically, / Only with words . . ." (OP 41). As she knows the inevitable nature of this love,

> Why care I for their quick sterile sting while
>
> My body's wisdom tells and tells again
>
> That I shall find my rest, my sleep, my peace
>
> And even death nowhere else but here in
>
> My betrayer's arms... (OP 41)

Even if the lover turns out to be a betrayer of his mutual responsibility, she would find 'my rest, my sleep, my peace / And even death nowhere else but here in / My betrayer's arms... .' There is a veiled imploration here to her male partner not to be a betrayer, for such betrayal is synonymous with 'death' for her.

Kurup interprets the poem based on a conflict in the narrator persona's sensibility between the need for escape and a tendency for enslavement:

> . . . . a woman cannot escape from her basic need of love and security. Thus the feminine self is the combination of the need for domestic security and the desire for independence. This predicament, which, by and large, is common to the modern woman, leads to the confessions of the inescapable such as "That I shall find my rest, my peace/And even death nowhere else but here in/My betrayer's arms". (138)

But this hasty manner of arriving at the conclusion that the poet is pining for 'domestic security' and 'independence' simultaneously, striking an echo that 'domestic security' and 'independence' are antithetical to each other, is absolutely unfounded. It is not exactly independence that she is talking about here. On the other hand, she is imploring actually for a strong mutual dependency on each other, in the absence of which her lover would turn out to be a 'betrayer,' and her union with him is a matter of 'death' for her, not literally but figuratively. As a matter of fact, instinct at all as a propelling force of desire, whether physical or emotional, is an equally compounded quality in both men and women. She is merely indicating that love as a universal instinct must be shared with equal mutual responsibilities. There is a widespread purist comprehension, more prominently in men, that physical desire in women should be checked or crushed at any cost. All the religions have dubbed physical desire as a sin; and the men-folk conveniently interpreted this sinful component in their favour by way of dubbing that it is a thing unwanted in woman, forgetting the simple fact that it is the same instinct and desire that force them to seek the companionship of woman.

Another picture of the defeated self, striking a reconciliatory note appears in "Morning at Apollo Pier." Here the shelter of the lover is 'absolute as the tomb' and a 'flawed beauty,' but the woman predestines herself to take "refuge" even in this flawed beauty:

> I hide my defeat in your
>
> Wearing blood, and all my fears and shame.
>
> You are the poem to end all poems,
>
> A poem, absolute as the tomb,
>
> Your flawed beauty is my only refuge.
>
> Love me, love me, love me till I die... (TSR 15)

In the folk songs and literature such profound poetical effects of love partners teasing and accusing each other is a widespread commonality. Moreover, the critics never comprehended the figurative nature of most of the poems of Kamala Das, with all its folk vigour and pathos. In the *Bhaktimarg* 'devotional path' of ancient India, nine types of devotional variations are earmarked, amongst which 'hatred' too is counted as one way of devotion. The negative manner in which Das is showing her devotion towards her male partner should be understood as a profound folk-poetical stroke. It is through such accusations that the partners try to induct reason and good sense into their counterparts. The delicate 'lovers' quarrel' that she makes is unfortunately comprehended by critics as an unabashed exposition of her 'body's wisdom.'

In both these poems the perception is that the gregarious existence of humans depends on the principle love, for loneliness is the most fearful augury of being-in-the world. Loneliness as such is a matter of paralysing anxiety. To dispel and extricate oneself from the intricacies of inevitable loneliness in being a person, man and woman are under a certain psychological compulsion to hurdle themselves into a togetherness. Even if they are averse to each other in the social interactive counters, in the naturalistic context they have to be together in order to carry out the primaeval plans of nature. Togetherness that is the essence of gregarious instinct is in itself a matter of offering the most needful exquisiteness on ecstasy to the individual persons in the primordial unit of man-woman relationship. When that magical 'something' happens to man and woman as constituting units in that togetherness, the constituent persons are not just persons, but they are mutually sought after persons. In this mutual gregarious seeking process both man and woman are equal co-sharers of the experience itself in its phenomenon of acquiring heights. Moreover, in the mutuality of desiring power there is something magnetic, and in that magnetism itself there is that promise of perfection. When that wanting of perfection is mutually aimed at, the very object of our own selves, which is outside of ourselves, creates a titillation, a thrill, and this thrill itself is a psycho-physical experience that involves our mind and the senses.

Naturalistically speaking, togetherness is a minimal necessity for survival. What all is important to be noted here concerns with man being a gregarious social animal, and the minimal gregarious unit, in this context, is the whole-hearted readiness of man and woman to be such gregarious partners, at the outset. Man is not entitled or capable to override the principal aims of nature. In whatever way he vies to acquire the (unavailable) existential heights, he cannot transcend the all-encompassing principle of his creaturely survival as is designed by nature for its own evolution. In that blue-print of nature he is only an animated being conducting his journey from the unknown past to the unknown future. Man and woman are just beings in the process of perennial becoming. Mutual incompatibilities between man and woman are a fact in nature where man grudges woman and vice-versa. But it is for them to realise that by being-in-the world humans cannot expect totality or consummation, as they are only a particle in the cosmic whole. In the poem "Mortal Love," Das clarifies this:

> Fidelity in love
> Is only for the immortals,
> The wanton Gods who sport in their
> secret heavens and feel
> no fatigue. For you
> and me, life is too short
> for absolute bliss and much too long
> alas, for constancy. (OSK 132)

In relegating fidelity as a mere phoney coinage Das is actually pointing towards the ever-changing, never-resting phenomenal manner of a personality performing itself. Personality is not a mechanical block to be encumbered and frozen in certain mechanical spatio-temporal parameters. Very often the personality formula in itself cognate with freedoms and choices undergoes changes in the instance drastically altering the personality. In this context 'fidelity' as a property has no real meaning. The very companionship of male and female is not merely encumbered with just two personalities. Sigmund Freud is supposed to have statistically enumerated at least six personalities taking alternative stances in the intimate relationship of man and woman.

Libido ("life instinct") and *Mortio* ("death instinct") are certain given properties to all the living beings. In the humans the urgency to do and perform, that too beautifully, is born of the consciousness of impending death. Therefore, in his poem "Sunday Morning" Wallace Stevens says, "Death is the mother of beauty" (L. 63). On the same analogy Das introspectively comprehends that we the mortals are under a certain urgency to acquire for ourselves the requisite pleasures of life. Therefore, she says, 'life is too short / for absolute bliss.' The 'absolute bliss' that she talks of is a spiritual property called *Brahman*, a happiness that emerges out of the self's unification with the Supreme self. Since this 'absolute bliss' is given only to a chosen few, what all is available for us mortals is an intermediary manner of acquiring the foretaste that the man-woman instinctive entanglements might provide. It is important to note here that instincts themselves perform instantaneously. So the instinctive operation being only a moment's given, it is certainly too short in its practical operations.

At the same time, Das quite antithetically arrives at the conclusion that life is 'too long' for 'constancy,' implying that the very feel of constancy itself is a matter of momentary operation in the phenomenal manner of experiencing. Life as an intermediary between birth and death has in itself a relative extended temporality, in the context of which constancy is an impossible acquirement. Constancy cannot stretch itself to the length of life since we are ever changing, never-resting personalities in action.

Thus the poet's concept of love transcends the flesh and enters a more philosophical state where man and woman should find the foretaste of bliss in being equal partners in the act of lovemaking. For her, love is a vital element for mankind for sustaining itself in the eternal march of time. It is founded on mutual compassion and concern emerging out of the gregarious context of human existence. In the social historical context women have been considered to be dependent on men, and the modern feminist thinkers of the West wanted women to be independent of men in thoughts and actions. But Kamala Das adds a third dimension to this love-hate tangle. For her, woman is neither dependent on man nor is she independent of him; both man and woman are equally interdependent agents, and this interdependence will go to fulfil the nature's purpose of self preservation and preservation of the race. Thus in the union of man and woman she aspires to visualize the contingence of existence, as against mere subsistence or survival. Even here, the supremacy of femininity as a principle is ascertained in nature ('Yes, / It was my desire that made him male / And beautiful'). It is quite ironic in being a fate that within the togetherness there is ground prepared for difference, distinction, and mutual accusations. If this were to be the practical way of life, the poet is absolutely frustrated and scared of being left alone without being provided with a conscious feel of rest and ease in being a woman. Therefore, her poetry is an attempt for clarifications, the most necessary property in sharing life.

Towards Other Precincts

Kamala Das as a poet was considered by many as running a mere feminist poetic feud against men folk by way of violently and even pornographically trying to settle the scores. Although the most important tenet of her poetry is her aspirations as a woman, she vibrantly diffuses her poetic art also to innumerable other vistas of life. There is a way of understanding this poetic diffusion of Kamala Das as a matter of poetic digression undertaken to give a broader canvas for her poetic breadth. This broader canvas popularly extends to the poet in relation to nature, fellowmen (other than lovers), and in relation to her own self. In the sensitive poetic manner of considering her self's poetic demands, both physical and metaphysical, it becomes clear that she considers human life as a blend of painful orgies. It is just possible that this note of painful burden in her poetry is born of that inevitable and unavoidable existential crisis that constantly and continually grows and stares into the very eyes, and scares the very being with all sorts of fears and dreads. These fears and dreads in Kamala Das are not born of any supernatural visitations. On the other hand, they are born of frustrated hopes and fractured desires to gain for her a relative life of calm and quietude in the human set. But, as had already been discussed, the most necessary calm and quietude of life always eluded her; and life, for all her poetic introspective purposes, turned out to be a sort of unendurable existential agony. It is in this context that Kamala Das can be termed as a hate poet poetically capturing the vehement hatefulness of life in its available creaturely dimensions and unavailable existential heights.

Kamala Das fervently stands for pulsating primitive animism, in the context of which the human relations in a given society are required to be potentially informed by the sincere and transparent affections born of gregarious instinctive curiosity. A social system, in order to be a viable humanistic entity, cannot afford to disregard the primal affections by way of resorting to deviating and marginalizing the individual freedoms and choices of others. Most of her poems, particularly in the later stages of her poetical career, have extended consideration for all the social and ethical norms of life. These norms are usually informed by enchanting human affections towards everything in nature and fellowmen. So far as her love for self is concerned, the entire corpus of her poetry is replete with the outcries of a stricken self particularly in the patriarchal traditions and taboos. In this context her poems having the themes of naturalistic beauties and social significances—poems such as "Forest Fire," "The Wild Bougainvillea," "Nani," "Honour," "The Flag," "Terror," "Inheritance," and the Colombo poems—are highly important. From these poems, it perspires that she is not a mere dogmatic feminist trying to expose the formidable enemies of feminine freedoms and choices. However, Kamala Das will be remembered by the future generations as a revolutionary feminist poet who had undertaken a fervent feud against all such patriarchal forces that dictate terms and conditions to the women-folk.

1. *Transcending the Ego*

In fact not much critical attention has been paid to the depth and significance of Das's many poems in which she rises above her obsessive preoccupations with gender concerns, and pilots her poetic imaginative flights to other vistas of life. Most of the criticism on her has been floating on the surface of her aggressive and open statements on love-acts and love-partner(s). In reality the plasticity of the structural properties of her poetry is more attractive to the readers than the real poetic implication centred in the thematic grounds of individual poems. Therefore, the readers arrive at an instant conclusion that sex and sexuality is all her themes. This may be so for a superficial reading. If we take the real animating forces of her poetic forms, it becomes clear that her intentions are deep-rooted in the very phenomenon of human heart that longs for a childlike comfort and protection.

However, it becomes pertinent to look at the direction in which Das's poetic concerns spread to embrace in its fold life's myriad colours, sounds, and smells; and also its fears, hopes, and vanities. In this regard Satchidanandan observes:

> Kamala Das's poetry shows a gradual widening of concerns over the years as she liberates herself from her initial obsession with her gender identity and extends her sympathies to entire sections of suffering humanity -the marginalised, the poor, the minorities, the fighters for justice, women, children, abandoned youth, victims of war and oppression. . . . This commitment, however, does not turn her deaf to the call of her inner self . . . (13)

The 'call of her inner self' is primary in her poetry while the 'obsession with gender identity' is only a typical initial explosive manner of her trying to express herself as a universal feminist medium. All other concerns as enumerated by Satchidanandan are strong attendant forces towards 'the call of her inner self.' With such attendant concerns, Kamala Das certainly extends her poetic worth to a universal stature. Wherever there is exploitation, the intensity of her self becomes aggrieved and aggravated to a state of rebellion. The metaphysical extensions of her rebellion simultaneously maintain in themselves certain aesthetic niceties and vibrations, but not any final human solutions. She merely exposes and strategically formulates the question of happiness; she never answers it, for the answers are to be arrived at independently and individually by the readers, that too through a sort of metaphysical understanding. Kamala Das merely readies the readers' instinctive property for such metaphysical apprehensions.

It is, however, important to note that these different commitments of the poet eventually become a harmonious holistic blend, sublimating her poetic art towards a zenith of compassion. In the poem "Forest Fire," Das is very clear about her poetic intentions—her instinctive urgency of taking all spiritual experiences that come her way in her creative moments. She feels a

> . . . hunger
> To take in with greed, like a forest fire that

Consumes, and with each killing gains a wilder
Brighter charm, all that comes my way. (OP 39)

Her instinctive creative urge is an all-embracing phenomenon, which ruthlessly prevails 'like a forest fire that / Consumes' indiscreetly what all it meets upon its way. This act of consuming makes the sensibility not satiated; on the contrary, it leaves the sensibility more and more ravenous, which is a suggestion of the naturalistic fact of craving and cringing for more and more possession not knowing why. In the profound moments of poetic creation, she says,

My eyes lick at you like flames, my nerves
Consume; and, when I finish with you, in the
Pram, near the tree and on the park bench, I spit
Out small heaps of ash, nothing else. (OP 39)

The metaphor of 'eyes lick(ing) at you like flames' is reminiscent of Miltonic sublime 'tongues of flame' in the Satanic Hell. Further, if it is a matter of forest fire, it is bound to culminate into the most useless 'ash' cognate with 'signifying nothing.' She convinces herself that the poetic activity itself is a matter of great 'sound and fury' that comes to nothing. In the meantime the inflated vision of life that are presented for her experience compound in her a passionate desire to encumber them in her poetry. But the profound poetic moments that emerge out of practical experience of the world somehow slips out of the poetic grasp, as Wallace Stevens rightly observed, 'A poem comes to words as a tree comes to twigs.'

She, however, considers her passionate creative experiences ('To take in with greed, like a forest fire that / Consumes') more important for her artistic self than her created frameworks. As a result her poems are 'small heaps of ash, nothing else'. Therefore, we are compelled to put a serious insight into the heart of the poet in its vibrant compulsive moments of such poetic creation insofar as they are personal acquirements by the poet in her peak inner poetic activity. However, these 'small heaps of ash' give the poet only a brief moment of solace, a momentary relief each time she spits out. All the agonies and pleasures of the sights and smells and sounds will remain in the inner self of the poet forever. These experiences occur and recur in her mind as perennially conserved treasures:

> In me, the street-lamps
> Shall glimmer, the cabaret girls cavort, the
> Wedding drums resound, the eunuchs swirl coloured
> Skirts and sing sad songs of love, the wounded moan,
> And in me the dying mother with hopeful
> Eyes shall gaze around, seeking her child, now grown
> And gone away to other towns, other arms. (OP 39)

Looked from this angle, the creative urge in the poet is only an offshoot of a more aggressive urge to take and keep within her, life in all its colours and smells and sounds. These colours, smells, and sounds reappear, re-enter, and resonate in the inner self of the poet, which gives her more and more creative energy. Hence the poet 'with each killing gains a wilder / Brighter charm.'

In a very concerned manner Kamala Das provides here a continual catalogue of human acquirements that come to man on instances and leave him too on other instances of life. By and large it is the broad impermanence of the desired eventualities of life that ultimately culminate into a great sense of frustration through loss. Nothing is more painful than the abrupt and unwarranted loss of the given in the name of family affections. All affections vanish like 'forest fire' resulting into mere 'heaps of ash' and nothing more. Thus the poem "Forest Fire" is about the inevitable manner of all human desires and hopes and dreams getting burnt in the formal facets of life in its quick and rhapsodic passage.

In the poem "The Wild Bougainvillea" she writes about a dramatic change in her initial longings for "a man I had left behind, a man / from another town." Now her self turns towards the naked realities outside, and accepts the smell and stench of life:

> I smelled the stench of the dead and
> the heavier smell of the dying, and then
> walked on streets where the night-girls
> with sham, obtrusive breasts sauntered. (OSK 49)

The above lines confirm the inevitability of destruction of the given. In this destruction there is that contingent pain. Now the desiring self craves and cringes for permanence or at least a comparative constancy, but life does not provide such opportunity; it has to be lived in perennial and continual frustrations. Thus beneath this account of smell and stench of the rot, there lurks a calm and cool acceptance of life as it is, and her self becomes wakeful to the eternal cycle of myriad colours, sounds, and sights of the world around her. The dream walking of the poet is reminiscent of the fond desiring self pining for primal affections:

> I did see beside the oldest tombs
> some marigolds bloom and the red
> bougainvillea, climbing the minarets.
> I walked and I walked, the city then
> tamed itself for me, my hunger for
> a particular touch waned . . . (OSK 49)

This is a very significant realization. The co-mingling of contrasting images—the repellent ones like 'the stench of the dead,' 'the heavier smell of the dying,' 'night girls with sham obtrusive breasts'; and the gorgeous ones like the blooming 'marigolds' on the 'oldest tombs,' the red bougainvillea climbing the minarets'—definitely suggests at a realization that new life blooms from this 'stench of the dead,' and an acceptance of nature's eternal cycle of birth-growth-decay followed by rebirth.

The implicit Wordsworthian echoes are vibrantly available in the above two poems. Wordsworth concludes his "Immortality Ode" with the lines, "To me the meanest flower that blows can give / Thoughts that do often lie too deep for tears." On the same analogy, Kamala Das directs her poetic vision towards primeval naturalistic affections towards nature and fellowmen and her own self. Any gesture of love and affection emerging out of these counters gives her 'thoughts that lie too deep for tears.' Particularly in "The Wild Bougainvillea," we have such passionate poetic echoes which can be competitively adduced as poetic parallels for the Wordsworthian poetic excitations and exquisiteness. The lines 'I did see beside the oldest tombs / some marigolds bloom and the red / bougainvillea, climbing the minarets' poetically compound an idyllic picture of the bougainvilleas ultimately consoling and contributing for a sense of poetic complacency and conformity. The expressions 'some marigolds bloom' and 'red bougainvillea climbing the minarets' 'beside the oldest tombs' are suggestively symbolic of the ultimate victory of life over death. Here the poet arrives at the conclusion that happiness, as such, is not in the 'particular' experience getting concretised, but in evolving for oneself a profound conviction and manner of adjusting squarely both with positives and negatives. This is what can be called equanimity of attitude towards the positives and the negatives more or less in evoking a feeling of generous joy towards all things in life. It also gives her the ultimate balance of heart and the necessary courage to withstand the phenomenal manner of the antithetical properties of the world. Thus we find here a greater maturity of thought than what is usually available in her exclusive feminist poems speaking of feminine demands. This is exactly what the creative sceptics call *ataraxia* 'tranquillity of mind.' It is in this altered predilection of Kamala Das in some of her major poems that acquired for her a metaphysical stance. Ultimately she concludes that life has always to be lived with some reason or the other, whether it is good or bad, for the reason itself is compounded by human instinct in operation. When the reasons are good, it is physics; when they are bad, it is metaphysics; and if they are both good and bad simultaneously, it is life. So at any cost life as a given has to be experienced or suffered in accordance with the anomalous and discordant contextual 'particulars' converging into 'generals.'

The poems "Forest Fire" and "The Wild Bougainvillea," thus, set the tone of her overall poetic concerns on a wider perspective, corroborating a humanist's vision in her poetic sensibility, which, closely studied, assuages the charges against her of being a poet of only love and sex. However, the said poems merely set the tone of a broadening in Das's poetic concerns. For a more concrete evidence of her turning towards other precincts, it becomes pertinent to look at the poetic detouring of her self in certain important poems.

2. *Violence against Feudal Traditions*

A singled out reading of Kamala Das's nostalgic poems like "My Grandmother's House" (CP 120), "A Hot Noon in Malabar" (BK 18), "Composition" (D 29), "Blood" (OP 16), "No Noon at My Village Home" (CP 31), "Evening at the Old Nalapat House" (CP 38) might impress the reader that she always travels back in time and space to reach her ancestral home (Nalapat House) for reminiscence of a comfortable world of childhood. But this is far from true. As a child she had also witnessed many disturbing scenes at her home, which remained unexplained in her tender mind. The poems "Nani" and "Honour" speak of the outrages of the Nalapat Nayars on the poor and lower caste people in the immediate surroundings. "Nani" looks on philosophically at the discrimination even death can hold out to the poor. The poem narrates an incident when their housemaid ['Nani'] committed suicide:

> Nani the pregnant maid hanged herself
> In the privy one day. For three long hours
> Until the police came, she was hanging there
> A clumsy puppet. . . . (OP 40)

It seems that the child-poet and other children of the house could not feel the terror or grief that normally accompanies such an incident. Because what they felt was, "Nani / Was doing to delight us, a comic / Dance" (OP 40). The expression 'comic / Dance' not only suggests at the innocence with which children perceived the whole episode, but also there is an intended suggestion at the casual way in which the superior class looks at the death of the lower masses. The whole incident happened when the poet was a small child. Therefore, Nani's death does not compound a telltale misery or agony in her mind. The extremely casual manner in which she looks at it has two important suggestions: one, tragedy or tragic visitation is only a matter of incomprehensible thrill for children; the other implication is in fact more heart-rending. 'Nani' is only a maidservant. In the feudal aristocratic conceptual formulas, the death of a servant is not at all a matter of any serious concern. It is in this suggestion that Kamala Das exposes the frail vanities of the feudal aristocrats. The childlike manner of looking at 'Nani' hanging herself is a poetic way of suggesting as to how innocently and ignorantly she could not evaluate the death of 'Nani.' There is a sense of inconsolable regret on the part of the poet for having looked at the death of 'Nani' in a slighting manner.

Quite naturally, the memory of the dead poor fades faster than time, for after a year or two when the child-poet asked the grandmother whether she remembers "Nani," a visibly upset grandmother poses a counter question, "Nani . . . who is she?" The child is startled and feels: "With that question ended Nani. Each truth / Ends thus with a query" (OP 40). For the child, Nani was a truth even after a few years of her death, but with the question from the grandmother, 'who is she?' the poet knew that the truth of 'Nani' ended among the living. The question 'don't you remember Nani?' and the counter question 'who is she?,' put together, is an encounter of the innocence with the feudalistic terror. The child poet's mind is in fact disturbed by the designed deafness of the elders, which kills the dead for a second time. The memory of 'Nani' is too short-lived in the mind of the grandmother who wantonly forgets 'Nani' and her untimely death. Here the poet is successfully exposing certain unfair attitudes of humanity in being what they are, particularly when they are divided into different classes, creeds, and the like. It is a poem that echoes a poetic sentiment that all lives are equally invaluable, and the death of 'Nani' had put a lifetime trauma on the authentic self of the poet. The trauma itself is more concerned with the callousness of some towards the beauty of life. The death of the other is only an inconsequential phenomenon for many who do not know the invaluable nature of life and its given lively moments. The poem as a whole is a far-reaching poetic reflection on the callous and casual attitudes of people towards the preciousness of life as a given.

The poem "Honour" is an attack on the unjust feudal situation that prevailed among her own community (Nayars). The poet now stands bearing the burden of sins of her ancestors. She sees herself as "born out of that uneasy soil, nourished / By sweat, semen, blood, the juice of the placenta, and the / Strangled babe" (CP 47). All these repelling images suggest at her ancestors' histrionics and cruelties in the darkness because "Honour was a plant my ancestors watered / In the day, a palm to mark their future pyres" (CP 47). The undercurrent of sarcasm which runs through the whole poem reaches the target more powerfully than if expressed directly.

Kamala Das's poems on death, and the feudalistic attitudes towards death itself are expressive of the insensibility of human races towards pain and evil. Very often this insensibility is formally implanted in the people's psyche as it happened in the 'Nayar' community. But the incidental manner of indicting the 'Nayar' community really strikes at the widest spread generality of callousness towards the death of the other in the entire humanity in one form or the other.

3. *Violence Against State and Communal Exploitations*

The predicaments that the modern man is subjected to are by-products of the so-called socio-political institutions which, in their impatience to impose ominous strictures, perennially attempt to restrict the freedom of their members. The method in which these strictures work in a particular sovereignty is termed by Camus as 'State Terrorism.' But no revolution in human history, either bloody or peaceful, could preclude itself from degenerating into a distorted way of unleashing the 'State Terror' on its subjects. In Camus' own words, "The prophetic dream of Marx and the over-inspired predictions of Hegel or of Nietzsche ended by conjuring up, after the city of God had been razed to the ground, either a rational or irrational State, but one which in both cases was founded on terror" (148). In the modern context, where mostly the so-called democracy is in vogue, these strictures are very dexterously administered on the people under the camouflage of appealing terms like nationalism, patriotism, and the like. According to Kamala Das, all the responses by the people to this state-sponsored propaganda are fear-driven, and not born of any real attachment to the modern political systems. Her poems "The Flag" and "Terror" talk about the hypocrisy of nationalism. In the poem "The Flag," she forthrightly exposes the paradox in the conceptual and perceptual contexts of the national flag. Each shade of the flag should conceptually give a message of progress, prosperity, and peaceful coexistence. But in reality:

> Dear
>
> Flag, look, beneath you, the scarred limbs of this
>
> City sprawl, scarred, so
>
> Emaciated... (OSK 50)

This 'scarred' and 'emaciated' look of the 'City' beneath the 'flag' compels the poetic sensibility to further probe into its dark and remote corners; the sights are disquieting:

> Rich men dance with one another's wives and
>
> Eke out a shabby,
>
> Secret ecstasy, and poor old men lie
>
> on wet pavements and
>
> Cough, cough their lungs out. (OSK 50)

The horrifying images of life beneath the proudly flying flag expose the contrast between its conceived message and the perceived realities. The flag has lost its pride and purpose. The condition of the city where the flag flies defeats its very meaning, and fails the false hopes it gives to the people. There is no point in its staying there with its false pride: "Poor flag, dear one, / Your pride is lost, it's time to leave the sky / And fall, fall . . ." (OSK 50). The Flag image symbolizes the emblematic manner of representing a nation's sovereignty. But this sovereignty, insofar as it is a protective mechanism of the nation itself, has a profound appeal and feel of heights. But the very manner of this sovereignty and the emblematic hegemony of the flag, when inverted towards the people of the nation itself, become questionable. In a world which is trying to become unified into that laudable concept of 'one world, one nation,' all other splinter nationalisms and their national flags not only become superficial but also do not augur well for the humanity as a whole. In "The Flag" Das goes to the extent of questioning the very validity of the national prerogatives, in the name of which main attractions are perpetrated. The flag is addressed to as if it is an anthropomorphized being with a sense of discretion. Insofar as the flag is only an inanimate symbol, it cannot really comprehend the evil and rot that goes under its own nose. In fact according to the poet, the flag in being a unifying emblem of a nation, only contributes for all kinds of wretched and inhuman deeds resorted to by the people who constitute themselves as a veritable nation.

The poem "Terror" expresses the poet's concern and anxiety over the growing political institutional clutches on the individuals. The hypocrisy of nationalism, emerges from fear, nothing else:

> Fear
> is our leader, leading us into
> high exitless hills, standing tall
> as a mountain goat upon the snow, and
> all the languages paralyzed
> on our tongue. (OSK 41)

The existential fear of time slipping out of grip, as suggested in the poem "The Fear of the Year" (CP 108), now changes into the pervading fear of political impositions 'leading us into / high exitless hills.' The expression 'exitless hills' portrays the inescapability of the modern political subjects from the chambers of false ambitions in which they remain captives. The concluding lines expose bluntly and with pungent sarcasm the facade of national pride and the inherent tyranny of political institutions:

> Terror hides behind
> thickets of pubic hair, all men are
> impotent, all women barren, the sky
> is taut like the face of a drum. We
> go round and round singing the national

nursery rhymes, we are kids with souls
tied into tight hypnotic knots.
We are happy, we are free, we are padmashree. (OSK 41)

The whole poem is an ironic echo of the poet's human concerns which received an irreparable damage and impairment in the hands of the people who in a self-appointed manner enact themselves as the so-called trend-benders of the human civilization itself. In the name of governance of a nation, they impose on the people a great sense of fear instead of endowing in them a humanistic impulse and feel of love. Therefore, she says: 'Fear / is our leader.' In fact the poem is reminiscent of the pain in the mind of the poet about the atrocious manner in which the rulers wielded their powers against their own subjects, as well as on the whole humanity itself. The poet looks at the very concept of nationalism from a far-reaching critical angle, and declares it unworthy of dispensation for the real human dignities. Somehow, the very notion of nationalism breeds in its people a dogmatic irrationalism, in the context of which all the human niceties and dignities are wilfully violated in one form or the other.

In the poem "Inheritance," the topic is communalism which is "an ancient / Virus that we nurtured in the soul." For her, "the muezzin's high wail sounded from / The mosque," the "chapel bells" announcing the "angelus," and "the brahmin's assonant chant" from the temple, are all synonyms of hatred (OP 20). In the heart of hearts all know:

That it was our father's lunacy speaking
In three different tones, babbling: Slay them who do not
Believe, or better still, disembowel their young ones
And scatter on the streets the meagre innards. (OP 20)

The macabre images of communal antagonism and the ensuing violence inherent in each prayer of the institutionalised religions cannot be better expressed. The economy of words with which these powerful images are constructed is really admirable. The concluding lines in the form of a prayer, full of irony, indicts the mute(d) God:

> Oh God,
> Blessed be your fair name, blessed be the religion
> Purified in the unbeliever's blood, blessed be
> Our sacred city, blessed be its incarnadined glory. (OP 20)

S.C. Harrex observes that these lines are born of a tension in the poet's sensibility between religious idealism and social reality:

> Social criticism and spiritual questing are important, and not incompatible forces in this poet's personality. Hence the tragic perception of the discrepancy between the religious idealism and factional, homicidal reality . . . emulates both prayer and Shakespearian soliloquy, vision and violence, Brahma and Macbeth. (168)

In fact Harrex is not exactly right in concluding that 'Social criticism and spiritual questing are important and not incompatible forces in this poet's personality.' He appears to have not taken the ironic tone of the poet into serious critical consideration. In stating 'Blessed be your fair name, blessed be the religion / Purified in the unbeliever's blood,' the poet is categorically evoking a sense of disgust, if not hatred towards the dogmatic manner of religions asserting their sway on humanity. All religions are supposed to have sustained in the 'unbeliever's blood.' Again, coming to 'social criticism,' Kamala Das is vibrant enough as to how the power-wielding religious leaders and trend-benders allow no place of sustenance for people in the programmes and systems of religions if they are not believers of their cult. Therefore, practically speaking, 'social criticism and spiritual questing' are substantially incompatible in being antagonistic and exploitative of each other.

However, these occasional poetic outbursts against social, political, and communal wrongs and terror seem to signify a growth in the otherwise egocentric poetic sensibility of Kamala Das, and also a shift of the centre of concerns. This wider recognition of life outside the poet's private self, though occasional, has its own meaning and significance in understanding her overall poetic property. The inward and outward journeys, after all, serve the purpose of perceiving the world through the inner eye, and also of comprehending the self through responding to the external realities, thus establishing a one to one contact of the self with the outside world. The humanistic concerns are manifested in the self's attempt to "take in with greed all that comes my way" ("Forest Fire" OP 39), i.e. conveying the general to the particular by holding the self face to face with the external objective realities; and also in resolutions like "all men are / impotent, all women barren, the sky / is taut like the face of a drum" ("Terror," OSK 41), i.e. comprehending the particular through the general.

4. **Violence against Ethnocide**

For a poetic sensibility like that of Kamala Das, discrimination in any form is unbearable and something to be abhorred. The whole poetry of Das in one way or the other voices against discriminations in the political, social, and cultural contexts of human interactions. The fact that she lends it a personal mood and colour is her own manner of creating powerful poetic images for the purpose of inviting the attention of the world. As had already been discussed, in Das, one can trace back the source of violence against discrimination to her childhood experience of maltreatment of the 'Brown children' by the Whites in the primary school. As this was her first experience of prevalent social inequities hot embers of the unbearable agony caused by such experiences lay hidden in her mind, ready to manifest themselves on the first encounter with any such situation. Her Colombo poems are sketches of extraneous over-doings inflicted by the Sri Lankan army on the resident Tamils. Whatever be the political reasons behind the conflicts in Sri Lanka, the poet only looks painfully on the pervasive atmosphere of terror unleashed by the army, hating and suspecting every Dravidian to be a militant. After all, the whole racial fight is meaningless in the sense that the ideology behind these fights is only a self-generated suspicion of one race overpowering the other, both living on the same land. In the poem "Smoke in Colombo" Das presents the most tragic picture of the aftermath of each fight. Only smoke welcomes and smoke follows the visitors, which was there:

> . . . in the rubble and the ruins,
> Lingering on as milk lingers on
> In udders after the calves are buried,
> Lingering on as grief lingers on
> Within women rocking emptied cradles. (OSK 58)

These expressions are heart-rending examples of the perpetration of inhumanity. Such inhumanity is the ultimate result of all ethnic conflicts which are usually flared by certain egocentric interested parties in order to hold their sway on the affairs of the nation and culture. The seething violence in the poet's mind towards such racial hatred and ethnic fights finds very powerful expression in the poem "The Sea at Galle Face Green," where she asks, "Did the Tamils smell so / Different, what secret / Chemistry let them down?" (OSK 59).

The poem "After July" presents yet another dreadful picture of ethnic violence. Here, the enormity of the cruelty and terror is personified as a tyrant and a racial fanatic:

> Hitler rose from the dead, he demanded
> Yet another round of applause; he hailed
> The robust Aryan blood, the sinister
> Brew that absolves a man of his sins and
> Gives him the right to kill his former friends. (OSK 75)

The poet uses her experience of visiting Sri Lanka during the peak days of the racial violence to unravel her bitterness over racial domination of any kind. In the poem "A Certain Defect in the Blood?" the poet recalls with a shudder the fear of ethnocide, which had overpowered her in Sri Lanka:

> Fear had warped our movements. Like spiders exposed
> To a water jet we curled ourselves into
> Tight balls, preparing to escape, to escape,
> Into sleep and its wide freedoms of the soul. (BK 135)

The 'fear in a handful of dust' as suggested by T. S. Eliot is manifested throughout Kamala Das's poems in many forms. While in "The Fear of the Year" it is the existential fear that "has warped us all" (CP 108), in "Terror" it is the fear of political terror, where "Fear / is our leader, leading us into / high exitless hills" (OSK 41). But in "A Certain Defect in the Blood," the fear of ethnic killing and bloodshed makes her shudder, and she tries to 'escape into sleep and its wide freedoms of the soul.' This fear triggers her to think that all this violence and bloodshed is the outcome some very old hostility of Aryans and Dravidians for each other, for she says:

> It was a defect
> In our blood that made us the land's inferiors,
> A certain muddiness in the usual red,
> Revealing our non Aryan descent. (BK 135)

The ethnic tragedies of Colombo as visualized by Kamala Das take a sublime agonizing form of poetic outcry. She only means to imply that in the true belief of the metaphysics of a nation there should be no place for violent conflicts and perpetration of atrocities. But in the overall assessment of her concerns one finds that any kind of oppression and discrimination is unbearable for her sensibility. As Nair rightly says:

> The Colombo poems are a part of Kamala Das's perpetual attempt to free her consciousness from the oppression of tyranny, despair and neglect. She is always in sympathy with souls in distress whether it is a case of woman mutilated by the onslaught of male lust or a people mutilated by the onslaught of racial venom. (74)

Kamala Das as a fervent feminist poet has spoken at length about the tragic end results of racial conflicts, particularly when man and woman are comprehended as belonging to two different and even antagonistic races. It is the same kind of odd racial polarization in the context of Sri Lanka that awfully shatters her poetic sensibility. Neither men and women are of two different races nor are the Sri Lankans and Tamilians enemies of each other. Only a little bit of humanistic understanding is likely to contribute for a glorious difference. Again, the ethnic differences, to the extent that they are universal and equally available in every nation and state, have certain far-reaching inhuman implications. They go to contribute for an irreparable damage on the humanity itself. If so, Das's Sri Lankan poems are a timely poetic warning to the inhabitants of Sri Lanka about the atrocious nature of their conflicts, particularly when looked from the gregarious instinctive angle of comprehending the entire humanity and all the living beings as invaluable creation of nature in its phenomenal operations.

The whole purpose of examining Kamala Das's poems on humanitarian, social, political, and communal themes is to exorcise the demons of criticism around her of eroticism as the only end of her poetic exercise, and to establish the fact that her poetic sensibility is not narrowed down to the themes of love and sex. It is true that such objective pathetic pictures as portrayed in these poems (Poems such as "Nani," "Honour," "The Flag," "Terror," "Inheritance," and the poems on Sri Lankan ethnic violence) are a rarity in the whole poetic endeavours of Kamala Das, and her poetry is more or less completely suffused in the vast interiorities of subjective experiences. Even then, such rare surfacing of the self out of the private world, and its intercourses with the objective realities definitely add to the human flavour of her poetic property. As a result, the tedium of overall egocentric imagery is suspended at least for a while, and the images of daughter, wife, lover, mother, and even woman, coalesce into an archetypal human figure as the prime protagonist of her poetic outcries.

Those who rebel physically and those who rebel metaphysically, though their spheres vary, have the same chromosome of violence and passion in their psyche against oppression and injustice. Such violence is not always founded on egoistic reflections. It can also spring from outside the private experiences of the one who rebels. In such cases it results at times from an identification of oneself with the oppressed, and at others even from an element of intolerability in oneself, of other people being insulted. This view finds support with Camus when he says, "When he rebels, a man identifies himself with other men and, from this point of view, human solidarity is metaphysical"

(23). When we evaluate the poems of Kamala Das, we should invariably keep in mind this 'human solidarity' embedded in her poetic violence. She is undeniably a rebel poet who rebels against the forces of oppression and injustice in all the counters of human social interactions. She is very much aware that the philosophy working behind the gender discrimination in human society does originate from the same malevolent male-egocentric mindset that spreads its tentacles to other spheres of human life, and causes vices such as social iniquities, racial discriminations, political suppressions, and communal extravaganzas. This awareness makes her turn chiefly against injustice on women, of which she too is a direct victim. When she sees that her experiences as a woman in the familial and social environments are similar to that of other women, or when she considers others' experiences as her own, what Camus termed as 'metaphysical human solidarity' comes into play. As and when this element of 'human solidarity' enters her very neurons, there emerges violence towards all the forces of suppression, mostly towards man and his autocratic, self-emanated, self-sanctioned, and selfish formulas of traditions and conventions. Das in an interview with Iqbal Kaur reflects upon this 'metaphysical human solidarity':

> Whether something happened to me or to another woman is immaterial. What really matters is the experience, the incident. It may have happened to another woman who is probably too timid to write about it. I wanted to chronicle the times we lived in and I had to write about the experience." ("I Needed" 165)

It is this personal nature of her poetry that ultimately compounds a feeling and sense of human psyche in its restless moments of existence. Love for her is a must; hatred in all probability must be crushed if only humanity wants to survive as a dignified and glorious entity on the earth. Her poetry formally puts an invitation for a judicious re-consideration and re-assessment of all that happened to humanity in the traditional context which impoverished its enthusiasm, and for finding means and ways to subsist and survive as a humanistic whole. Thus the philosophy arousing the phenomenon of violence in her poetry can be attributed to the 'collective unhappiness' of all those who endure any type of oppression, discrimination, and wrongs in their socio-cultural milieu.

The sources of philosophical violence ultimately land Kamala Das into the phenomenal properties of aesthetic violence, in the context of which her poetic emotions take a leap from the conventional aesthetic standards by way of re-defining the very concept of aesthetic involvement of man with the world. In this context, her poetry opens up new blinds, and focuses upon certain aesthetic novelties of her own personal emotions and feelings. These aspects will be taken up for discussion in the next chapter.

6

Aesthetics of Anger

The poetic formula of philosophical violence leads to the aesthetic formula of Kamala Das rediscovering herself through the medium of her poetry. For her a far-reaching ego-consciousness is the sum and substance of every emotive experience. This ego-consciousness is the real agent of all her volitions in seeking the experiment. In this context the words of Krishna Chaitanya are very important: "The ego abides and develops because the fundamental principle of being is the self's love of itself. *Atma-rati* or *Atma-kama*" (407). In the case of Kamala Das, it can be considered as the ego of the individual who had reached the highest level of culture. Therefore, human nature takes the form of perfection in her poetry through experiencing and expressing all the humiliations of surviving in a biased society. The particles of primitive animistic complexities of self-love constitute the basic reality of Das's poetry. This self-love inspires the ego to seek higher and higher levels of self-affirmation and self-realization. In general there are two fundamental aspects of this self-love and emergence of ego. Aristotle makes it clear in the *Nicomachean* ethics: "The good man ought to be a lover of self, since he will then act nobly . . . but the bad man ought not to be a lover of self, since he will follow his passions" (qtd. in Chaitanya 407). In a way, the subtle difference is between 'act(ing) nobly or follow(ing) passions.' As regards her tirade and criticism of male authoritarianism and chauvinism, Das appears, merely appears, as following her 'passions'; but the fact is that she is acting very 'nobly' in exposing, intimating, and reforming the traditional attitudes of men towards women in almost all the patriarchal systems. In order to call oneself a modern in the real sense, he has to look at others in the same manner as he or she looks at him/her-self. Das is invoking the haughty and dogmatic men-folk for introspection as to how it looks like being an exploited woman in the social context. This sort of introspection is possible only in the primaeval gregarious perspective of human life. So the "inward path" that she is talking about in the following lines is as important as (if not more important than) the outward one for her, in order to be poetically relevant:

> The longest route home is perhaps
> the most tortuous, the inward
> path you take that carries you step
> by weary step beyond the blood's
> illogical arrogance . . . ("Anamalai Poems VIII," OSK 110)

This 'inward path' takes her 'beyond the blood's / illogical arrogance' to the primitive animism where only life's primary concerns interest her. Thus the best criteria to evaluate Kamala Das's aesthetic parameters emerge as to how seriously she is fundamentally pre-occupied with absolute primary concerns as against the wicked secondary concerns. The secondary concerns which weigh most in the minds of the men-folk are in a way not only harmful, but even dangerous to the body politic in a given social system founded on equality, equal dignity for all, and equal mutual sharing of pleasures and pains. Since Das insists upon the needful phenomenon of equality and equal mutual perception between men and women, she is often thought to be running a one-sided feud against the men-folk. It is a fact that educating men and preparing them to be honest and honourable citizens is one thing, and to expose their drastic shortcomings and ignorance is altogether another thing. But in the potential manner in which Kamala Das exposes the men-folk and the lack of concern in their behaviour towards their women, she only aims at divining a 'man-thinking,' to borrow the expression of R. W. Emerson. The thinking man of the traditional context must renew himself as a powerful 'man-thinking.' It is only then that real happiness becomes available for the humans. The pursuit of this real happiness through self-love conforms Kamala Das to apprehend the other into a sense of passionate interpersonal love; and she expects the same kind of intensity of love from the men-folk in a given society.

Aesthetic Experience as the End of Poetry

All said and done the all-important place of poetry lies in the fact that its chief function remains in aesthetically elevating the reader's mind. Defining the term "aestheticism" J. A. Cuddon says, ". . . the term *aesthetic* has come to signify something which pertains to the criticism of the beautiful or to the theory of taste. . . . And a*estheticism* is the term given to a movement, a cult, a mode of sensibility. . . it entailed the point of view that art is self-sufficient and need serve no other purpose than its own ends" ("aestheticism"). Therefore, without an all-pervasiveness of aesthetic quality, a poem will definitely degenerate into a mere treatise in verse and a catalogue of cultural properties, irrespective of any amount of social and cultural realism interwoven in it. While the thought in a poem is its vital principle, the immediate interest is its pleasure-giving ability. Emphasizing on the primacy of poetic delight, Paul Valery observes: "Thought should be hidden in the verse like the nutritive principle in a fruit. A fruit is nourishment, but it is seen only as relish. We perceive only the delight, but we receive a substance" (qtd. in Chaitanya 209). How the reader should absorb a poem into himself cannot be better expressed. The 'nourishment' of the 'fruit,' as Valery has put it, becomes an offshoot of the act of 'relish' itself. The substance of a poem, thus, enters the consciousness of the reader inevitably, while he delights himself with this 'relish.' If so, the chief interest of the reader remains this immediate 'relish,' during the course of which the 'nourishment' gets into his blood and nervous system. This 'relish' is in fact nothing but the aesthetic pleasure. This quality of aesthetic pleasure is known as *rasa sidhi* ("acquiring juicy relish") in the Eastern poetics; and as the tenets of sublime pleasure principle involved through 'transport,' in the Western aesthetic theories. The modern psychologists designate this aesthetic pleasure quite cryptically as 'aha' experience. Whatever be the name given for this kind of pleasurable relief, insofar as a poet consciously maintains it constantly and consistently, the poetic endeavour becomes worthy of critical regard and recognition.

Indian aestheticians have categorized human motivations into three types: They are *Tamasic* ("blind impulsions of unconscious instincts"), *Rajasic* ("conscious extrovert action"), and *Satvic* ("poised, untroubled participation in the world's life"). Out of the above three types of motivations, "aesthetic experience," comments Krishna Chaitanya, "cannot be *Tamasic,* because it is not instinct-impelled or unconscious; it needs a heightened consciousness. It is not *Rajasic* because it is not utilitarian in its motivation. It is *Satvic* because it is a mood of poised, tranquil relishing" (211). Schopenhaur describes this 'tranquil relishing' as "the painless state Epicurus prized as the highest good and the state of the gods; for we are for the moment set free from the miserable striving of the Will; we keep the sabbath of the penal servitude of living; the wheel of Ixion stands still" (qtd.in Chaitanya 211). Any work of literature, since it is literature, has to have this quality of making 'the wheel of Ixion stand still' at least for that much time during which the reader relishes it. This momentary suspension of 'the miserable striving of the Will' is the aesthetic experience, and according to W. Basil Worsfold:

> It is the characteristic quality, which poetry shares with its sister arts, the quality of giving pleasure-aesthetic pleasure, that is, pleasure which arises neither from a consciousness of right conduct nor from an expectation of material profit, but which consists in a sense of enjoyment that is purely self-sufficing and disinterested. (21)

However, aesthetic pleasure, to the extent that it 'consists in a sense of enjoyment that is purely self-sufficing and disinterested,' is derived not necessarily from the experience of a pleasant situation; but it can invariably happen in an encounter with the tragic, or from the reflections of any human emotion, be it love, hate, happiness, pity, fear, anger, violence, sorrow, anxiety, agony, dread, and even nausea. This arousal of aesthetic pleasure from the tragic happens due to a situation to which Bullough gives the name "aesthetic distance." Citing an instance of "aesthetic distance," Cuddon says, ". . . one may deplore Iago's motives and actions and the thoughts he expresses but at the same time receive considerable satisfaction from the way he does things or expresses himself, as well as from *what* he expresses" ("aesthetic distance"). It is here that the real scope for argument lies in the context of modern literature which invariably encounters only the tragic. Creativity itself, in the modern context, is a quality of encountering the tragic and transmuting the tragic phenomenally into aesthetic experience. This is made possible in the creative process by stimulating the pure static thoughts and animating them into rhythmic becoming. Since this becoming is a process of transmutation and creation of beauty, the experience of this becoming is aesthetic. If, during the process of poetic creation, the creative mind experiences a relief from emotions, it invariably brings forth in the reader's mind also a similar effect which is his [the reader's] aesthetic relish. This is also popularly called attribution of sympathetic experiencing of the process. In this context Vaghbhata (the Elder), the twelfth century critic, says,

> The content of poetry must be drawn from actual life, but it should also be judiciously idealised. The purpose of the idealisation is two-fold. In the first place, it is that, having its source in the poet's imagination, it may appeal to the same faculty in others and not to their intellect merely. In the second place, the purpose is that particular things of common experience may thereby be transformed into general ones, and thus readily induce a detached attitude in the reader or spectator which is the essential requirement of aesthetic experience. (qtd. in Chaitanya 214)

When poetry, 'having its source in the poet's imagination,' appeals 'to the same faculty in others,' the reader may identify himself to be in the same suffering situation as that of the poet, thereby attaining an equal degree of emotional state to which the poet must have been put through while writing the piece, for a good piece of poetry "blesseth him that gives and him that takes," to borrow a Shakesperean expression. In this twice blessed state, as Chaitanya observes, the "emotion first experienced by the poet is private, a state of his being. If it is to be transferred, the only way is to make the spectator or reader live through the same experience and feel the same emotion. This ideal revival is possible because human nature and experience are generally identical" (32). What undeniably haunts us in the literature of our times is this aesthetic experience born out of the writers' perpetual encounter with the tragic and the ominous; and the transmutation of the particular experiences into general ones. Thus for a complete evaluation of the poetry of any poet, it is imperative to examine whether it serves, along with other social and cultural objectives, this aesthetic purpose; whether it makes 'the wheel of Ixion stand still' for the reader, and whether the reader is 'for the moment set free from the miserable striving of the Will.'

In the case of Kamala Das this identical nature of human experience extends to both men and women even when they are put apart as mutually rivaling entities in the blissful act of life. As a matter of fact, the contingent restlessness created by the rival factions contending with each other becomes the very tissue of her poetry. In being so, the poetic content of Das touches the highest levels of aesthetic experience. As a modern feminist poet, she constantly and successfully creates in the minds of the readers the characteristic emotions of our times such as anger, anxiety, angst, dread, fear, and nausea. As Anisur Rahman rightly says: "The poet experiencing the pain herself makes more than a personal suffering, a common feminine predicament. Herein lies the true feminine sensibility expressed in a form where Kamala Das the woman and Kamala Das the artist coalesce into one and transcend each other" (8). Thus, when the emotion is predominantly tragic, it becomes the reader's suffering too; and it is through this vicarious suffering of the reader that her poetry is universalized.

Modern feminist liberation movement that took its initial roots in the revolutionary tracts and fictional writings of Simone de Beauvoir and Virginia Woolf in the twentieth century added a particular judicious sympathetic wave towards woman and her downgraded status of survival almost up to the nineteenth century. There is certainly a point of potential argument in the essential manner in which the creative writers took up the cause of the feminist liberation as a privileged fundament of woman's prerogatives by adopting a violent tractarian approach towards highlighting women's special importance in being an equal creative agent along with men in all the prevailing social systems.

Since the tone and tenor of the feminist poetry and fiction took the form of violent machismo reactions, the ultimate tug of war turned out to be a macho-machismo feud in its operations. In this feud of extraordinary verbal dimensions, there is at bottom a humour born of incongruous mutual attitudinal surmises. In cognitively understanding the rebellion and violence, there is pleasure, sublimation, and even exasperating moments of inflating the momentary mutual emotional surges. After all, the whole feminist violence and rebellion emerges out of the 'lovers' quarrel' (to borrow the phrase of Robert Frost), which has its own sweetness and light in enhancing the intellectual horizons of man, and in combating his inbred ignorance and lack of transparency. When one of the parties in their quarrels, one finds, is the 'central intelligence' (to borrow the Jamesian formula) of woman herself as the mouthpiece, the whole violence and rebellion in operation takes the form of a literary strategic trait to be eschewed by a judicious reader in his own personal silences.

Thus in the European feminist writers and the American poets like Sylvia Plath and Anne Sexton, the very manner of violence took the form of exulting aesthetic exuberance. The introduction of a new challenging verbal idiom used for the purpose of expressing this violence progressively contributed for the language of violence and rebellion in the hands of the poets and fiction writers. This tone of anger and challenge then contributed for the strife between men and women taking upon itself almost the form of par-excellence epical dimensions. The poetic and creative mouthpieces of this war and its epical dimensions are substantially prominent in offering certain revolutionary modes of creative and literary expositions even when they are less important when aesthetic pleasures and sublimations are taken into consideration. In order to make their message prominent and promptly attended to, they attribute for their tracts a tone of violence, and this violence in itself has the tenets of aesthetic excellence.

The whole corpus of the feminist literature, thus, becomes

an added aesthetic ornament in the literary dimensions. Therefore, the violence in the woman writers is a spacious aesthetic formula that becomes all too important particularly in our times of innumerable vexing problems concerning decisively destructive arms and armaments of atomic weaponry and unceasing covetousness of the nations for decisive wars. Feminist aesthetic propositions prominently act as momentary needful dimensions from the irretrievable hopeless situations in which man is involved in our times. The modern feminist poetry is a prime example of how anger and anxiety can be converted into texts with par excellence aesthetic dimensions both in form and spirit. Creation of new and exclusive idioms for the expression of anger and angst with challenging tonalities in the feminist confessional poetry has definitely enriched literary aesthetic experience in our times. Also it had vibrantly opened up altogether a new way of looking at the basic essences of human relations from the point of view of a pleasurable operation of the human intellect.

It is here that Kamala Das's poetry, as a feminist confessional document, becomes relevant insofar as it is an aesthetic formula of expressing the angst and violence of a hurt feminine psyche. Thus there is a way of interpreting her poetry from the vantage point of the *Rasa* theory ("theory of aesthetic emotions") of the Sanskrit aesthetics. As has already been discussed, the production of *rasa,* or the emergence of 'juicy relish experience,' is the ultimate purpose of all aesthetic approaches. The ancient Eastern *rasa* theory formulates nine *rasa* ("aestehtic emotions") viz., *Sringar* ("the erotic"), *Veer* ("the heroic"), *Roudra* ("the furious"), *Karuna* ("the piteous"), *Hasya* ("the comic"), *Bhayanak* ("the fearful"), *Beebhatsa* ("the repulsive"), *Adbhul* ("the marvellous"), and *Shant* ("the peaceful"). It is interesting to note that, on a conscious perusal of the body of her poetry, most of the emotions enumerated in the *Rasa* theory are prominently attended to by Kamala Das on instances. Even on the point of repetition, a few lines can be quoted to illustrate this point. To start with, the following lines can be quoted from the poem "For S after Twenty Years," for 'the erotic':

> The fountain in chilly winter, blossoming ice blue,

And he shy, rose skinned, glossy haired, selfconsciously
Kneeling to take my photo. That noon a carousel for
Strong lusts, the sun tanning our pimpled cheeks,
The woodwasps on
Every tree, the shadows, green rugs at our feet, you singing
(TSR 23);

for 'the fearful,' from "The Fear of the Year":

. . . fear has warped us all; even
In the freedom of our dreams, it
Thrusts its paws to incarnadine
The virgin whiteness (CP 108);

or from "Terror":

Fear
is our leader, leading us into
high exitless hills (OSK 41);

for 'the repulsive,' from "The Testing of the Sirens":

On the old
cannon-stand, crows bickered over a piece
of lizard-meat and the white sun was there
and everywhere ... (BK 58);

or from "The Dance of the Eunuchs":

They
Were thin in limbs and dry, like half-burnt logs from
Funeral pyres, a drought and a rottenness
Were in each of them (CP 106);

for 'the comic' (which, in her poetry, is invariably satiric) from the poem "Next to Indira Gandhi":

Next to Indira Gandhi my father I feared the most.
. . . .

> You chose my clothes for me
>
> My tutors, my hobbies, my friends,
>
> And at fifteen with my first saree you picked me a husband (OSK 118);

and for 'the peaceful,' from "The Wild Bougainvillea":

> I walked and I walked, the city then
>
> tamed itself for me, and then my hunger for
>
> a particular touch waned. I sent him roses
>
> and slept through a dreamless night. (OSK 49)

Nevertheless, the most prominent type of aesthetic experience that Kamala Das offers emerges out of observing the painful nature of the pageant of the world in its unequal and humiliating disbursement of pains in the name of pleasures. If so, the predominant *rasa* of her poetry is *Roudra* 'the furious,' which is a manifestation of her metaphysical violence against her constrained freedom as a being. In the case of Das, it is a kind of tragic fury that manifests itself throughout her poetry, like in the following lines of "A Losing Battle":

> Men are worthless, to trap them
>
> Use the cheapest bait of all, but never
>
> Love, which in a woman must mean tears
>
> And a silence in the blood. (OSK 48)

or in the following lines of "The Freaks":

> Can this man with
>
> nimble fingertips unleash nothing more
>
> alive than the skin's lazy hungers? (OP 11)

or in the following lines of "Conflagration":

> Woman, is this happiness, this lying buried
>
> Beneath a man? It's time again to come alive,
>
> The world extends a lot beyond his six-foot frame. (D 20).

Other emotions—be it *Sringar, Bhayanak, Beebhatsa, Hasya,* or

Shant—that emerge in her poetry are the attendant forces, only to intensify the manifestation of *Roudra* as the ultimate spirit of her poetry.

Poetry as the Medium of Personal Experience

"I see poetry in an experience," says Kamala Das in an interview with P. P. Raveendran ("Of Masks," 149). Poetry itself becomes boiling pot of emotions and feelings when such experiences are forced upon the incumbent by the institutions, systems, and the authoritarian onslaughts of others. In Das's poetry the encounter with the tragic and the ominous, and the transmutation of the tragic into creation of beauty invariably take place against the backdrop of personal experiences. The exclusivity of private phrases and the marvel of personal idioms are so harmonized with the experience itself that the 'matter-manner' conundrum in her poetry alleviates itself to a point where all experiences become exulting, and, at the same time, poetry becomes the medium of personal experiences. As had already been discussed, the paramount emotions in her poetry are anger and fury of a woman who, being thrown into a cultural context where life becomes awfully crumpled and suffocative, seeks life each moment with the 'necessary courage to be' in a world full of formalistic cultural obsessions and objections. Poetry for her, as it is for Wallace Stevens, is a medium of personal experience, where the mediating ground of poetic tissue is not less personal. Naturally, such poetry is bound to be of a personal nature, though in a broad spectrum analysis, it is universal in the sense that experience as a woman in a given cultural milieu is not very different from that of other women. But the fact that anyone or everyone is not gifted with a capacity to present such experiences to the world in a style that is aesthetically satisfying places the poet above others. In other words, experiences are universal and it is the style of expression that differentiates the aesthetically lofty from the ordinary, the sublime from the banal. Literature is the reflection of experiences in a particular style. If so, Kamala Das's poetry is born out of her own private experiences, and, at the same time, out of a perception that they are also someone else's experiences, who may have been subjected to a similar life-situation. The archetypal image of woman whose voice rises representing "a million, million" voices is beautifully presented in her poem "Someone Else's Song":

> I am a million, million people
> talking all at once, with voices
> raised in clamour, like maids
> at village wells. (BK 40)

These lines are reminiscent of Walt Whitman's lines in his poem "Song of Myself": "Do I contradict myself? / Very well then I contradict myself / (I am large, I contain multitudes)" (L. 1324-26). In the case of Kamala Das also, it is this multitudinous constitution of her personality that makes her poetry a formula of 'million, million people / talking all at once.' The image of 'maids at village wells' fittingly serves the purpose of representing feminine grievances, as it is generally at the wells that village girls exchange their pains and pleasures with each other. The poet's voice becomes an amalgam of tongues muted for centuries entering into a single mouthpiece and talking all at once. The concluding lines of the poem clarify this representation of muted tongues:

> I am a million, million silences
> strung like crystal beads
> onto someone else's
> song. . . (BK 40)

This is somewhat ironic. It is in fact allowing 'a million, million silences' to string onto the poet's own song and become a single rhythmic voice. As she confirms in "Anamalai Poems V," she only enters others' dreams to steal their thoughts:

> My songs echoed in strangers' dreams, in unease
> they stirred in their sleep and sighed. Yes, often, poets
> gatecrash into the precincts of others' dreams
> as Gods and Goddesses do many a time
> in unsolicited magnanimity. (OSK 109)

It is this attempt to 'gatecrash into the precincts of others' dreams' to ascertain her own identity or lack of it with that of others, and become an archetypal voice, that makes her metaphysically significant and aesthetically lofty. This is what Camus means when he says, "... from the moment that a movement of rebellion begins, suffering is seen as a collective experience" (28). Taking this way, any voice of protest representing a class of its own becomes metaphysical. This 'metaphysic' in Kamala Das's poetry is made possible by the poetic sensibility's 'gatecrash onto the precincts of others' dreams,' and as Kurup observes, in her poems "she articulates the universal angst of the modern feminine sensibility rather than being self accusing and morbid and emerges as a rebel genius whose stance as a poet is even more important than her poetry" (144). In stating that 'My songs echoed in strangers' dreams, in unease / they stirred in their sleep and sighed,' the poet vibrantly suggests that quite unconsciously as though through the medium of the 'collective unconscious,' she poetically captured the impulses of multitudes, and comprised them in her poetry as invaluable offshoots of the conscious expression of her own experience. She in fact suggests that human consciousness or authenticity is not at all an exclusively private property of the incumbent. In the human set, the very presence of consciousness is a non-thetic phenomenon of unifying all the humans under one umbrella called humanity. So every particular conscious experience is a reflection and refraction of the universal consciousness. If so, according to Kamala Das, every living moment in our life, and thereby every poetic moment, is a mutually shared complexity. But at the same time, insofar as the experience itself passes through one's particular personality, it has all the apparent invaluable preciousness of being one's own personal experience. It is unfortunate that instead of being properly and sympathetically understood, Kamala Das is regarded as a raving virago in certain critical circles in India. The necessity of sympathetic understanding of her poetry emerges out of the universal concern that she maintains as a central point of her poetic experiences and expressions. In fact, the fundamental nature of the pain she experiences and expresses in her poetry is universally acknowledgeable as a certain principle of evil that haunts the entire humanity. The personal-most expressions and charges in her poetry assume for themselves a par excellence universal status, if only they are comprehended as the expressions of the innermost grievances of almost all women in the world.

Poetic Alternatives

The poetry of Kamala Das cannot be separated from her life. Though the element of generality is prominent towards conclusion of almost every poem, yet its birth takes place in the en-situational poetic sensibility. Thus each poem of hers is an encapsulation of her closefisted encounter with life in a particular situation. In fact, there is a veiled attempt to relive through memory play, the circumstances that had passed through her life. When life's hopes are not fulfilled, and when all encounters eventually end up in disillusionment, the autistic imaginative sensibility unfurls its canvas and starts sprinkling painful colours of imagination on it so that the half-lived moments of life attains a fulfilment through poetic strategy. Kamala Das visualizes her own ideal world and even creates it around her in imagination, just like all the romanticists and confessional poets do, where she reads aloud her own rules of love and life, and plays queen like a gold fish in an aquarium. Thus in the world of poetic imagination the poet seems to seek alternatives for life's prime moments that were slipped out of her hands in real life. Elsewhere in an interview with Irshad Ahmed, Das elaborates on this fantastic world:

> I believe that each of us must live in two worlds existing close to each other like substance and shadow – one, the world visible to us and therefore, called real, and the other invisible, existing in the sixth and inaccessible dimension which we fill with fantasies. The revelations picked up from the real world must strengthen our existence in the shadowy world – and likewise the vitality gained from our sojourn in the world of fantasy must contribute to our strength in the real world. Each world must benefit the other, as one's personality is the sum total of one's knowledge, dreams and fantasies; our poetry will gain from our honest portrayal of it. ("I have Kept" 80)

Das is trying here to bring together poetic imagination and

fantasy born of autistic splendour. She calls this autistic splendour as 'shadow.' Needless to say, a shadow is two dimensional in nature, and in being so, it eludes and keeps the depth unexplored. This 'shadowy' nature of the world of fantasy is invariably a part and parcel of everybody's experience. Therefore, 'each of us must live in two worlds existing close to each other' simultaneously. However, the 'sojourn in the world of fantasy' is not a mere imaginative escape; it is an attempt to attribute upon oneself a deviated actor's trunk, and look at the relative differences and deficiencies from a third party angle. Here, then, creation becomes an attempt to capture unity in imagination, as the poetic sensibility tries to substitute the incomplete universe with a complete one in imagination, and fulfil the unfulfilled hopes through poetic creation. In fact, it is in that shadowy world 'existing in the sixth and inaccessible dimension' filled with 'fantasies' that life's fulfilment is made possible. It is a two-way process in the sense that 'the revelations picked up from the real world' that is past, incomplete, and lost, lends the poetic sensibility the requisite knowledge and ingredients for achieving a wholeness and unity in the 'world of fantasy. And 'the vitality gained from . . . the world of fantasy' reciprocally contributes to the poet's 'strength' in the real world, which is her poetry. Ahmed also sees this as an "attempt to achieve a sense of completeness through writing and to re-live the imperfectly lived or half-lived moments of life," which "bears testimony to her unifying and unified vision of life as a literary artist" (Reflections 130). This 'unifying and unified vision of life' is invariably supplemented with and supported by innumerable colours of imagination. It is these colours of imagination that work as the cementing forces of confectioning the consciously 'lived' and instinctively 'half-lived moments of life' into elaborately structured artefacts of poetry. As instinct is momentary both in operation and disappearance, the recapitulation of the 'lived' and 'half-lived moments' brings a sort of formal stylistic perfection in her poetry. This can be further clarified by what Camus comments upon rebellion and creativity:

> Through style, the creative effort reconstructs the world and always with the same slight distortion which is the mark of both art and protest. . . . When the most agonizing protest finds its

> most resolute form of expression, rebellion satisfies its real aspirations and derives, from this fidelity to itself, a creative strength (239).

The 'same slight distortion' that Camus mentions is what gives this imaginary world the status of artistic creation. The redistribution of elements ['picked up from the real world'] in the imaginary world, as the poetic sensibility envisions it, makes it unified and complete as well as aesthetically satisfying. At the same time, this process of unification in the world of fantasies has a soothing effect on the creator, which can be considered as a sublime reliever. This relief is made possible by two things: one, by giving vent to the pent up suffocative agonies through the outlet of poetic creation, and the other, through the sense of achievement of a better world albeit in imagination. Through each of her poems, Das tries to recapture the 'unfulfilled' or 'half-lived' instinctive moments of suffering she has undergone as a girl, as a woman, as a wife, and as a beloved. As a wife she has undergone the neglect of her husband in the prime most times of her life. In the poem "An Introduction" she has very clearly stated about this neglect. Added to the confusion and quandary prevailing at the very young stage of womanhood, the early marriage that too with an uncaring man made things worse for her. Here she talks about how painfully she found herself an unwanted entity with her own man:

> When
> I asked for love, not knowing what else to ask
> For, he drew a youth of sixteen into the
> Bedroom and closed the door. He did not beat me
> But my sad woman-body felt so beaten.
> The weight of my breasts and womb crushed me. I shrank
> Pitifully. . . (OP 26)

There is an abundant suggestion about the personal pain she experienced when her man 'drew a youth of sixteen and closed the door.' Her man's preference for a sixteen-year youth of his own sex as against the presence of his woman (wife) certainly has a reference to some hateful incident in her personal life. The following lines from her *My Story* suggest at the probable incident of a homosexual preference and indulgence of her husband:

> At this time my husband turned to his old friend for comfort. They behaved like lovers in my presence. To celebrate my birthday, they shoved me out of the bedroom and locked themselves in. I stood for a while, wondering what two men could possibly do together to get some physical rapture, . . . I felt then a revulsion for my womanliness. The weight of my breasts seemed to be crushing me. (110)

The above instance may be very private and personal in being a biographical incident. But these insufferable biographical incidents in a general way compound in women an awful sense of being neglected, abandoned, and declared unwanted. The expression: 'When / I asked for love, not knowing what else to ask / For' clearly suggests at the emotional turmoil and the loneliness she has felt at her encounter with male indifference towards her initial longings for companionship. The felt ecstasy at the initial stage of growing into adulthood all of a sudden transforms into a vacuum, and the edifices of adolescent dreams about love relationships crumble together. In the ultimate analysis, Kamala Das vibrantly suggests at a fundamental fact about the very nature of woman: Woman wants to be possessed and favoured affectionately. Even the slightest gesture that derides her hopes for possession and affection creates in her an inconsolable introspective agony, as a result of which she considers her very feminine credentials as absolutely useless (symbolized here by the expression 'my sad woman-body felt so beaten / The weight of my breasts and womb crushed me') in keeping her partner as an exclusively possessed property for herself. It is this gregarious-born possessive instinct that gets mollified on suddenly feeling and experiencing that her male counterpart is not attending to her in the hoped-for manner. On the contrary, his extra-normal dramatized intimacy with his male friend in the very presence of his spouse compounds in her a great revulsion coupled with an utter hatred. Needless to say, her companionship with a partner who has no concern for her is literally a shattering experience. Her possessive instinct receives a shattering blow here, and she becomes inconsolable.

It is at this point that the poet felt a compulsion to defy all the customary ingredients of gender dichotomy and differentiation. The subsequent lines in the same poem confirm this, which reveal a desperate effort on her part to run away from the reality of being a woman: "Then I wore a shirt and my / Brother's trousers, cut my hair short and ignored / My womanliness" (OP 26). This desire on the part of the poet to assume upon herself manliness just by wearing 'a shirt and my / Brother's trousers' and cutting her 'hair short' speaks for her innocence. It is not at all a matter of dress code that determines man and woman. The intentional ground reality of both male and female partner is to arouse themselves to the occasion in order to be equally sharing the mystic joys of love-play through sublimation (man) and through orgasm (woman). The innocent manner in which she expresses herself to be manly by way of wearing a 'shirt and her brother's trousers' and cutting 'her hair short' is her vibrant poetic stylistic gesture to suggest at one important point: In the matter of love-play, woman is not really a passive agent. She, as a woman, too breeds in herself an impossible desire to enact herself as an active agent like a male in the love-play. But then, to the extent that nature itself had conformed her to the passivity, there is always the trauma of unfulfilled desire to be as active and even virile as man is. She has as much inherent fire in herself as man seemingly appears to have or pretends to have. Insofar as it is a mere invitation for an equal recognition of woman's needs in love-play, the poet's purpose lies in reminding man that her physical posture is not at all really passive. It is for her man to understand the possible availability of concealed active state in his feminine counterpart in the naturalistic sense. But will he ever understand her? Or, will she ever meet a man who understands her? The answer is 'No' and 'Yes.' 'No,' in the sense that the perfect man that she is looking for throughout her life, and is talking about throughout her poems, is only an idealised entity and cannot be a being-in-the-world. 'Yes,' because in the dual world complexity as explained earlier, i.e., one's existence in the 'real world' and 'the world of fantasy,' whatever is not attained in the 'real world' is 'realized' in the creative self's 'sojourn' in the 'world of fantasy.' In "An Introduction" she vibrantly reveals this realization:

I met a man, loved him. Call
Him not by any name, he is every man
Who wants a woman, just as I am every
Woman who seeks love. (OP 26)

The expressions 'every man / Who wants a woman' and 'every / Woman who seeks love' themselves explain the needful state of each other in a gregarious sort. Here the meeting is not between two worldly persons, but between the idealised states of man and woman who are mutual invitees for comprehending the other. 'And this union between the ideal lover and ideal beloved, both living in the 'sixth sense,' constantly and consistently takes place in a dreamy state of mind. The poet considers this union more important and more legitimate than any worldly commitments.

Kamala Das confers on this 'ideal lover' a mythical framework in many of her poems, and calls him the archetypal 'Krishna,' that mythological god who had been considered as the universal lover of all in the world. Due to the employment of 'Krishna' symbol, to a great extent, her poetry is interpreted as 'transcendental' on the lines of the Indian *Bhakti* 'devotional' cult of poets. For instance, Mohanlal Sharma while evaluating the theme of love in Das's poetry, comments:

> In a final summing up of the predominant theme of love in the poetry of Kamala Das, we may say that through the varied experiences of love and hate, pain and joy, slowly but surely, the poetic persona (who is primarily identical with the author) progresses towards a transcendence of the lusts of the body, the physical hungers. . . . Throughout her multifarious relationships, she was in quest of her spiritual paramour, the eternal companion of her soul, the Divine Mate, her Krishna. (103-104)

Kurup also comments in a similar tone, "Not only the poems directly dealing with the Radhakrishna theme, but almost every poem of Das' poetry and each chapter in her autobiography stands testimony to the fact that sensual and religious elements are inseparable in her work from the start" (288).

At the outset, there is no transcendence in the poetry of Kamala Das in the sense of approaching a higher reality through conscious preparation and practices of mind. All this metaphysical babble of transcendence is only a matter of critical gibberish. Talking about the 'progresses towards a transcendence of the lusts of the body, the physical hungers,' is quite untenable in the context of Kamala Das's poetry. The strict sacrosanct Indian traditions of religions consciously relegated the pleasures of love to lust as though that is something unwanted and peripheral for the purpose of the spiritual good of the being. Interpersonal love has been traditionally depicted as a source of destruction in the course of *Mukti* ("spiritual salvation"), which in all probability is the ultimate goal of being human. Needless to say, all this is practically unviable in the naturalistic context where the protection of the self and propagation of the race are the prime movers of evolution itself. Therefore, for a realistic poet like Kamala Das, how far this transcendence transpires could be a subject for debate. For the same reason it becomes instantly pertinent to try to clarify the ever-brewing myth of spiritual transcendence in her poetry.

The Myth of Transcendence

Whenever Kamala Das talks about her 'Krishna' or the 'eternal lover,' one should keep in mind the 'dual world-dual personality' complexity already discussed above. Rather than a 'spiritual paramour,' she is all through seeking an 'ideal paramour' who will bestow on her all that she has missed in her lived life, and who in a sweep can exorcise the loneliness of her life. In fact, for Kamala Das, 'Krishna' is a mere icon standing for the profile of an equal and sympathetic love partner. 'Krishna,' for her, is as ideal as a perfect humanistic agent, the reflection of her self's mere longing to reach for the unfathomable. So her 'Krishna' is not the mythological figure with all the mythomaniacal antiques, but he is her own alter ego poetically conceived and objectivized in a sort of vibrant figurative vicarious entity. This kind of poetic figuration of her private-most 'Krishna' into a public figure is born of her gregarious instinctive necessity of an exclusively dependable other for the self in order to withstand the doubts, difficulties, and mysteries of the worlds. Thus her 'Krishna' is her supporting agent, who introduces into her a kind of hymnal unification of the self with the other. The 'Krishna' figure in her poetry, therefore, should be looked at only as a poetic ploy to convey a desire, a longing to be one with a perfect masculine being that is unreal, and also one that will not be realized in the practical world of things. Therefore, the association of the mythological 'Krishna' with her 'ideal lover' itself turns out to be a myth. The following statement of the poet, in an interview with P. P. Raveendran, will confirm the above point of view:

> I think I decided to wear a disguise. That was why I shifted to poems that seemed metaphysical. Because many people used to advise me that I should write about the love between Radha and Krishna and escape criticism from people rather than write about my own affairs, if there were any. ("Of Masks" 148-149)

The above statement of Kamala Das firmly establishes that the mythical framework in some of her poems is only an attempt to give them a transcendental look, and the mythological figures of Radha and Krishna are a mere subterfuge to escape social criticism. All this in a broad parlance is only a visionary manner of confectioning for oneself a state of imaginary circumstance, since talking of such subjective desires as personal properties amounts to resorting to verbal expressions without en-situational gravity. So imaginatively and poetically dramatising the self and the other in the mythic extensions and distances solves the whole problem of the poet.

Even if we do not take her above statement at its face value, a close analysis of her 'Radha-Krishna' poems would reveal that while an awareness of the possibility of transcendence does exist in her sensibility (it is certainly not 'transcendence of the lusts of the body' as Mohanlal Sharma puts it), the real barrier is not smashed off, and always her journey ends on the frontier and not beyond. As she says in "Feline," the perception of "a sea wailing beneath the sea, / a sky behind the taut drapes of our firmament, / a rain that rains hard and long within the summer-rain" (OSK 35), is merely a cognition which does not necessarily mean that her poetry unravels a full-fledged faculty to culminate in to that 'sky behind the taut drapes of our firmament.'

The metaphysical concept of possible heightening experience very often comes because of strong interference of instinctive imagination. Transcendence as a spiritual or romantic phenomenon is always a matter of personal experience. It is always unique without any parallel reference to make whether it is the experience of intimate relationship in love or it is the experience of self-supposedly acquiring and concretising for oneself, imaginatively of course, the relevant feel of elevation and heightening. To the extent that these experiences are exclusively personal, enthusing, and elevating, they have in them a kind of mythical and mystical composition that eludes all logo-centric paradigms. As a matter of fact, the practical impossibility of achieving them to the complete and total satisfaction on the one hand, and the possibility of putting abstract imaginative insights into the phenomenon itself on the other automatically turn these experiences into certain myths. These myths, in order to be what they are, always depend upon contraries and antitheses. Contradiction being the life of a myth, the very possibility of asserting favourably or otherwise always depends upon the state of mind on instance. The same spiritual transcendence or sublimation is most likely to remain as teasing riddles challenging the capacities of the incumbent to understand. Experience of course is there, and it is felt in all its intensity, but understanding the same or attributing some sort of objective meaning for it is not at all possible. Therefore, these experiences are required to be expressed as mere myths and archetypes, which have in themselves a kind of laconic versioning of drawn images into a graspable mythical entity. Since these dream images are constantly altering and performing themselves as evocative artefacts of certain experiences, they only contain in themselves a dream-like quality that always eludes reason and rational analysis. The experiences themselves being ecstatically inflated, we do not allow 'cold reason' (to borrow the expression of John Keats) to interfere and interpret. They have a sort of inexplicable and inexpressible quality of their own; and this quality can be poetically transmitted through what Malraux suggested as 'the universal dialectic of gestures.' Thus gestures and suggestions are mere pointers as a compass needle towards North. It is a well-known fact of experience that the mariner's compass needle just points towards the North but it never arrives at North. Such is the profound nature of the poetry of Kamala Das. In her poems, these gestures and suggestions are sometimes concretised through the mythical figures of 'Radha' and 'Krishna' or their innumerable forms suggesting at the possibility of man and woman acquiring a sort of transcendental plane in their ideal companionship.

However, while her ideal lover or 'Krishna' exists in her imaginative faculty, 'Radha' also lives as another person in herself, who is the reflection of her own abandoned self. This abandoned self continually whiplashes her from her interiorities. In the poem "Feline" she says:

> Another lives in me, I fear, a twin left unborn,
> unnamed, unacknowledged, bitter with defeat,
> and, she with her new-moon eyes stabs my face
> and turns me so often, half human,
> half feline. (OSK 35)

It is in fact a haunting experience of being perpetually condemned by another one living in the inner self. The expression 'a twin left unborn' is glaringly remindful of the vanquished self. This persistent haunting experience further impels the poet to seek an ideal lover or to idealise her love-experience. Her subjective mystical animations compound in herself the very icon of 'Radha' in the above lines. This 'another' who 'lives' in her is probably that 'Radha' figure; and the poet invokes the same to suggest at the needful immensity of experiencing love and its promises more or less in an archetypal manner. Both 'Radha' and 'Krishna' as conceived by her are charming archetypes, actually representing her own self's figurations. Therefore, the 'Radha-Krishna' composite that subsists in her poetic personality is only a matter of dreamy wish-fulfilment that provides a relief and a real fulfilment of having poetically completed a task. This is what she means when she makes the following statement in the interview with Raveendran:

> If I feel that my life is inadequate in some areas, I try to fill that—

> I try to perfect my life by adding things which may not really have happened. But for me they are real—they have happened. That is why sitting here in this armchair I can still write of murders or of brothels. ("Of Masks" 150)

This is exactly what can be called 'autistic imagination' and 'dialectic thinking' in the language of the psychologists. But, however, it is the par excellence manner in which a cornered and constrained child imagines for itself a world where nothing of the practical world intrudes to confine it and curtail its imaginative freedom. In such moments the child virtually lives in two different worlds altogether different from each other: one, the desired imaginary world, and the other, the practical detestable world for one reason or the other. The ultimate purpose of two felt worlds for a child envisages the child's concerned manner of revenging the practical forces, again, in its own confused projects. Just like dream is not a solution, and yet it is a human experience, in the same way the autistic poetic imagination is a certain fact of the manner in which human mind works.

In the case of Das the continuous act of perfecting her life 'by adding things which may not really have happened' is in fact the manifestation of her creative faculty and her imaginative power. So not only 'of murders' and 'of brothels,' she can also dream of her 'Krishna' and her innumerable meetings with him. Hence, in the poem "The Maggots," 'Radha' (here an image of the poetic persona) does not morally hesitate to lie with her husband after having made love with her 'Krishna':

> At sunset, on the river bank, Krishna
>
> Loved her for the last time and left . . .
>
> That night in her husband's arms, Radha felt
>
> So dead that he asked. What is wrong,
>
> Do you mind my kisses, love ? and she said,
>
> No, not at all, but thought, What is
>
> It to the corpse if the maggots nip ? (D 22)

In the above lines we have two distinctly contradictory personal experiences the poet had undergone: one is a total and complete fulfilment, and the other is a total and complete shattering. Here Das is poetically proposing two states of experience in their relative dimensions of fulfilment versus unfulfilment. The affair with 'Krishna' is a living experience, whereas the affair with her own husband is cognate with death in the sense that there is no pulsating animation. It is very interesting to note that such moments of drastic variation and opposition are very common in the lives of women. But the vicarious figurative manner of 'Krishna' figure put side by side by the poet brings out a very interesting property of experiencing. She is comparing here the unavailable Heavenly bliss with the practically available detraction and disaffection in the real life. The desired plenty is contrasted with the available nothing. One is life and the other is death. When the abandoned self ('Radha'), wandering in the world of imagination and fantasy, already establishes an ideal relationship with the perfect masculine being ('Krishna'), everything else in the practical world dissipates to a state of nothingness. Therefore, after having had her creative self's flights to the self-supposed heights of exquisiteness and ecstasy, she returns to the practical world completely exhausted and almost 'dead.' So the husband's kisses on her body are not at all even felt by her as they turn out to be as good as if 'maggots nip' on 'the corpse.' The expression 'if the maggots nip' vehemently suggests at the nauseating experience of the woman persona in the practical world where she is fated to drag her own dead self and present it to her exterior paramour who persistently feeds on her 'dead' body as 'maggots' feed on the 'corpse.' In considering herself as a corpse, the expression of unfulfilled desires comes to the forefront as a detestable and nauseating experience. It is as good as death itself. In "Maggots" Das portrays her powerful world of poetic imagination, treading which all worldly things become dead, decadent, and repulsive. In spite of their thematic relevance, the images of 'Radha' and 'Krishna' gradually fade away, and what is eventually projected is the self's annoyance in being bothered by external interventions when it wants to luxuriate in the upshot of satiety gained from the imaginative bond with the ideal.

The image of eternal lover again appears in the poem "A

Man a Season" where the poetic persona indicts him for having made her wander like a vagabond looking for an ideal relationship in this shadowy world. Eventually she realizes:

> A man is a season,
> You are eternity,
> To teach me this you let me toss my youth like coins
> Into various hands, you let me mate with shadows,
> You let me sing in empty shrines, you let your wife
> Seek ecstasy in others' arms. (CP 80)

The dilemma of man-woman relationship is always irresolvable in the sense that man's moment of ecstasy comes to a flare and finish in the manner of a 'season' in its own appointed moment. But the emergence of ecstasy and resolution in woman is a continual tangle of events experienced in series of consecutions. The whole poem suggests at the simple fact that there are distinct variations in the processes of experiencing sublimations in man and woman. In man it emerges in the manner of 'a season' and blows off, giving way to another 'season.' But in the case of woman the demands of pleasurable relief are invariably many. In a fitful consecution they operate in woman's inner experience. The lifelessness of her real-life love affairs is hinted at in the expression 'mate with shadows.'

But in effect, these mating with 'shadows' made her aware of the male-universe in which each figure resembled her eternal lover's "blurred image," and even "The words and gestures seemed familiar" (CP 80). These interactions with the shadows could never take her out of her loneliness: "Yes, I sang solo, my songs were lonely" (CP 80). While the body sings 'in empty shrines,' the self wanders through thick forests of loneliness in search of the mysterious 'idol' which is the ideal. Finally, the ecstasy of becoming one with the ideal is attained through poetic imagination and writing of poetry. This is what she mentions in "Anamalai Poems III":

> If I had not learnt to write how would

I have written away my loneliness
or grief? Garnering them within my heart
would have grown heavy as a vault, one that
only death might open, a release then
I would not be able to feel or sense... (OSK 108)

So writing of poetry, for her, is writing 'away' her 'loneliness' that gathers itself, 'heavy as a vault' that 'only death might open.' Unlike 'a release' offered by death, which 'then / I would not be able to feel or sense,' the poet invariably experiences the 'release' offered by writing poetry. If so, writing poetry itself is an escape mechanism from the hard realities in the world that constrains the individual from the four walls of morality, ethics, religion, and tradition. Freedom in its abstract sense implies an absolute manner of asserting that 'since it is my life, I live it the way I like it.' Thus each poem offers her a 'release' of the emotions that weigh heavy in her heart, and if so, the overall effect of the realization of the ideal through creative process is a matter of instant leap rather than a process of transcendence. In other words, what is accomplished does not reach a transcendental plane in terms of the mythological *Radha-Krishna* or *Meera-Krishna* relationships, but it is surely and purely a non-thetic, self-emanated, self-satisfying dream phenomenon. As a result it is a greater achievement in terms of exquisiteness and ecstasy gained through aesthetic dimensions.

Thus some critics, reading spiritual transcendental motifs in the 'Radha-Krishna' poems of Kamala Das, read too much in between the lines. The real formal felicity of her 'Radha-Krishna' poems echoes the nuances of folk love-poetry, in the context of which the lover and the beloved enter into a hot lovers' quarrel. All her 'Krishna' poems envisage this omniscient delicate charm of the folk love songs which are available in any language. The invocation of the 'Krishna' icon is not at all for what the spiritualists call mystical transcendence. On the other hand, the 'Krishna' icon is an imagined poetic property, and the kind of total immersion and sublimation that is suggested in the companionship of 'Krishna' is only a cosmetic dream vision. But then, this cosmetic dream vision, to the extent that it offers a total and complete fulfilment, is to be comprehended as the phenomenal exquisiteness of heights that is aspired by woman in the companionship of man. Otherwise, invocation of 'Krishna' myth is only a mere poetic sublime height of fulfilment. 'Krishna' is poetically invoked just to suggest how pathetic and low the companionship of mortal man would be. The grievance and violence of Kamala Das lies in this fact and not in the unfounded imaginary exquisite ecstasies as she experiences in the companionship of 'Krishna.' There are goodly reasons why she invokes 'Krishna' icon in her poetry. While Lord Krishna is an ideal mythic lover in the Hindu mythological context, he is just used by her as a passionate suggestion of the so-called dreamy aspiration of fulfilment. These fulfilments are more felt in their absence rather than in their achievement. However, the absence of dream-vision fulfilment functions here as a gross parallel to the absolute realistic absence of joy and fulfilment in the companionship of ordinary mortals.

One who closely studies Das's poems that prima facie seem to be mythological would conclude that unlike in Sarojini Naidu, the 'Radha-Krishna' relationship in her does not have a divine framework. In Sarojini Naidu, 'Radha,' the seeker, is human; and 'Krishna,' the sought, is always that divine elusive figure. The relationship between them is that of the creator and the creature, and not of two equally ideal lovers like Das's 'Radha' and 'Krishna.' In fact Naidu's 'Krishna does not promise a one to one meeting, but he tells her, "I am of thee, as thou of me, a part / Look for me in the mirror of thy heart" ("Songs of Radha-The Quest" 156). But on the other hand, in Das's quest for her ideal lover she always meets him and secures herself within him, as is suggested at in the poem "Krishna":

> Your body is my prison, Krishna,
>
> I cannot see beyond it.
>
> Your darkness blinds me,
>
> Your love words shut out the wise world's din. (CP 75)

In this context, what P. Mallikarjuna Rao says is pertinent:

> In Sarojini Naidu the Radha-Krishna relationship is a metaphor for that between Atman and Brahman; in Kamala Das the relationship, though one of ideal lovers, is realized in human terms, and as such it does not rise to "the divine level." Sarojini Naidu's Radha is not anti-sexual, yet sex is not the primary concern in the Radha poems. But in Kamala Das sex implies a "deep and intense relationship" which is not devotional: it is very much human in its concern. (66)

Kamala Das is a stark realist. She is not at all a mystical transcendentalist. A poet pursuing the path of transcendence cannot say,

> Do not thrust upon me
> the scriptures compiled by sages
> wise and celibate
> or pacifying philosophies.
> I have held a man
> between my legs and have
> brought forth goodnatured sons (OSK 120)

She does not believe in the real divine interferences in the affairs of man and woman. Lord Krishna would not be really available even for imagined companionship. It is only in the *Bhakti* ("devotional") cult of poets like Meerabai, this transcendental phenomenon can be felt. In the poetry of Kamala Das, it has a negative suggestion in being a phenomenal unavailable consequence in the mortal companionship. There ends the purpose of 'Krishna' metaphor in her poetry.

In fact, in Das's poetry we sense a moan from her cognitive self that remains hard-fixed between the watery edge of this world and the 'sea wailing beneath the sea'; we hear in it an inner cry of failure to establish any firm bond either with the eternal or with the temporal. Her self's numerous attempts to enter that 'sea wailing beneath the sea' invariably culminate in its indecisiveness in this world and the aspired transcendental heights of the other world, the poet perennially suffers a dilemma. This is what is suggested in her poetic *tête-à-tête* with the external sea in the poems "The Invitation" and "The Suicide." In "The Invitation" the self is trying to pull back from the incessant and tempting call by the 'sea':

> Come in,
>
> Come in. What do you lose by dying, and
>
> Besides, your losses are my gains. (D 14)

But the state of the poet's self is different. It cannot so easily give up this life owing to many associations. So the self's response to the sea is:

> Oh Sea, just leave
>
> Me alone. As long
>
> As I remember, I want no other.
>
> On the bed with him, the boundaries of
>
> Paradise had shrunk to a mere
>
> Six by two . . . (D 14)

Here the poet is aware that she is in the entrapment of creaturely avidities. The reference to the carnal bed as 'the boundaries of / Paradise' is notable for its irony. The outer sea is but in no mood to hold back its invitation: "End in me, cries the sea. Think of yourself / Lying on a funeral pyre / With a burning head . . ." (D 14). The conflict is now more conspicuous. The 'Paradise' of 'Six by two' now becomes 'a funeral pyre' where the poet is lying with 'a burning head.' But at the same time, an understanding of the inevitable nature of this entrapment makes her reject the sea's continuous plea: "No. I am still young / And I need that man for construction and / Destruction. Leave me . . ." (D 15).

Here the poet autistically declares the victory of life over death, knowing it fully well that death comes to all in its own way and in its own time. In the meantime life asserting itself as a victorious champion is only an ironic matter in the ultimate sense. The poet's self, like the sea waves, is vacillating between the sea of life and the reality of death. The 'sea metaphor' exactly stands for the sea of life whose eddies are invariably compounded in death. The invitation of the sea and the contingent response of the incumbent not to enter the sea provides us a very interesting imaginary drama of life and death that constantly play hide-and-seek on the conscious plane of everybody and anybody in one form or the other. This hide-and-seek dramatic entanglement of life and death gets re-enacted in the sensibility of the poet in a typical mock-serious manner, particularly in view of the fact that death comes to all in its own appointed time, and any refusal to succumb to death is only an evocative passionate desire to have more and more life for oneself. However, presently there is no possibility or hopes of transcending these 'whiplashes of memories' of 'Lying on a funeral pyre / With a burning head.' Ultimately the self returns to its own shell of 'Six by two' losing all hopes of escape.

Even in the poem "The Suicide" the poet gives an impression of entering the sea "deeper," and finds,

> The sea's inner chambers
> are all very warm.
> There must be a sun slumbering
> At the vortex of the sea (D 2),

But there is a graceful withdrawal to life and its agonies:

> I tell you sea,
> I have enough courage to die,
> But not enough
> Not enough to disobey him
> Who said: Do not die
> And hurt me that certain way. (D 1)

However, at the end, the self consoles itself and gets ready to take the dip in the sea. But only "Take in my naked soul / That he knew how to hurt" (D 4). This request to 'Take in my naked soul' is in perfect harmony with the opening lines of the poem "Bereft of my body / My soul shall be bare" (D1). This suggests at some sort of incompleteness even in 'soul' without 'body.' So the concluding lines of the poem "The Suicide," "Only the soul knows how to sing / At the cortex of the sea" (D 4) remains a mere awareness, and are never meant to communicate the possibility of a total transcendence. In this context, what Sunanda P. Chavan says is worth quoting:

> . . . the sea still remains an important metaphor to communicate the ordeal of the self instead of providing a condition to transcend the self and reach the ultimate knowledge. The sea incorporates the soul's yearning for the impossible ideal of love. Hence, the consolatory note on which the poem ["The Suicide"] ends . . .seems rather to echo the helplessness of despair in the recognition of impossibility to achieve fulfilment on the levels of body and soul simultaneously. (The Unity 147)

It is this 'recognition' makes the poet hold back herself from entering 'the sea's inner chambers' and live her life in this world with all its agonies, anxieties, and pleasures, even when she knows that there is a 'sun slumbering / At the vortex of the sea.' This may also be the only factor that restrains the poet from a physical self-elimination. As has already been discussed in detail, the poetic sensibility of Kamala Das has not been transcendental like that of Avvayyar or Mirabai. It has also not been fatal like that of Anne Sexton and Sylvia Plath, for whom death seemed to be the only way out, if not their mission. The impassioned manner in which they pursued death is evident in their poems. For instance, Sexton writes in "Wanting to Die": "But suicides have a special language. / Like carpenters they want to know which tools. / They never ask why build" (142). And Plath's "Lady Lazarus" says, "Dying / is an art, like everything else. / I do it exceptionally well" (245).

In the case of Kamala Das also there are confessions to a few suicidal attempts in her autobiography. In the poem "The Suicide" she solemnly expresses her wish to die:

> O Sea I am fed up
>
> I want to be simple
>
> I want to be loved

And
If love is not to be had,
I want to be dead, just dead. (D 2)

While many critics feel that this suicide wish is a mere pretence in Kamala Das, according to Nair, "In Kamala Das the suicide-wish has always been strong but not precipitate because of her essentially spiritual psyche and deep sensitivity" (97). The spiritual psyche that Nair talks of is only a secular inner authentic particular. It does not have anything to do with mythical traditions, or metaphysical dimensions. Kamala Das believes only in one religion i.e. the religion of being human; and the inner spirit in this human context is the necessary radar and indicator of the poetic path that she has to divine for herself. Therefore, her poetic self does not accept a defeat; and she does not resort to the suicidal tendencies. Life is a precious given for her, and she wants to live it to the ultimate leagues of depth.

However, probing into the real cause of such self-restraint and abstention from self-elimination, one finds the presence of a more sacrificial and pitiful form of self-killing instinct in her. In Kamala Das it is present as an impulse not as an unfounded desire of physical elimination, but annihilation of her other [social] self by means of dying many deaths. By defying everything that is socially imposed, and by vying for everything that is naturally suggested, she has deliberately made herself a misfit in the honorific traditions of social systems. Thus every creative moment becomes a moment of death for her social existence, be it as a mother; a wife; a daughter; a beloved; or even as a so-called civilized being. So the seemingly absent suicidal instinct in the poet is owing to an intuitive urge to represent and present through poetry the agonies and sufferings of the self in being a woman-in-the world, even risking an existential conflict with the immediate social surroundings.

Chaitanya recalls an instance where Ignazio Silone suggests at two different roads in life in the context of "post-Nieztzschean and existentialist literature": one ends in killing oneself, "the recognition that life is not worth the trouble . . . . The other road leads to the discovery of some valid meaning to existence" (223). In the modern context the suicides of Virginia Woolf, Anne Sexton, and Sylvia Plath can be accountable to their accepting the first road. Even according to Kamala Das this 'life is not worth the trouble.' But what holds her back is an empathetic psyche towards the world and its beings. Looked from this angle, Das comes very to the 'metaphysician Camus' who said, "The world in which I live repels me, but I feel with its inhabitants" (qtd. in Chaitanya 223). For Das death offers no great solution, for, as she says in the poem "A Requiem for a Son,"

> Death is
>
> Ordinary. To live on an earth built upon layers and
>
> Layers of bone requires an extraordinary
>
> Courage, to walk the corridors of this prison and note with
>
> A quiet joy the saplings bursting from the cracks in stone and
>
> Know for certain that life will go on. (CP 29)

Kamala Das's love poetry is absolutely down to earth and comprehends the very grassroots of being human. The par excellence humanistic instinctive phenomenal forces of being-in-the-world compound in her a psychological tendency to aesthetically exact for her rightful properties as a living being, and she ventures to channel her psychic energy towards self-elevation and aesthetic expression of all the suffering, anxiety, and violence. It is evident from the above discussion that all the aesthetic dimensions of Kamala Das and the violence thereof are emerging out of her inner most personal agonies and questionings that have no available answers or solutions.

Conclusion

In the foregoing chapters a modest critical attempt has been made in order to highlight the greatness of Kamala Das as a poet. In fact the essential loss of adventure, surprise, and sense of wonder from life as a whole, as the ultimate result of industrial revolution, compounded in Kamala Das certain typical feminine demands which acquired for themselves a par excellence poetic form. It is very important to note that the basic tenets of violence in Kamala Das emerge out of the widespread insufficiencies of life catered by the above significant losses. The industrial man had suppressed the naturalistic man; and this negative influence of industrialisation and mechanization turned her into a feminist rebel. So Kamala Das is prominently addressing her poetry to the social and cultural systems that are on the road to ultimate perfection. In this act of pursuing perfection of the human aspirations, dispositions, and attitudes, she prominently questions certain kind of ignorance and incapacities to understand. Offering the most needful understanding of the feminine nature and needs being the whole purpose of her poetry, her poetic exquisite indulgence into the audio-visual screenplay has to be understood in its proper spirit. It is an objectivized screenplay with all the ultimate purpose and design of making humanity somewhat more intimate, freer, more frank, and more transparent. Listen to Kamala Das in the poem "Wood Ash":

> in this new world i lack coherence
> listen differently for what i have to tell
> let your blood listen and from within
> your descendants shall hear me. (OSK 28)

It is with this hope of the reader listening 'differently' that she conducts her poetic activity. Kamala Das is a gross feminist without any confusions and complacencies of being a traditional woman in the third world. In her as a person there is a full-grown trait of feminine individuality akin to a stern matriarch or an enlightened feminist. To the extent that she draws her inheritance from the Nair community of Kerala, the matriarchal component of her personality is understandable. But it is her pure love and passion for the feminist liberation movement of the West that conforms her as a restless mouthpiece of the suppressed femininity, particularly as it is in the Indian context. Equality and equal opportunity for women to be what they are, is the minimum that she demands in the social and cultural distributional parameters of life. In the naturalistic context she is profoundly conscious of the superior nature of femininity as the creative prime mover. Denial of equal opportunities to women for centuries together almost fossilized them, and it is this fossilization that Das rebels at. Since the fossilizing agents are the autocratic and chauvinistic men-folk, her fury against them categorically evolves into a profound poetic fury extending to an irresolvable feud. The very essence of her poetry is the wildness of the expression of this irreconcilable feud. Biological oppression and exploitation of women leading to psychological atrophy, and psychological oppression and exploitation of women culminating into biological atrophy are the two fundamental grounds of Kamala Das's creative activity. Glaring examples of biological exploitation and oppression can be traced to the acts of rape and forced sexual congress. So far as the psychological exploitation and oppressions are concerned, they are broadly born of the patriarchal composition of male superiority and female inferiority. The discriminative and denying factors of sublimation for women are traceable to these two kinds of exploitations born of sheer ignorance. Greater the psychological feel of the exploitative modalities, higher the poetic pitch of her voice, very often extending to extraordinarily challenging intimidations. Therefore, her poetry is a potential emblem of feminine individuality asserting itself as an intellectual formula pleading for a gracious and graceful recognition of woman as equal individuals in a given social system.

That she takes a fighter's stand in conducting a feud against the blinkered and blindfolded attitudes and dispositions of men towards women is only a matter of stylistic conformities. In fact there is no fight intended. Yes, the war cry-like poetic challenges are very much there in the very corpus of her poetic forms. She becomes a feminist rebel poet, particularly in the Indian context, and quite strongly exposes the aetiological damage that man perpetrated and perpetuated upon woman during all these centuries. But behind the ostentatious fury of this war cry, there is always hidden a conscious persuasive mode of pleading for an understanding of woman's point of view. There is in her poetry an opening up of vibrant insight into the psychophysical dimensions of woman as a matter of additional knowledge. With this mission of offering knowledge and insight in mind, Das makes certain instinctive poetic efforts of squarely, transparently, and uninhibitedly discussing, determining, and defining the most personal needs of woman in being an equal gregarious partner with man. Therefore, her conscious avidity towards the exposure of the feminine needs should not be mistaken as cheap and peripheral imaginative attempts at confectioning pornography and obscenity. In the man-woman confidential relationship of privacy there is no place for the ideals of pornography and obscenity.

At the outset, it is not at all a romanticized or plasticized view of the feminine angle that becomes all-important in Kamala Das's poetry. If the exciting plasticity of the feminine human postures is vibrantly presented by Das, it is only with a mind to express the extent of restlessness and humiliation of being a secondary slave-like citizen. She certainly does not mean to imply that love and love-play amongst the humans is an uninhibited exhibition of the animalistic posture and dimensions of man and woman. But when a spacious cognisance of the need of creaturely survival in the naturalistic context is taken into consideration, certain in-camera visualization of animalistic orgies becomes not only inevitable, but also right on instances where such instances are exclusive personal moments of interactions. Since they are poetically offered to the readers, the preciousness of the personal manner of outpouring one's grievances and concerns becomes poetically established and aesthetically received. For a close-camera reading, the picturesque pornographic dimensions that she offers become the primary quickening forces for establishing a potential insight into the exclusive needs and necessities of women as love-partners. Thus again, the pornographic dimensions of her poetic images have to be sensibly taken into personal consideration, just like one looks at oneself as a primal unsophisticated being-in-the-world, particularly when he/she stands face to face with his/her life-size mirror.

For the same reason, the male generations have to read her poetry as a matter of private confidential and explicit confessional poetic outpourings, which in all probability are most likely to challenge and question the settled ethico-moral dimensions of the traditional thought and action. This challenge is an intended stylistic device poetically adopted by Kamala Das in an exclusive atmosphere of freedom and choice. She talks about all her feminine demands, exercising no reservations and restraints, which speaks for her adaptation of innocence and naïvete as proper educable modes of offering real insights into the depths of femininity.

However, the dominating and autocratic tone and tenor of her poetry, which is a mere stylistic strategy of drawing arrestingly the attention of the reader's mind, was popularly mistaken as a sort of bacchanalian orgy, and unwanted excesses of talking more than what the social decencies can withstand. But when the social decencies that are objectively and forcefully imposed upon woman become the very bone of her poetic contentions, the only way for absolute transparency is an unabashed expression of anxiety and concerns through equal violence. Thus her poetry and intriguingly imparts a pristine sensibility that at bottom every particular individual is a person, or should be a person in order to live one's own life with the ultimate satisfaction of having lived it for purpose, the purpose being the achievement of liberation of the self through freedom, and freedom of being through liberation, and freedom and liberation though sublimation.

But unfortunately her initial critics and reviewers as well as average readers just made a surface peripheral attempt at understanding her poetry. For all such readers and reviewers, the pornographic imagery had become the target of levelling a sort of destructive and negative critical charges upon her. Many of the critics of Kamala Das indicted her for out and out pornographic poetic effects. For instance, one of her critics says, "With Kamala Das love is a disease, being mixed with an overdose of sex" (Raphael 136). Love is certainly not a 'disease' in Kamala Das. Love in one form or the other is a universal demand that emanates out of the primal gregarious instinct. If the famous Bergsonian concept of *élan vital* ("life force") is taken into consideration, it becomes easy to understand and appreciate the essential point of view of Kamala Das as a poet of love.

Further, the question of 'overdose of sex' or pornography in art comes to the forefront; and the prolific critical discussions for and against the so-called exhibitionistic indiscretions ever remains inconclusive. But as the old adage goes, pornography or indecency is very often in the eyes of the onlooker, and not in the object poetically presented. It is true that many of the poems of Kamala Das are full of intimidatory imagery verging upon the pornographic dimensions; but then, pornography is not at all her poetic aim. Pornographic imagery is an incidental poetic phenomenon taken up by her in order to give vent to the feminist fury on being exploited and subjugated. As a matter of fact, she writes exclusively personal poetry to be read and pondered deep in a personal way. But by close critical reading and appreciation, this charge of 'overdose of sex' on her is altogether unfounded. In fact, pornographic imagery is the handy medium for her to highlight the innermost sufferings of woman in a social system that had never inculcated and awarded a place for individualism and other human dignities associated with it.

The ultimate poetic manner in which she exacts for the pleasures of flesh and blood might appear to some as questionable properties from all the angle of morals and civic decencies. But then, the reality of being human, to the extent that it is inextricable from the concomitance of sex, conforms in her a par excellence poetic urge to bare all her wears without any fear or inhibitions. In this context she is a lone voice that has the rare courage to call a spade a spade, in order to assert that sex is sex; and to insist upon its inevitability in the human set. The moralists, the religionists, and the so-called watchdogs of culture may not agree to the ways and means in which she performs herself as a poet. But they cannot deny that what all she says is the essential truth of life and not a criticism of life.

In order to critically solve the puzzling problem of charging Kamala Das with pornography, the readers must bear in mind that in the Indian mythology, sexuality has been celebrated for its vitality and importance for healthy mind and body. Sexual love is the vital force of the primary function of nature–continuity through evolution. Ancient India had recognized sexuality and sex as a vital principle in life, which, rather than being suppressed or hidden, gets manifested amply and aesthetically in the classical literatures, paintings, and sculptures. For instance, if one thinks of the great Vatsyayana of the "Kamasutra," or the out and out 'pornographic' sculptures in the Indian temple architecture, it is very difficult to consign one's thoughts and imaginations that either Vatsayana or the ancient Hindu temple architects were votaries of pornography. On the same analogy, the content of pornographic interpersonal relations are there in the poems of Kamala Das as poetic artefacts meant to arrestingly involve and engross the reading public into the kind of inhuman and wicked dimensions in which women are held as mere usufruct, unfeeling objects meant to serve the carnal purposes of macho men. Of course, she pretty violently proposes her poetic thoughts and imagery in a challenging manner. Exhibitionism and sensuality are not the real themes of Kamala Das; they are just metaphoric incidentals in her poetic structural strategies. As a feminist, she visualizes the very love-hate tangle from exclusive woman's point of view; and, insofar as she is making wide analytic confessions of the feminine needs and demands of love, there is only a place and opportunity to gauge the intensity of love itself as a primitive animating fundament in woman. Love for man is an act whereas for woman it is the very basic stratum of generation and evolution of nature in all its fundamental modes of operation in the world. Unless and until one is capable of sympathetically understanding the rhetorical onslaughts of Western radical feminist writers like Simone de Beauvoir, it may not be possible for him to put an insight into the sources of violence in Kamala Das. This point had prominently been clarified in the foregoing chapters.

Everybody has an urgency to be himself or herself in accordance with the naturalistic potential and cultural dispensation of justice and dignity. The entire poetic tissue of Kamala Das emerges out of this urgency to assert herself for her conscious experience as a potential being-in-the-world. Her exact feminine problem lies in the harrowing manner in which she conducts an extended introspective self-search concerning the importance of being a woman. In spite of the fact that this feel of self-importance is an unfounded subjective, innermost predilection, any obstruction and impediment for this conscious feel of self-importance becomes worth denouncing. It is Kamala Das's poetic convenience that conforms this apprehended oppositional force in the metaphor of male counterpart. The presence of this insurmountable male counterpart ultimately serves her poetic purpose of a standing mute wall on which she goes on banging, quite revengefully of course, with the ultimate purpose of momentarily declaring for herself a fleeting instance of victory. She says in "Composition,"

> Grovel at my feet,
> remove your monkey-suits and dance,
> sing Erato Erato Erato,
> yet I shall be indifferent. (D 31)

Even if such kind of victory in making the male oppressor into a grovelling victim is just momentary and instantaneous, it serves well her purpose of declaring her victory even in defeat, that is, declaration of success in failure itself. The poetic metaphor of man in her poetry is certainly not conquerable because it is irrational without any transparency or fair play. So far as the absence of transparency, clarity, and fair play are concerned, all humans are equally deprived. It is here that Das has a wide poetic scope for generalizing the eternal grievances. They are not feminine grievances; they are in effect universal grievances affecting both men and women more or less equally. In fact pleasure or happiness of the sort that Das poetically comprehends as the due naturalistic province of women, should be a given for all living beings. But then, as had already been suggested, nature offers no pleasure or happiness-offering shop to the subsisting species. On a ıight perception, life does not counteract man as a given. It only establishes the possible chance encounters as promises. The realization or otherwise of the promises is a matter of innermost subjective conformity. The modern existentialists designate life as a given, but Kamala Das, with all her supreme poetic sensibility, considers it as a promise, a promise that perennially eludes the capture. But it always stares into her eyes from an enticing distance.

The out and out virago rhetorical dimensions that Kamala Das attributes to her poetical tones brought forth many bitter ones amongst her critics who contingently turned to levelling personal charges on Kamala Das, which of course are gross violation of decencies in rhetoric. Contending that all the problems poetically inflated by Kamala Das are her personal problems, and that they do not in any way concern with the generality of public, is tantamount to blinkered critical vision with all the negative purpose of declaring her as an uncontrollable feminist virago. But in all the poetic sound and fury of her tirade against men, her essential purpose is to give vent to the inner most hitherto consciously suppressed counters of the feminine freedoms and choices. In this context she becomes a wide vocal articulator of the problems of all women insofar as they are concerned with the negligence and rejection in the minds of their own so-called loving counterparts.

Yet while probing into the confessional mode of Kamala Das's poetry, there has been a predilection among critics of Kamala Das to trace her inheritance of Nayar lineage of Kerala. For instance, M. Elias thinks that Das's confessions are merely "the Nayar maiden unburdening her collective nightmare" (18). He adds, "Kamala Das's sexual philosophy is thus located in her own cultural heritage deriving from the South or Dravidian India" (22). Here the critic miserably fails to discover the paradigmatic resonance pulsating beneath the personal 'I' in her writings. Considering her confessions as a representation of the 'Nayar maiden unburdening her collective nightmare' is the result of a far-fetched critical meandering. In her poems it is rather the 'collective feminine unconscious' (as Jung has put it) that unfolds its nightmarish experiences. In this context G. B. Sajjan rightly asks, "When it is plain that Kamala Das stands for the universal type, the eternal woman waiting in search of her man . . . why should she be equated with a representative Nayar woman unbaring her psychic sore?" (53). After all, even a Nayar woman is a woman at the outset; and the most general manner in which Das poetically inflates the real feminine problems have nothing to do with the erstwhile matrilineal dimensions of the Nayar community. But one has to agree to the point that her Nayar heritage had given her the necessary courage to stand up as a significant voice in a world that mercilessly suppresses all the personal voices and freedoms of women.

Further, A. G. Khan, in a very cursory estimate of Das's writings, comments, "A Nair woman might enjoy certain freedom of sex: but when it is depicted by Kamala Das, it might suggest that all Indian women enjoy promiscuity!" (36). It is true that Kamala Das's ancestors practised the matrilineal traditions of inheritance, in which women used to have the maximum freedom when it comes to the matters of inheriting properties and their own marriages. What Fawcett writes about the very matrilineal system [of Nayars] is very pertinent here: "Equality of the sexes in all sexual matters, the man and woman being on terms of equality, having equal freedom, is certainly an uncommon merit in the *Marumakkattayam* 'matrilineal' system (Italics mine)" (237). This has to be considered as a matter of extended freedom to the individual rather than an advance of callousness in choice, or 'promiscuity.' In fact, Khan's very painstaking exposition grossly slips out his primal ignorance of human psychology and its endemic attachment to the concept of freedom. The psychological inward of humans performs itself very often in an autistic manner and in gross contravention to the well-founded and established morals, traditions, and ethics. The far-reaching freedom of imagination, to the extent that it is a human virtue, conforms itself as a potential and lone free voice in the poetry of Kamala Das. Her confessions are neither 'the Nayar maiden unburdening her collective nightmare,' nor are they a treatise on 'promiscuity,' as the above critics have concluded. Her confessions are her attempts to explore the inner authentic self in her quest to know herself, as she clarifies in "Composition":

> . . . by confessing
> by peeling off my layers
> I reach closer to the soul
> and
> to the bone's
> supreme indifference. (D 33)

However, Elias, Khan, and such other critics would have drawn a blank had they looked for such racial chromosomes at work in other confessional poets like Sylvia Plath, Anne Sexton, as well as the modern novelists like Katherine Annporter, Flannery O'Conner, and the enviable dramatist Lillian Hellman, who immensely handle feminist themes such as extra marital affairs, marital discord, love, sex, and frustration, with a delicate sense of humanistic sanctity. As a matter of fact, such personal charges and ominous remarks, camouflaged in the garbs of literary criticism, point to one simple fact: the conventional roots still embedded in the philosophy of Indian literary criticism, its mindset, and methods compel its practitioners to blindly use the same formalist yardstick everywhere–to evaluate either a medieval morality play or the modern feminist literature. As a result, the intrinsic philosophy of the modern women's writings and the subtle nuances of the very sensibilities that express them, invariably go unnoticed; and the pragmatic dimensions of its manifestations are consciously shrouded. Such criticisms laden with personal and racial prejudices eventually turn out to be a mere but deliberate subterfuge to digress from the main point of discussion, i.e., the feminine demands. It also amounts to waylaying the critical rhetoric into a marginalized periphery.

Very few critics denounced her language and its poetic fervency. But a majority of them have raised their critical cudgels against her forward ideals and ideologies as though they are dangerous for the social and cultural health and harmony. This kind of negative attitude towards Das results from a sort of prudish self-consecrated manners of people who evaluate themselves as proper authorities on all matters. In fact all the critics that railed against Kamala Das had attacked her from personal angle of their taste and temperament, but not from any judicious appreciation of her arresting poetic craft. Creating arresting and controversial sensibility is part and parcel of the par excellence poetic strategy of Kamala Das. Initially she inflates the retaliatory sensibility of the reader, and then poetically resolves its content as a mere universal establishment of human desires to substantiate themselves as the necessary ground truths and realities of life.

While Elias and Khan try to trace the roots of only the negative dimensions of 'Nayar' heritage in Das's poetry and prose, her women critics lash at her on other accounts. Vimala Rao blames her for the weak and deliberate 'eroticism.' In Rao's words, "The flagrant eroticism loses its strength and becomes a weakness in her art as it is bound to become in life. As a result, Kamala Das appears to be a poet of decadence, a poet who is a victim of the inadequacies of her life, failing to gain control even over her art" (88). Since Rao obviously overlooks the poetic sublimation of Kamala Das, her charges are far too personal in nature. The brash manner in which Rao concludes that Kamala Das is a failure both in life and poetry confirms the fact that Rao could not somehow put her proper insight into the universal nature of interpersonal relations, which always remain on a threatening threshold of temptation and withdrawal. It is unfortunate that critics like Rao obviously misunderstood Das's poetic fury as mere celebration of 'eroticism.' Kamala Das is certainly not a 'poet of decadence.' If exacting for a due consideration for women and their happiness is the real theme of her poetry, there is no decadence here.

Further, naming her as 'a victim of the inadequacies of her life' amounts to dwindling critical activity to a personal plane of disagreement. So far as the adequacies or otherwise are concerned, it is all purely a personal matter of judgement. When her art is fervently concerned with the overall present 'inadequacies' in the social surroundings in which we survive, it is not possible to pooh-pooh her poetry as fallout of personal inadequacies. Rao in the above lines speaks like mere critical mouthpiece trying to acquire for herself a critical superior importance as a woman over and above Das.

It should have been better if Rao ventured to consider Das's poetry from the standpoint of a woman sailing in the same boat as the poet herself. On a close scrutiny, it perspires that such negative charges on Kamala Das are born of some inexplicable personal animosity, which they take upon themselves as self-appointed guardians of the so-called traditions and morals. Ethics and morals are certainly important; they are important for Kamala Das also. But then, as she appears to suggest, the real sweetness of life lies in doing away with all the formalities at least in a poetic moment, if not in life altogether. In this acquiring for oneself the real sweetness of life, the morals and ethics should not become impediments. Thus Das's poetry is amoral in its initial perception, but it is not immoral in the God's world of things. The amoral streak compels one to think about the validity or otherwise of the traditional morality itself in confining woman and her freedoms to certain ranges of social, cultural and domestic environments. The aggressive manner in which she exercises innumerable poetic licences to assert her choices and freedoms as a woman, automatically turn out to be ideological challenges indicting traditional man as responsible for the irreparable damage and injury done to femininity.

Among other women critics of Das, Monika Varma feels that the initial promise of vigour and violence in Das's poetry loses its strength even before it takes off. Verma sees Das's poetry as "dusty trivia snuffling under the munched-up spat-out remnant of chewed-up cud and chopped-up sugar cane stalks." She adds further, "It began life green, it was sweet and full of sap and juice, but what we get is snippets of trivia" (26). As a poet herself, Varma's grudges against Das are quite understandable. The immense vibrancy and force of Das's poetry and its immediate effect on the readers of Indo-Anglian poetry are evident from the fact that in Iyengar's book [*Indian Writing in English*, 5th ed., 1990] her name gets mentioned in as many as fifteen pages, which is a far greater recognition than what is given by him to any other contemporary Indian women poet. No sensible reader would ever think that Iyengar, as a literary critic and literary historian, is a chronicler of the 'spat-out remnants of chewed-up cud,' and that any amount of 'snippets of trivia' would fascinate him. Further, M. K. Naik creditably observes, "While there are more than thirty modern women poets with more than one collection each to their credit, the work of few of them possesses the individuality and power of Kamala Das's verse."

The hostile critics of Kamala Das often take objection to her feminism compounded with her open emotionalism, the large verbal gestures which seem to them mere rant, the rapt pleasures in raving at men-folk, and above all the bawdy tone. But her bawdy tone is more preferable to the modern reader than the dry impassionate discourse of the Indian romanticists. There is certain amount of robust physicality in Das's poems duly supplemented by musical sounds and immensely visual images. Her contempt for rational meaning and behaviour as compounded in the patriarchal male counters actually counts for the enormous success of Kamala Das as a poet. It is a fact that dislike for Kamala Das derives from an orthodox fear of male-superiority and male-domination being eroded. Even the ardent admirers of Kamala Das sometimes confess to the moments of uneasiness that her poems create. This uneasiness emerges because of the fact that she strains her poetic language beyond bearable limits. The basic themes of her poetry are very simple: a love of paternal home, an obsessive concern with anatomy of sex, the inter-involvement of men and women as partners in love, and almost a profound love for primitive animistic pleasure. It can always be said that progress in her poetry is achieved through intellectual development, verbal play, wit, and incantation of fury. If one wants to search for any great ideas in her poetry, he is likely to be disappointed. Her rhetoric powerfully derives forward very often in anguish and rage. She makes a desperate attempt to overcome the near extinction of femininity in the male-machinations and exploitations. Her idea of life is very simple; it has to be lived to the best of one's own satisfaction and happiness. Anything that comes in the way of such satisfaction and happiness is wildly resented and retaliated by her.

Honesty, stunning frankness, and aggressive antagonism to institutional prerogatives in her poetry place Kamala Das directly amongst the modern feminist confessional poets like Anne Sexton and Sylvia Plath. Generally, the use of the first person singular by the confessional writers puts themselves at the centre of their works. As a result, their poems gain an autobiographical tone and authenticity. But, on the other hand, this also leads many readers and critics to take it for granted that the protagonists of these works are the authors' own overt caricatures. For the same reason, many critics have based their studies on Das's fictional autobiography "My Story" for evaluating her poems. As T.N. Dhar rightly warns, "excessive reliance on her life-story has led many critics to accept her position on several things in categorical terms about which she is ambivalent in her poems" (36). True, owing to the autobiographical tone and tenor of Das's poetry, many critics have always looked at her confessions with suspicion. The poetic violence unleashed by Das through her various women protagonists, no doubt, evinces oneness between her life-experiences and her creative visions. But this fact should not mislead the reader to conclude that it is the poet in person everywhere with her promiscuous sexual encounters. In such a case, her poems would have degenerated into mere personal commentaries upon her life. But this does not happen at all. The personal frame of her poems is her stylistic manner of protesting against the condition of women in general. In this context what Arlene Zide observes is worth mentioning:

> The crude reality of her personal experience may not have literal counterparts for every woman, especially those in the "more modern" Western world, but it is most definitely and completely of this world. We cannot help but empathize with the girl whose "weight of breasts and womb crushed" her; it is perfectly translatable into the realization for any woman, anywhere, of what being a woman means; not merely from the sexual point of view but rather from the universal experience of women . . . . the realization that to be a woman inevitably entails some sort of psychological shrinking. (240)

In Kamala Das's poems her protagonists invariably assume more dimensions than one; but in whatever attire they appear, including her own, they are global victims of social conditioning, gender dichotomy, and male chauvinism. But during the course of a poem, at certain points the poet dexterously makes the personal details withdraw into the background, and what takes their place is a universal quality in the thematic concerns. Like for instance, the poem "An Introduction" starts with a purely personal note: "I don't know politics," but when the poem culminates, the poetic persona transforms herself into an archetypal woman:

> I am sinner,
> I am saint, I am the beloved and the
> Betrayed, I have no joys which are not yours, no
> Aches which are not yours. I too call myself I. (OP 26)

Vijayshree very pertinently comments:

> The subject in Kamala Das's poetry is always 'woman' and the content is female experience whether it is the trauma of an unhappy marriage, or humiliation of a desireless surrender in sex, or disgust at the male domination. This should not be taken as one woman's experience in which case it becomes a stray incidence of individual misfortune. In fact, she clearly hints at the archetypal nature of her experience when she says: '...I am every/Woman who seeks love' [An Introduction]. (139)

Yet in intervals the personal 'I' peeps through the curtain, and then again withdraws. This hide-and-seek technique often deceives the reader who struggles to differentiate between the personal 'I' and the archetypal 'I'. In fact, while responding aggressively to the traumatic experiences of her life as a woman, the poet, in order to unmask her hurt female psyche, put on masks of many personae. The masks are, however, pro-tempore; the real self of the poet ultimately identifies with each of the protagonists owing to the commonality of the situations a woman confronts in being-in-the world. Her representative stances are amply made clear in the poem "The Summing Up":

> Change the world with
> rhetoric? Never.
>
> . . . .

Life spreads its moulting
wings to sicken me but do not judge
me harshly, I am your kith and kin
I gathered your laments into a song. (OSK 127)

These lines very evidently dispels the darkness around the conundrum of 'I' in her poetry, as they illumine the truth that even at the stage of 'Life spread(ing) its moulting / wings to sicken' the poetic power, the poet's assurance of a collectiveness is strong and convincing. With this assurance only she says, 'I am your kith and kin.' The idea of the presentation and representation of life's 'laments' in being a woman-in-the-world gains strength by the expression: 'I gathered your laments into a song.'

Thus the modern Indian poetry with all its aggressiveness and violence in articulating the feminine concerns begins with Kamala Das, and culminates into a compelling poetic voice contending for the naturalistic feminine superiority. She is a crusader on behalf of all women and every woman all over the world where the institutional exploitation of women are the widest spread generality. The poetic strategic tone of challenging manner is only a matter of impressing upon the need to resolve and dissolve all the grounds of antagonism and rivalry between man and woman in an atmosphere of poetic heights and artistic transparency and sublimation. For all the practical purposes, life has to be lived by both man and woman in a naturalistic social and cultural atmosphere of harmony and happiness. She threateningly pleads that man should not consider himself as a self-appointed authority in deciding and designating the fate of woman, particularly in the context of achieving pleasure and happiness for her in being a woman. This achievement of happiness and pleasure even at the point of creaturely survival requires loving and understanding co-operation of man. Thus she writes with a social and cultural commitment in order to instruct and educate men about the propriety or otherwise of their behaviour towards women, and the needful sanctity of complete transparency and freedom in expressing the feminine concerns and prerogatives.

However, the poet nurtures a fond hope of immortality for

the very fervent spirit of being human. The following lines of her poem "Composition" evidently displays a sparkle of optimism in the heart of her hearts:

> The ultimate discovery will be
> that we are immortal;
> the only things mortal being
> systems and arrangements,
> even our pains continuing
> in the devourers who constitute
> the world. (D 35)

Generations may come and generations may go; the 'systems and arrangements' perennially inflict a gross sense of failure on the very spirit of being human, and haunt the humans even while the elements devour them. But at the same time, the 'systems and arrangements,' purely temporary, may outdate the earlier ones in chronological order. Somehow, she holds a strong faith that humanism ultimately champions by way of becoming a certain good in the ages to come, even if it is threatened in the present. Very simply, all her desire is for the human society to be more and more humane in being immortal.

Thus the content of violence in the poetry of Kamala Das has a vibrant mission of educating men to be more and more humane in his relations with women. She is of a confirmed view that the very feminine fonts of happiness have been crushed and smashed for centuries together, and the feminist fury in her takes the form of rebellion and violence. The compounded fury of this rebellion and violence is mainly addressed to the finer sensibilities of men. Even if it is aesthetically unpalatable to some of the traditional readers, particularly men-folk, so far as the universal validity of her arguments is concerned, one has to acknowledge her poetic vibrancy and finesse as a profound artistic achievement.

Works Cited

PRIMARY SOURCES

Poetry

Das, Kamala. *Collected Poems.* Trivandrum : Kamala Das, 1984.

__________, *Only the Soul Knows How to Sing: Selections from Kamala Das.* Kottayam: D.C. Books, 1996.

__________, *The Best of Kamala Das.* Kerala: Bodhi Publishing House, 1991.

__________, *The Descendants.* Calcutta: Writers Workshop, 1967.

__________, *The Old Playhouse and Other Poems.* Bombay: Orient Longman, 1973.

Das Kamala and Pritish Nandy. *Tonight this Savage Rite: The Love Poems of Kamala Das and Pritish Nandy.* New Delhi: Arnold Heinemann, 1979.

Prose

Das, Kamala. "I Have Kept Myself Away From Books In Order To Preserve My Independent Original Voice." An Interview with Irshad Ahmed. *Perspectives on Kamala Das Prose.* Ed. Iqbal Kaur. New Delhi: Intellectual Publishing House, 1995. 79-81.

Das, Kamala. "I Needed to Disturb Society." An Interview with Iqbal Kaur. *Perspectives on Kamala Das's Poetry.* Ed. Iqbal Kaur. New Delhi: Intellectual Publishing House, 1995. 157-68.

Das, Kamala. "My Instinct, My Guru." *Indian Literature* 33.5 (Sept-

Oct 1990): 155-62.

Das, Kamala. "Of Masks and Memories." An Interview with P. P. Raveendran. *Indian Literature* 36.3 (May-June 1993): 144-61.

Das, Kamala. *My Story*. New Delhi: Sterling Publishers, 1978.

Suraiya, Kamala. *The Path of the Columnist*. Calicut: Olive Publications, 2000.

SECONDARY SOURCES

Ahmed, Irshad. "Reflections on the Mind and Responsibility of Kamala Das." *Perspectives on Kamala Das Poetry.* Ed. Iqbal Kaur. New Delhi: Intellectual Publishing House, 1995. 129-33.

Allport, G. W. *Personality: A Psychological Interpretation.* New York: Holt, Rheinehart, & Winston, 1937.

Beauvoir, Simone de. *The Second Sex.* Trans. and Ed. H. M. Parshley. England: Jonathan Cape, 1956.

Brewster, Anne. "The Freedom to Decompose: The Poetry of Kamala Das." *The Journal of Indian Writing in English* 8.1-2 (Jan-July 1980): 98-107.

Camus, Albert. *The Rebel*. Trans. Anthony Bower. London: Hamish Hamilton, 1956.

Chaitanya, Krishna. *Sanskrit Poetics: A Critical and Comparative Study.* Bombay: Asia Publishing House, 1918.

Chavan, Sunanda P. *The Fair Voice: A Study of Indian Women Poets in English.* New Delhi: Sterling Publishers 1984.

__________, "The Unity of Vision in the Poetry of Kamala Das." *Perspectives on Kamala Das's Poetry.* Ed. Iqbal Kaur. New Delhi: Intellectual Publishing House, 1995. 142-49.

Cixous, H'ele'n. "Castration or Decapitation?" Trans. Annette Kuhn. *Contemporary Literary Criticism: Literary and Cultural Studies.* Eds. Robert Con Davis and Ronald Schleifer. 2nd ed. New York: Longman, 1989. 479-91.

Cuddon, J. A. *A Dictionary of Literary Terms.* London: Andre Deutsch; New Delhi: Indian Book Company, 1977.

Dass, Veena Noble. "Feminism and Literature." *Feminism and Literature.* Ed. Veena Noble Das. New Delhi: Prestige Books, 1995. 9-12.

Davis, Robert Con, and Ronald Schleifer. "Feminism." *Contemporary Literary Criticism: Literary and Cultural Studies.* Eds. Robert Con Davis and Ronald Schleifer. 2nd ed. New York: Longman, 1989. 449-56.

De Souza, Eunice. "Kamala Das." *Indian Poetry in English: A Critical Assessment.* Eds. Shahane Vasant A. and M. Sivaramakrishna. Madras: Macmillan, 1980. 41-47.

Dhar, T.N. "Eros Denied: Love in the Poetry of Kamala Das." *Contemporary Indian-English Poetry.* Ed. Atma Ram. Calcutta: Writers Workshop, 1989. 21-31.

Dwivedi, A.N. *Indo-Anglian Poetry.* Allahabad: Kitab Mahal, 1979. 297-98.

Elias, Mohamed. "Kamala Das and Nayar Heritage." *The Journal of Indian Writing in English.* 6 (July 1978): 15-24.

Eliot, T. S. *The Waste Land.* Madras: Macmillan, 1986.

Empson, William. *Seven Types of Ambiguity.* England: Penguin, 1977.

Ezekiel, Nissim. "Poet, Lover, Birdwatcher." *Journal of South Asian Literature.* 11.3-4 (Spr-Sum 1976): 75.

- - -. "Poverty Poems—2." *Indian Poetry in English.* Eds. Harimohan Prasad and Chakradhar Prasad Singh. New Delhi: Sterling Publishers, 1986. 29-30.

Fawcett, F. *Nayars of Malabar.* 1901. New Delhi: Asian Educational Services-Reprint, 1990.

Flieger, Jerry Aline. "The Purloined Punchline: Joke as Textual Paradigm." *Contemporary Literary Criticism: Literary and Cultural Studies.* Eds. Robert Con Davis and Ronald Schleifer.

2nd ed. New York: Longman, 1989. 351-68.

Frye, Northrop. "Literature and Linguistics Scholarship in a Post Literate World." *Myth and Metaphor: Selected Essays.* Ed. Denhem Robert. London: Virginia UP, 1991.

Gilbert, Sandra. "Life's Empty Pack: Notes Toward a Literary Daughteronomy." *Contemporary Literary Criticism: Literary and Cultural Studies.* Eds. Robert Con Davis and Ronald Schleifer, 2nd ed. New York: Longman, 1989. 492-516.

Harrex, S.C. "The Strange Case of Mathew Arnold in a Sari: An Introduction to Kamala Das." *Kamala Das: A Selection With Essays on Her Work.* Eds. S. C. Harrex and Vincent O'Sullivan Adelaide: Centre for Research in the New Literatures in English, 1986. 155-77.

Hess, Linda. "Post-Independence Indian Poetry in English." *Considerations.* Ed. Meenakshi Mukherjee. New Delhi: Allied Publishers, 1977. 23-42.

Hocking, W. E. *Types of Philosophy.* London: Charles Scribner's Sons, 1939.

Iyengar, K. R. Srinivasa. *Indian Writing in English.* 5th ed. New Delhi: Sterling Publishers, 1990.

Jain, Manju. *T.S. Eliot: Selected Poems and A Critical Reading of the Selected Poems of T. S. Eliot*. New Delhi: Faber & Faber-Oxford UP, 1996.

Keats, John. "Happy Insensibility." *The Golden Treasury of the Best Songs and Lyrical Poems in the English Language.* Ed. Francis Turner Palgrave. London: Oxford UP, 1964. 191.

_______, "Ode to a Nightingale." *The Poetical Works of John Keats.* Ed. H. Buxton Forman. London: Oxford UP, 1946. 230-32.

Khan, A. G. "Liberated or Libidinous: Women Writing in English." *Indian Women Novelists.* Set 3: Vol. 1. Ed. R. K. Dhawan. New Delhi: Prestige Books, 1995. 33-38.

King, Bruce. *Modern Indian Poetry in English.* New Delhi: Oxford UP, 1987.

Kohli, Devindra. "Kamala Das." *The Literary Criterion.* 12.2-3 (1976): 173-86.

______, "Virgin Whiteness An Interpretation of the Poetry of Kamala Das." *The Literary Criterion.* 7.4 (1967): 64-79.

Kurup, P.K.J. *Contemporary Indian Poetry in English.* New Delhi: Atlantic Publishers and Distributors, 1991.

Lim, Shirley Goeklin. "Terms of Empowerment in Kamala Das's My Story." *Perspectives on Kamala Das's Prose.* Ed. Iqbal Kaur. New Delhi: Intellectual Publishing House, 1995. 87-111.

"Modernism." *Hutchinson Educational Encyclopaedia.* CD-ROM. Oxford: Helicon Publishing, 1999.

Nabar, Vrinda. *The Endless Female Hungers: A study of Kamala Das.* New Delhi: Sterling Publishers, 1994.

Naidu, Sarojini. "Song of Radha-The Quest." *The Golden Treasury of Indo-Anglian Poetry.* Ed. Vinayaka Krishna Gokak. New Delhi: Sahitya Akademi, 1995. 155-56.

Naik, M. K. *A History of Indian English Literature.* New Delhi: Sahitya Akademi, 2006. 210.

Nair, K.R. Ramachandran. *The Poetry of Kamala Das.* New Delhi: Reliance Publishing House, 1993.

O'Sullivan, Vincent. "Whose Voice is Where? On Listening to Kamala Das." *Kamala Das: A Selection With Essays on Her Work.* Eds. S. C. Harrex and Vincent O'Sullivan. Adelaide: Centre for Research in New Literatures in English, 1986. 179-94.

Parthasarthy, R. "Homecoming." *Indian Poetry in English.* Eds. Harimohan Prasad and Chakradhar Prasad Singh. New Delhi: Sterling Publishers, 1986. 73-77.

Pascal, Blaise. "Quotations." *Hutchinson Educational Encyclopaedia.* CD-ROM. Oxford: Helicon Publishing, 1999.

Plath, Sylvia. "Lady Lazarus." *The Collected Poems.* Ed. Ted Hughes. New York: Harper, 1981. 245.

Radha, K. *Kamala Das.* Madras: Macmillan, 1986.

Rahman, Anisur. "Expressive Form in Kamala Das," *Expressive Form in the Poetry of Kamala Das.* New Delhi: Abhinav Publications, 1981. 3-36.

Rao, P. Mallikarjuna. "Body and Beyond: Love Poetry of Kamala Das." *Kakatiya Journal of English Studies* 8 (1987-88): 60-68.

Rao, Vimala. "Kamala Das-The Limits of Over Exposure." *Studies in Contemporary Indo-English Verse (A Collection of Critical Essays on Female Poets).* Ed. A. N. Dwivedi. Vol: 1. Bareilly: Prakash Book Depot, 1984. 87-96.

Raphael, R. "Kamala Das: The Pity Of It." *Indian Literature* 22.3 (May-June 1979): 127-37.

Saha, Subhas C. "The Dance of the Eunuchs." *Insights.* Subhas C. Saha. Calcutta: Writers Workshop, 1972. 13-26.

Sajjan, G. B. "Kamala Das Writings: A Challenge to Literary Interpretation." *Journal of the Karnatak University Humanities:* 23 (1979): 52-56.

Satchidanandan, K. "Transcending the Body: On the Poetry of Kamala Das." *Haritham* 7 (1996): 79-89.

Scott, Wilbur. Introduction. "The Sociological Approach." *Five Approaches of Literary Criticism.* Ed. Wilbur Scott. New York: Collier Books, 1962. 123-27.

"Self." *Hutchinson Educational Encyclopaedia.* CD-ROM. Oxford: Helicon Publishing, 1999.

Sexton, Anne. "Wanting to Die." *The Complete Poems.* Boston: Houghton, 1981. 142.

Sharma, I. K. "The Irony of Sex: A Study of Kamala Das's Poetry." *Contemporary Indo-English Poetry.* Ed. Bijay Kumar Das. Bareilly: Prakash Book Depot, 1986. 41-49.

Sharma, Mohan Lal. "The Road to Brindavan: The Theme of Love in Kamala Das's Poetry." *Studies in Contemporary Indo-English Verse. (A Collection of Critical Essays on Female Poets).* Ed. A.N.

Dwivedi. Vol. 1. Bareilly: Prakash Book Depot, 1984. 97-111.

Shelley, Percy Bysshe. *Poetical Works.* Ed. Thomas Hutchinson. London: Oxford UP, 1967. 577-79

Showalter, Elaine. "Feminist Criticism in the Wilderness." *Contemporary Literary Criticism: Literary and Cultural Studies.* Eds. Robert Con Davis and Ronald Schleifer. 2nd ed. New York: Longman, 1989. 457-78.

Singh, Susheela. *Feminism: Theory, Criticism, Analysis.* Delhi: Pencraft International, 1997.

Stevens, Wallace. "Sunday Morning." *Concise Anthology of American Literature.* Ed. George Mc Michael. 2nd ed. New York: Macmillan, 1985. 1658-60.

Varma, Monika. *Facing Four.* Calcutta: Writers Workshop, 1973. 25-33.

Vijaysree, C. "The Art of Memory: A Note on Kamala Das's Poetry." *Perspectives on Kamala Das's Poetry* Ed. Iqbal Kaur. New Delhi: Intellectual Publishing House, 1995. 134-41.

Whitman, Walt. "Song of Myself." *Concise Anthology of American Literature.* Ed. George Mc Michael. 2nd ed. New York: Macmillan, 1985. 914-59.

Woolf, Virginia. "Quotations." *Hutchinson Educational Encyclopaedia.* CD-ROM. Oxford: Helicon Publishing, 1999.

Wordsworth, Williams. "Ode on Intimations of Immortality." *The Golden Treasury of the Best Songs and Lyrical Poems in the English Language.* Ed. Francis Turner Palgrave. London: Oxford UP, 1964. 308-13

Worsfold, W. Basil. *Judgment in Literature.* 2nd Ed. Ludhiana: Lyall Book Depot, 1968.

Zide, Arlene R.K. "Rev. of The Old Playhouse and Other Poems." *Journal of South Asian Literature.* 16.1 (Win-Sept 1981): 233-41.

Select Bibliography

Primary Sources

Poetry

Das, Kamala. *Collected Poems.* Trivandrum : Kamala Das, 1984.

_________, *Only the Soul Knows How to Sing: Selections from Kamala Das.* Kottayam: D.C. Books, 1996.

_________, *The Best of Kamala Das.* Kerala: Bodhi Publishing House, 1991.

_________, *The Descendants.* Calcutta: Writers Workshop, 1967.

_________, *The Old Playhouse and Other Poems.* Bombay: Orient Longman, 1973.

Das, Kamala and Pritish Nandy. *Tonight this Savage Rite: The Love Poems of Kamala Das and Pritish Nandy.* New Delhi: Arnold Heinemann, 1979.

Prose

Das, Kamala. *The Alphabet of Lust.* New Delhi: Orient Paperbacks, 1976.

_________, "I Have Kept Myself Away From Books In Order To Preserve My Independent Original Voice." An Interview with Irshad Ahmed. *Perspectives on Kamala Das Prose.* Ed. Iqbal Kaur. New Delhi: Intellectual Publishing House, 1995. 79-81.

_________, "I Needed to Disturb Society." An Interview with Iqbal Kaur. *Perspectives on Kamala Das's Poetry.* Ed. Iqbal

Kaur. New Delhi: Intellectual Publishing House, 1995. 157-68.

_________, "My Instinct, My Guru." *Indian Literature* 33.5 (Sept-Oct 1990): 155-62.

_________, "Of Masks and Memories." An Interview with P. P. Raveendran. *Indian Literature* 36.3 (May-June 1993): 144-61.

_________, *My Story*. New Delhi: Sterling Publishers, 1978.

_________, *Padmavati, The Harlot and Other Stories*. New Delhi:Sterling Publishers, 1992.

_________, *The Sandal Trees and Other Stories*: Trans. V. C. Harris and C. K. Mohamed *Ummer*. Hyderabad: Disha Books, 1995.

Suraiya, Kamala. *The Path of the Columnist*. Calicut: Olive Publications, 2000.

Secondary Sources

Agrawal, Ishwar Nath. "The Language and the Limits of the Self in the Poetry of Kamala Das." *Indian Writing in English*. Ed. Sinha Krishna Nanda. New Delhi: Heritage Publishers, 1979. 138-46

Ahmed, Irshad. "Reflections on the Mind and Responsibility of Kamala Das." *Perspectives on Kamala Das Poetry.* Ed. Iqbal Kaur. New Delhi: Intellectual Publishing House, 1995. 129-33.

Allport, G. W. *Personality: A Psychological Interpretation.* New York: Holt, Rheinehart, & Winston, 1937.

Ash, Ranjana. "Autobiography in the Poetry of Amrita Pritam and Kamala Das." *Aspects of Commonwealth Literature:* Vol. 2. London: University of London, 1992. 46-52

Asnani, Shyam. "Kamala Das, Judith Wright and Margeret Atwood as Poets of Love: A Comparative Study." *Perspectives on Kamala Das's Poetry.* Ed. Iqbal Kaur. New Delhi: Intellectual Publishing House, 1995. 69-88

Ayaz, Nasreen. "Concept of Love in the Poetry of Kamala Das." *Perspectives on Kamala Das's Poetry*. Ed. Iqbal Kaur. New Delhi: Intellectual Publishing House, 1995. 107-12.

Barat, Urbashi. "Forms of Feminine Protest: Rebellion within Marriage in Sita Devi's *The Wedding Dress* and Kamala Das's *A Little Kitten*. *Indian Women Novelists:* Set III; Vol.7. Ed. Dhawan R.K. New Delhi: Prestige Books, 1995. 99-108.

Barche, G.D. "Anger Expression in Kamala Das's Poetry: A Study in Klesa Vritti." *Indian Writing Today : Essays in honour of Professor L.S.R. Krishna Sastry.* Ed. C. R. Visweswara Rao. New Delhi: Indian Association for English Studies, 1996. 48-55.

Barhard, John. "The Poet's Audience," Rev. of *Summer in Calcutta,* by Kamala Das. *Journal of Commonwealth Literature.* 5 (Jul 1968): 116-18.

Beauvoir, Simone de. *A Very Easy Death.* England: Penguin, 1969.

__________, *The Second Sex.* Trans. and Ed. H. M. Parshley. England: Jonathan Cape, 1956.

Begum, Jameela. "Female Consciousness and the Short Story form: Uncertainties and Diversifications in Kamala Das's Stories." *Perspectives on Kamala Das's Prose.* Ed. Iqbal Kaur. New Delhi: Intellectual Publishing House, 1995. 37-43.

Bharucha, Nilufer E. "Women Poets and Feminist Critics." Rev. of *The Endless Female Hungers: A Study of Kamala Das,* by Vrinda Nabar. *Indian Horizons.* 44.3 (1995): 295-99.

Bhattacharji, *Sukumari. History of Classical Sanskrit Literature.* Hyderabad: Orient Longman, 1993.

Brewster, Anne. "The Freedom to Decompose: The Poetry of Kamala Das." *The Journal of Indian Writing in English* 8.1-2 (Jan-July 1980): 98-107.

Brooks, Peter. "Freud's Masterplot." *Contemporary Literary Criticism: Literary and Cultural Studies.* Eds. Robert Con Davis and Ronald Schleifer. 2nd ed. New York: Longman, 1989. 287-299.

Cambon, Glauco. *The Inclusive Flame.* Sudies in Modern American Poetry. Bombay: Popular Prakashan, 1969.

Camus, Albert. *The Rebel.* Trans. Anthony Bower. London: Hamish Hamilton, 1959.

Chaitanya, Krishna. *Sanskrit Poetics: A Critical and Comparative Study.* Bombay: Asia Publishing House, 1918.

Chakravarty, Joya. "Manifestations of Kamala Das's Poems in her Autobiography 'My Story.'" *Contemporary Indian Writings in English.* Ed. Jaydipsinh Dodiya. New Delhi: Atlantic Publishers and Distributors, 1998.

Chambial, D. C. "Kamala Das: The Poet as an Iconoclast." Rev. of *Kamala Das: Treatment of Love in Her Poetry,* by D. Murali Manohar. *Indian Book Chronicle News and Reviews.* 25.6 (June 2000): 16.

Chander, K.M. Rev. of *Kamala Das and Her Poetry. The Literary Criterion.* 20.4 (1985): 112.

Chavan, Sunanda P. *The Fair Voice: A Study of Indian Women Poets in English.* New Delhi: Sterling Publishers 1984. 60-71.

__________, "The Unity of Vision in the Poetry of Kamala Das." *Perspectives on Kamala Das's Poetry.* Ed. Iqbal Kaur. New Delhi: Intellectual Publishing House, 1995. 142-49.

Cixous, H'ele'n. "Castration or Decapitation?" Trans. Annette Kuhn. *Contemporary Literary Criticism: Literary and Cultural Studies.* Eds. Robert Con Davis and Ronald Schleifer. 2nd ed. New York: Longman, 1989. 479-91.

Cuddon, J. A. *A Dictionary of Literary Terms.* London: Andre Deutsch; New Delhi: Indian Book Company, 1977.

Daniel, Susan. Rev. of *Kamala Das and her Poetry,* by A. N. Dwivedi. *The Literary Criterion.* 20.4 (1985): 91-93.

Daruwalla, Keki N. "Confessional Poetry as Social Commentary: A View of English Poetry by Indian Women Poets." *Contemporary Indian English Poetry.* Ed. Atma Ram. Calcutta:

Writers Workshop, 1989. 9-20.

Das, Bijay Kumar. "Kamala Das And the Making of the Indian English Idiom." *Indian English Writing: 1981-1985 (Experimental With Expression).* Ed. R. K. Singh. New Delhi: Bahri Publications 1987. 91-98.

________, "The Poetry of Kamala Das." *Modern Indo English Poetry.* Bijay Kumar Das. Bareilly: Prakash Book Depot, 1982. 44-54.

Dass, Veena Noble. "Feminism and Literature." *Feminism and Literature.* Ed. Veena Noble Das. New Delhi: Prestige Books, 1995. 9-12.

Davis, Robert Con, and Ronald Schleifer. "Feminism." *Contemporary Literary Criticism: Literary and Cultural Studies.* Eds. Robert Con Davis and Ronald Schleifer, 2nd ed. New York: Longman, 1989. 449-56.

De Souza, Eunice. "Kamala Das." *Indian Poetry in English: A Critical Assessment.* Eds. Vasant A. Sahane and M. Sivaramakrishna. Madras: Macmillan, 1980. 41-47.

________, "Kamala Das, Gauri Deshpande, Mamta Kalia." Quest, No.74 (Jan-Feb 1972): 84-87.

________, "Kamala Das." *Osmania Journal of English Studies.* 13.1 (1977): 19-27.

Dhar, T.N. "Eros Denied: Love in the Poetry of Kamala Das." *Contemporary Indian-English Poetry.* Ed. Atma Ram. Calcutta: Writers Workshop, 1989. 21-31.

Dwivedi, A.N. "Kamala Das's *Alphabet of Lust* (1976): An Appraisal." *Papers on Indian Writing in English*: Volume II. Generes Other than Poetry. A. N. Dwivedi. Delhi: Amar Prakashan, 1991. 118-25.

________, *Indo-Anglian Poetry.* Allahabad: Kitab Mahal, 1979.

________, *Kamala Das and Her Poetry.* Delhi: Doaba House, 1983.

________, "Kamala Das: My World Defleshed, Deblooded." *Creative Forum*. 5.1-4 (Jan-Dec 1992): 65-72.

Elias, Mohamed. "Kamala Das and Nayar Heritage." *The Journal of Indian Writing in English*. 6 (Jul 1978): 15-24.

Eliot, T. S. *The Waste Land*. Madras: Macmillan, 1986.

Empson, William. *Seven Types of Ambiguity*. England: Penguin, 1977.

Ezekiel, Nissim. "Poet, Lover, Birdwatcher." *Journal of South Asian Literature*. 11.3-4 (Spr-Sum 1976): 75.

________, "Poverty Poems—2." *Indian Poetry in English*. Eds. Harimohan Prasad and Chakradhar Prasad Singh. New Delhi: Sterling Publishers, 1986.

Fawcett, F. *Nayars of Malabar*, 1901. New Delhi: Asian Educational Services-Reprint, 1990.

Fischer, William F. *Theories of Anxiety*. New York: Harper & Row, Publishers, 1970.

Flieger, Jerry Aline. "The Purloined Punchline: Joke as Textual Paradigm." *Contemporary Literary Criticism: Literary and Cultural Studies*. Eds. Robert Con Davis and Ronald Schleifer. 2nd ed. New York: Longman, 1989. 351-68.

Frye, Northrop. "Literature and Linguistics Scholarship in a Post Literate World." *Myth and Metaphor: Selected Essays*. Ed. Denhem Robert. London: Virginia UP, 1991.

Gangoli, Geetanjali, "Men Do Not Revere But Fear Women." The Speaking Tree. *Times of India* 2 Oct. 1999: 11.

Gibaldi, Joseph. *MLA Handbook for Writers of Research Papers*. 4th ed. New Delhi: Affiliated East-West Press, 1996.

Gilbert, Sandra. "Life's Empty Pack: Notes Toward a Literary Daughteronomy." *Contemporary Literary Criticism: Literary and Cultural Studies*. Eds. Robert Con Davis and Ronald Schleifer, 2nd ed. New York: Longman, 1989. 492-516.

Grewal, Omprakash. "The Poetry of Kamala Das-A Critical Assessment." *Indian Writing In English.* Ed. Krishna Nanda Sinha. New Delhi: Heritage Publishers, 1979. 128-37.

Hairston, Maxine. *A Contemporary Rhetoric*. Boston: Houghton, 1974.

Harrex, S.C. "The Strange Case of Mathew Arnold in a Sari: An Introduction to Kamala Das." *Kamala Das: A Selection With Essays on Her Work.* Eds. S. C. Harrex and Vincent O'Sullivan Adelaide: Centre for Research in the New Literatures in English, 1986. 155-77.

Hess, Linda. "Post-Independence Indian Poetry in English." *Considerations*. Ed. Meenakshi Mukherjee. New Delhi: Allied Publishers, 1977. 23-42.

Hocking, W. E. Types of Philosophy.. London: Charles Scribner's Sons, 1939.

Hutchinson Educational Encyclopaedia. CD-ROM. Oxford: Helicon Publishing, 1999.

Iyengar, K. R. Srinivasa. *Indian Writing in English.* 5th ed. New Delhi: Sterling Publishers, 1990.

Iyer, Sharada. "Split-Self in the Poetry of Kamala Das." *Indian Writings in English.* Ed. Manmohan K. Bhatnagar. New Delhi: Atlantic Publishers and Distributors, 1999.

Jain, Manju. *T.S. Eliot: Selected Poems and A Critical Reading of the Selected Poems of T. S. Eliot.* New Delhi: Faber & Faber-Oxford UP, 1996.

Jayachandran, Laila. "Kamala Das's The Dance of the Enuchus: A Study based on Indian Poetics." *Littcrit.* 19.1 & 2 (June, Dec 1993): 117-23.

Jha, Pashupati. *Sylvia Plath.* New Delhi: Creative Publishers, 1991.

Jones, Dorothy. "Freedom Became My Dancing Shoe: Liberty and the Pursuit of Happiness in the Works of Kamala Das." *Kamala Das: A Selection With Essays on Her Work.* Eds. S.C.

Harrex and Vincent O'Sullivan. Adelaide: Centre for Research in the New Literatures in English, 1986. 195-215.

Joseph, Annamma. *Feminism and the Modern American Poetry.* New Delhi: Prestige Books, 1996.

Jussawalla, Adil. "The New Poetry." *The Journal of Commonwealth Literature.* 5 (July 1968): 65-78.

Jussawalla, Feroza. "The Evolution of the Self." *The Journal of Indian Writing in English.* 10.1 & 2 (Jan-July 1982): 54-61.

_________, "The Iron of English Rings on My Tongue: Four Poets: Das, Ezekiel, Parthasarthy and Ramanujan." *Journal of South Asian Literature.* 22.2 (Sum-Fal 1987): 113-29.

Kalinnikova, Elena J. "New Poetry." *Indian English Literature: A Perspective.* Ed. K. K Sharma. Ghaziabad: Vimal Prakashan, 1982. 207-17.

Kanwadkar, M.M. "Motherly Sensibility in My Story." *Indian Women Novelists.* Set 2: Vol. 1. Ed. R. K. Dhawan. New Delhi: Prestige Books, 1993. 149-55.

Kaur, Iqbal. "Colonial Anguish in My Story." *Indian Women Novelists.* Set 2: Vol. 1. Ed. R. K. Dhawan. New Delhi: Prestige Books, 1993. 156-69.

_________, "Sexual Politics and Kamala Das." *Indian Women Novelists.* Set II: Vol. 1. Ed. R. K. Dhawan. New Delhi: Prestige Books, 1993. 102-40.

Keats, John. "Happy Insensibility." *The Golden Treasury of the Best Songs and Lyrical Poems in the English Language.* Ed. Francis Turner Palgrave. London: Oxford UP, 1964. 191.

_________, "Ode to a Nightingale." *The Poetical Works of John Keats.* Ed. H. Buxton Forman. London: Oxford UP, 1946. 230-32.

Khan, A. G. "Liberated or Libidinous: Women Writing in English." *Indian Women Novelists.* Set 3: Vol. 1. Ed. R. K. Dhawan. New Delhi: Prestige Books, 1995. 33-38.

King, Bruce. *Modern Indian Poetry in English.* New Delhi: Oxford UP, 1987.

Kohli, Devindra. "Kamala Das." *The Literary Criterion.* 12.2-3 (1976): 173-86.

__________, "Virgin Whiteness An Interpretation of the Poetry of Kamala Das." *The Literary Criterion.* 7.4 (1967): 64-79.

Kumar, Shiv K. "A Note on Contemporary Indian Poetry in English," *Commonwealth Literature: Themes and Techniques.* Eds. P. Rajan, K.M. George, Jameela Begum, and K. Radha. Delhi: Ajanta Publishers, 1993. 65-68.

Kumar, Sunil. "The Poetry of Kamala Das: A Women's Quest for Identity." *Creative Forum.* 5.1-4 (Jan-Dec 1992): 57-64.

Kurian, Elizabeth P. "Fading Out and the Female Psyche: Plath, Kmala Das and Sankranti." *College English Review.* 4.1 (January-June 2000): 19-20.

Kurup, P.K.J. *Contemporary Indian Poetry in English.* New Delhi: Atlantic Publishers and Distributors, 1991.

Lal, P. "Kamala Das." *Perspectives on Kamala Das's Poetry.* Ed. Iqbal Kaur. New Delhi: Intellectual Publishing House, 1995. 67-68.

Lim, Shirley Goek-lin. "Terms of Empowerment in Kamala Das's My Story." *Perspectives on Kamala Das's Prose.* Ed. Iqbal Kaur. New Delhi: Intellectual Publishing House, 1995. 87-111.

Love, Paul L. "Some Aspects of Kamala Das." *S.B. Academic Review* 6.1 (Jan-June 1997): 7-10.

Mathew, Molamma. "The Inward Journey: Search for Indentity in the Poems of Kamala Das." *S.B. Academic Review* 6.1 (Jan-June 1997): 37-40.

Mishra, Sanjit. "Kamala Das : Feminist or Otherwise." *Contemporary Indian Women Writers in English: A Feminist Perspective.* Ed. Surya Nath Pandey. New Delhi: Atlantic Publishers and

Distributors, 1999.

Mohanty, Niranjan. "Beyond Confession: Poetry of Kamala Das." *Malayalam Literary Survey* 12.1 (Jan-Mar 1990): 42-67.

_________, "Sublimation of the Femine Ego: Poetry of Kamala Das." *Malayalam Literary Survey* 14.1 (Jan-Mar 1992): 25-34.

Mokashi-Punekar, Rohini. "Scattered Arguments and Chatty Tone." Rev. of *The Endless Female Hungers: A Study of Kamala Das,* by Vrinda Nabar. *Indian Review of Books* 3.8 (May 16-June15 1994): 11-12.

Mokashi-Punekar, S. Rev. of *The Old playhouse and Other Poems,* by Kamala Das. *Journal of the Karnatak University Humanities* 18 (1974): 164-65.

Nabar, Vrinda. *The Endless Female Hungers: A study of Kamala Das.* New Delhi: Sterling Publishers, 1994.

Naidu, Sarojini. "Song of Radha-The Quest." *The Golden Treasury of Indo-Anglian Poetry.* Ed. Vinayaka Krishna Gokak. New Delhi: Sahitya Akademi, 1995. 155-56.

Naik, M. K. *A History of Indian English Literature.* New Delhi: Sahitya Akademi, 2006. 210.

Nair, K.R. Ramachandran. *The Poetry of Kamala Das.* New Delhi: Reliance Publishing House, 1993.

Nair, Vijay. "Memories of Childhood in the Poems of Kamala Das." *Changing Traditions in Indian English Literature.* Ed. P. K. Rajan. New Delhi: Creative Books, 1995. 111-19.

Narasimhaiah, C. D. "Makers of Indian English." *The Literary Criterion.* 34.1 (1999): 5-32.

Nayar, Pramod K. "Negative Poetics: An Approach to Kamala Das." *S. B. Academic Review.* 6.1 (Jan-June 1997): 27-31.

Nigam, Alka. "No More Masks: The Poetry of Kamala Das." *Perspectives on Kamala Das's Poetry.* Kaur Iqbal. New Delhi: Intellectual Publishing House, 1995. 99-106.

Nirmala, Mary. "The Theme of Death in the Poetry of Kamala Das." College English Review. 2.2 (April-June 1998): 28-30.

North, Marilla. "Watching Herself Watching Her Self: Kamala Das's Split Texts." *New Literatures Review*. 21 (Sum 1991): 42-57.

O'Sullivan, Vincent. "Whose Voice is Where? On Listening to Kamala Das." *Kamala Das: A Selection With Essays on Her Work.* Eds. S. C. Harrex and Vincent O'Sullivan. Adelaide: Centre for Research in New Literatures in English, 1986. 179-94.

Oxford Advance Learner's Dictionary of Current English. Eds. A.S. Hornby with A. P. Cowie. Delhi: Oxford UP. 3rd ed. 1985.

Pandeya, Prabhat Kumar. "The Pink Pulsating Words: The Women's Voice in Kamala Das's Poetry." *Indian Literature Today*. Ed. R. K. Dhawan. Vol. 2. New Delhi: Prestige Books, 1994. 66-77.

Parthasarthy, R. "Homecoming." *Indian Poetry in English.* Eds. Harimohan Prasad and Chakradhar Prasad Singh. New Delhi: Sterling Publishers, 1986. 73-77.

__________, "Indian English Verse: The Making of a Tradition." *Alien Voice: Perspectives on Commonwealth Literature.* Ed. Srivastava Avadhesh K. Lucknow: Print House Publishers, 1981. 40-52.

Perry, John Oliver. Rev. of *Kamala Das,* eds. S. C. Harrex and Vincent O' Sullivan. *World Literature Today.* 61.2 (Spr 1987): 348-49.

Plath Sylvia. *The Colossus*. London: Faber and Faber, 1967.

Prabha, M. "The Poetry of Kamala Das." *Indian Book Chronicle*. 22.11 (Nov 1997): 3-4.

Prabhu, Louella Lobo. "Kamala Das Soraya." *Indian Book Chronicle.* 25.3 (Mar 2000): 6.

Pritchard, R. E. *D. H. Lawrence : Body of Darkness.* London:

Hutchinson University Library, 1971.

Radha, K. *Kamala Das.* Madras: Macmillan, 1986.

__________. "Tributes(?) to Papas: The Attitude to Fathers in Some Indian Poems in English." *New Nations, New Voices: Essays on Commonwealth Literature.* Ramamurthy S. Tiruchi: 1994. 81-85.

Radhika, P. "Space-Time Co-ordinates in Madhavikutty's Writings." *S. B. Academic Review.* 6.1 (Jan-June 1997): 19-25.

Rahman, Anisur. "A Poet's Tale: A Doll for the Child Prostitute." *Response: Recent Revelations of Indian Fiction in English.* Bareilly: Prakash Book Depot, 1983. 274-82.

__________, *Expressive Form in the Poetry of Kamala Das.* New Delhi: Abhinav Publications, 1981.

__________,"Love is a Shadow: A Perspective on Sylvia Plath and Kamala Das." *Indian Journal of American Studies.* 22.2 (Sum 1992): 75-79.

Raizada, Harish. "The Confessional Note in the Poetry of Kamala Das." *Indian Poetry in English.* Ed. Hari Mohan Prasad. Aurangabad: Parimal Prakashan, 1983. 113-35.

Ramakrishnan, E.V. "Kamala Das a Confessional Poet." *Contemporary Indian English Verse*: An Evaluation. Ed. Chirantan Kulshrestha. New Delhi: Arnold Heineman, 1980. 201-7.

Ramanathan, Suguna. "Kamala Das's Composition: A Lacanian Interpretation." *Perspectives on Kamala Das's Poetry.* Ed. Iqbal Kaur. New Delhi: Intellectual Publishing House, 1995. 19-32.

Rao, Bhargavi P. "Kamala Das: Through A Different Lens." *Perspectives on Kamala Das's Poetry.* Ed. Iqbal Kaur. New Delhi: Intellectual Publishing House, 1995. 122-27.

Rao, P. Mallikarjuna. "Body and Beyond: Love Poetry of Kamala Das." *Kakatiya Journal of English Studies* 8 (1987-88): 60-68.

__________. "Love Poetry of Kamala Das." *Triveni* 58.2 (Apr-June 1989): 51-56.

Rao, Vimala. "Kamala Das-The Limits of Over Exposure." *Studies in Contemporary Indo-English Verse (A Collection of Critical Essays on Female Poets).* Ed. A. N. Dwivedi. Vol: 1. Bareilly: Prakash Book Depot, 1984. 87-96.

Raphael, R. "Kamala Das: The Pity Of It." *Indian Literature* 22.3 (May-June 1979): 127-37.

Raveendran, P. P. "History in the Anamalai Poems." *Perspectives on Kamala Das's Poetry.* Ed. Iqbal Kaur. New Delhi: Intellectual Publishing House, 1995. 150-56.

__________, "Kamala Das: The Ideology of Intimacy." *Changing Traditions in Indian English Literature.* Ed. P. K. Rajan. New Delhi: Creative Books, 1995. 81-91.

Reddy, K. Indra Sena. "Between the Fire and the Hungry Earth: A Note on Kamala Das." *Kakatiya Journal of English Studies.* 5 (1983): 61-68.

Roy, Sumita. "The Changing Contours: Paradoxes of Patriarchy : Feminist Motifs." *Between Spaces of Silence: Women Creative Writers.* Ed. Dinesh Kamini. New Delhi: Sterling Publishers Pvt. Ltd., 1994. 20-28.

Rumens, Carol. "Dislocated Carnality." Rev. of *The Best of Kamala Das,* by Kamala Das. Poetry Review 83.1 (Spr 1993): 35-36.

Saha, Subhas C. "The Dance of the Eunuchs." Insights. Subhas C. Saha. Calcutta: Writers Workshop, 1972. 13-26.

Sahayam, V. Sam. "The Feminist Stances of Margaret Atwood and Kamala Das." *Indian Literature Today:* Vol. 2. Ed. R. K. Dhawan. New Delhi: Prestige Books, 1994. 92-100.

Sajjan, G. B. "Kamala Das Writings: A Challenge to Literary Interpretation." *Journal of the Karnatak University Humanities:* 23 (1979): 52-56.

Sankaranarayan, Vasanti. "Passion and Oppression." Rev. of *The*

Best of Kamala Das, by Kamala Das. *Indian Review of Books.* 1.8 (May 1992): 43.

Satchidanandan, K. "Transcending the Body: On the Poetry of Kamala Das." *Haritham* 7 (1996): 79-89.

Saxena, D.C. "The Ambient View: 'Indianness' in Poetry of Sarojini Naidu and Kamala Das: A Prolegomena to Unity in Diversity." *Between Spaces of Silence: Women Creative Writers.* Ed. Kamini Dinesh. New Delhi: Sterling Publishers, 1994. 139-46.

Scott, Wilbur. Introduction. "The Sociological Approach." *Five Approaches of Literary Criticism.* Ed. Wilbur Scott. New York: Collier Books, 1962. 123-27.

Sharma S. D. *Thematic Dichotomy of Writings in Indian English: Indology and Culture.* Bareilly: Prakash Book Depot, 1985.

Sharma, I. K. "The Irony of Sex: A Study of Kamala Das's Poetry." *Contemporary Indo-English Poetry.* Ed. Bijay Kumar Das. Bareilly: Prakash Book Depot, 1986. 41-49.

__________,"Mary and Mira: A Study of Kamala Das." *Commonwealth Quarterly.* 3.10 (Mar 1979): 36-47.

Sharma, Mohan Lal. "The Road to Brindavan: The Theme of Love in Kamala Das's Poetry." *Studies in Contemporary Indo-English Verse. (A Collection of Critical Essays on Female Poets).* Ed. A.N. Dwivedi. Vol. 1. Bareilly: Prakash Book Depot, 1984. 97-111.

Sharma, S. D. "Kamala Das's Poetry: An Amatory Hiatus." *Indian Scholar* 14.1-2. (Jan-July 1982): 45-49.

__________, "Kamala Das's Poetry." *Perspectives on Kamala Das's Poetry.* Ed. Iqbal Kaur. New Delhi: Intellectual Publishing House, 1995. 1-18.

Shelley, Percy Bysshe. *Poetical Works.* Ed. Thomas Hutchinson. London: Oxford UP, 1967. 577-79.

Showalter, Elaine. "Feminist Criticism in the Wilderness."

Contemporary Literary Criticism: Literary and Cultural Studies. Eds. Robert Con Davis and Ronald Schleifer. 2nd ed. New York: Longman, 1989. 457-78.

Simms, Norman. Rev. of *Kamala Das and Her Poetry,* by A. N. Dwivedi. *The Journal of Indian Writing in English* 13.1 (Jan 1985): 76-78.

Singh, Mohinder. "My Favourite Reading: The Search for Feminine Integrity." *Indian Book Chronicle.* 6.1 & 2 (Jan 1918): 24-27.

Singh, R. K. "Voices of Anger and Sexuality: Some Recent Indian English Women Poets." *Indian Book Chronicle.* 20.5 (May 1995): 6-10.

Singh, Susheela. *Feminism: Theory, Criticism, Analysis.* Delhi: Pencraft International, 1997.

Sivadasan, C.P. "The Poetry of Kamala Das: A Lexical Perspective." *S. B. Academic Review.* 6.1 (Jan-June 1997): 11-14.

Spivak, Gayatri Chakravorty. "Imperialism and Sexual Difference." *Contemporary Literary Criticism: Literary and Cultural Studies.* Eds. Robert Con Davis and Ronald Schleifer. 2nd ed. New York: Longman, 1989. 517-29.

Srivastva K.C. "The Quest for Identity in the Novels of Kamala Das." *Indian Women Novelists: Set II: Vol. I.* Ed. Dhawan R.K. New Delhi: Prestige Books, 1993. 94-101.

Stevens, Wallace. "Sunday Morning." *Concise Anthology of American Literature.* Ed. George Mc Michael. 2nd ed. New York: Macmillan, 1985. 1658-60.

Sudipta, B. *The Novels of Virginia Woolf.* New Delhi: Prestige Books, 1990.

Sunitha, K. T. "All about Kamala Das." Rev. of *Kamala Das,* eds. S.C. Harrex and Vincent O' Sullivan. *The Literary Half-Yearly.* 28.1 (Jan 1987): 131-32.

Thomas, O.J. "Kamala Das: A Search for Home, Companionship and Love." *The Quest.* 5.1 (Jun 1991): 28-36.

Varma, Monika. *Facing Four.* Calcutta: Writers Workshop, 1973. 25-33.

Venugopal C.V. "Kamala Das: The Seeker After Truth." *Living Indian English Poets.* Ed. Madhusudan Prasad. New Delhi: Sterling Publishers, 1989. 143-47.

Vijaysree, C. "The Art of Memory: A Note on Kamala Das's Poetry." *Perspectives on Kamala Das's Poetry* Ed. Iqbal Kaur. New Delhi: Intellectual Publishing House, 1995. 134-41.

Wallace Crabbe, Chris. "The Loud Posters of Kamala Das." *Kamala Das: A Selection With Essays on Her Work.* Eds. S. C. Harrex and Vincent O'Sullivan. Adelaide: Centre for Research in the New Literatures in English, 1986. 217-24.

Weisbord, Merrily. "An Interview with C. R. Nambiar about Kamala Das." *College English Review.* 1.2 (Mar-Apr 1997): 11-13.

Whitman, Walt. "Song of Myself." *Concise Anthology of American Literature.* Ed. George Mc Michael. 2nd ed. New York: Macmillan, 1985. 914-59.

Williams H.M. *Indo Anglian Literature 1800-1970: A Survey.* Madras: Orient Longman, 1976.

Wordsworth, William. "Ode on Intimations of Immortality." *The Golden Treasury of the Best Songs and Lyrical Poems in the English Language.* Ed. Francis Turner Palgrave. London: Oxford UP, 1964. 308-13.

Worsfold, W. Basil. *Judgment in Literature.* 2nd ed. Ludhiana: Lyall Book Depot, 1968.

Zide, Arlene R.K. Rev. of *The Old Playhouse and Other Poems,* by Kamala Das. *Journal of South Asian Literature.* 16.1 (Win-Sept 1981): 233-41.

Index

***